POWER TOOLS

for
Cubase 7

Master Steinberg's Powerful Multi-Platform Audio Production Software

INCLUDES DVD-ROM!

Matthew Loel T. Hepworth

HAL LEONARD BOOKS
An Imprint of Hal Leonard Corporation

Published in 2013 by Hal Leonard Books
An Imprint of Hal Leonard Corporation
7777 West Bluemound Road
Milwaukee, WI 53213

Trade Book Division Editorial Offices
33 Plymouth St., Montclair, NJ 07042

All photos, screenshots, illustrations, and music examples by
Matthew Loel T. Hepworth

Book design by Kristina Rolander

Printed in the United States of America

Library of Congress Cataloging-in-Publication Data
Hepworth, Matthew Loel T.
 Power tools for Cubase 7 / Matthew Loel T. Hepworth.
    pages cm
1. Cubase. 2. Digital audio editors. I. Title.
 ML74.4.C8H47 2013
 781.3'4536--dc23
                                                2013030358

ISBN 978-1-4584-1368-0

www.halleonardbooks.com

POWER TOOLS

for
Cubase 7

Contents

CHAPTER 2
HARDWARE AND STUDIO CONFIGURATION

CHAPTER 3

LAUNCHING CUBASE
FOR THE FIRST TIME

CHAPTER 6
A PRIMER ON MIDI AND VIRTUAL INSTRUMENTS   95

CHAPTER 10
OVERLAPING EVENTS, COMPING, AND THE COMP TOOL

CHAPTER 15

EFFECTS, INSERTS, SENDS, AND FX CHANNELS

CHAPTER 16

MASTERING AND AUDIO MIXDOWN

Preface

DREAMING OF DIGITAL

Let me take you back to February of 1984. Once strictly reserved for classical music, audio CDs of pop music were just hitting the record-store shelves. As a fan of Peter Gabriel, I was thrilled to repurchase the CD version of his fourth album, known in the United States as Security. (For those of you in the know: yes, it is a West German "Target" disc.) As I stood at the checkout counter holding the shrink-wrapped package in my hands, I noticed a small pink band on the cover artwork that read, "Full Digital Recording." This was the first time I'd ever seen such a listing. It meant the music was digitized into a series of numbers, and only when the consumer played the CD was it reconstructed into the analog signal that my ears could hear. I couldn't fully grasp the concept, but it piqued my interest in recording music digitally.

It wasn't until I got home and listened to the CD (CD players didn't appear in cars until late 1984) that I started to understand the advantages of digital. First and foremost, there were no tape-noise artifacts. Since the multitrack recording was done with a digital recorder, there was none of the ubiquitous tape hiss that we'd all put up with for so long. Next, my amplifier and speakers were a little distressed by the upper limits of the dynamic range. Yet the quiet passages revealed subtleties once reserved only for those who could afford the most esoteric and expensive of phonographs. I thought to myself, "Someday I'll be able to make my own digital recordings."

"Someday" Only Took Eight Years

Throughout most of the '80s and '90s, I worked in music stores, selling keyboards and recording equipment. It was a great way to learn about the newest digital technology, and it left my nights free to play gigs. In 1992, we received our first shipments of a new product from Alesis known as the ADAT (Alesis Digital Audio Tape). It was the world's first affordable digital 8-track recorder. Suddenly, for just under $4,000, musicians and engineers alike could own a digital multitrack recording device. To say that it revolutionized the project- and home-studio market would be an understatement.

While it was the first, and therefore the most affordable, digital multitrack recorder on the market, I still needed a mixer, compressors, effect processors, and a 2-track DAT machine to mix down to. I also needed boxes of cables and S-VHS tape stock with which to feed the ADATs. While the ADAT made the dream of the digital home-recording studio a reality, it was still an expensive proposition.

The Dawn of the DAW

Music software has been around ever since the early '80s. In fact, I still have the music cartridges that in 1982 allowed me to sequence music on my Commodore 64 even before there was MIDI. (I still use my Commodore 64 computers with the MSSIAH MIDI cartridge from 8bitventures.com.) But in 1993, Steinberg released Cubase Audio. It allowed Atari Falcon (computer) owners to run Cubase MIDI tracks and up to eight digital Audio tracks simultaneously. I had been using Steinberg Pro16 MIDI sequencing software on my Commodore 64 for years, but didn't get into Cubase Audio until it became available on Windows in 1996. Together with my Yamaha CBX-D5 and CBX-D3 audio interfaces, I could play back just as many tracks as with my 8-track ADAT.

Time Becomes Nonlinear

Cubase Audio also allowed me to use the same digital editing techniques I'd been using on MIDI tracks for years. Suddenly I could cut, copy, and paste audio data from within the Cubase timeline. This kind of editing was unheard of on a single ADAT because of its tape-based format, which rendered its timeline linear. Not only did Cubase Audio allow me to move audio data around the timeline as easily as I could with MIDI data, it also did it nondestructively. In other words, all of the original versions of my Audio tracks were retained on the hard drive. The price of this computer-based system was even less than the ADAT technology.

The Real World Becomes Virtual with VST

Later in 1996, Steinberg created VST, or Virtual Studio Technology. VST created virtual signal processors (such as EQ, compressors, chorus, and reverb effects) right inside of the computer. My gigantic mixer and racks of external signal processors were quickly becoming obsolete. Within a few years, Steinberg added VSTi, or VST Instruments, to Cubase that created virtual synthesizers, samplers, and drum machines inside of the computer. At that point, my synthesizers and samplers were getting obsolete too. Fortunately, this was also when eBay hit the scene, and I used it to sell off my redundant hardware.

Cubase Is a Complete Recording Studio

Fast-forward to present day, and Cubase has become an entire recording studio right inside of your computer. Sure you'll still need mics, MIDI and audio interfaces, a few cables, instruments, speakers, and inspiration to make it all happen. But never before has the recording studio been more accessible to musicians and music enthusiasts alike. Consider this: Cubase LE and AI (limited editions of Cubase that ship with many third-party hardware products, Steinberg products, and Yamaha products) provide at least sixteen audio tracks. That's four times as many tracks as the Beatles ever had! We really do live in exciting times.

Be Careful What You Wish For

Now that you have an entire recording studio in your computer, learning how to use all of it can be a daunting task. Imagine you just walked into a state-of-the-art commercial recording facility and noticed all the buttons, switches, knobs, cables, and hardware that filled the control room. Now imagine you have to sit in the "big chair" and take charge of a recording session. Are you ready to do that? My guess is that you'd be besieged by the prospect of being thrown into the role of engineer and running all of that gear.

Well, by purchasing Cubase and running it on your computer, you are sitting in the big chair. I've had the advantage of gradually experiencing the digital revolution throughout its various stages. But if in 1984 I'd been thrown into a recording studio and told to record music, I'd have been completely overwhelmed and intimidated. I imagine that's how you feel right now. It might even be the reason you are reading this book.

HOW TO USE THIS BOOK

I have faith that you will be able to become an accomplished Cubase user and do things I could only dream of doing back in 1984. But to do so, I recommend that you learn Cubase as you would a new musical instrument. Many of you play some sort of musical instrument. Unless you are a prodigy, wrangling the first notes out of the instrument didn't meet world-class standards. However, through daily practice and learning from mistakes, you became a competent musician. Or at the very least, you've learned enough to allow the instrument and the music you make with it to enrich your life.

If you apply that same approach to learning Cubase, you will be able to record your music (or the music of others) on your computer in the comfort of your home, project studio, or commercial facility. To say that Cubase and digital music production have irrevocably augmented my musical experience, as well as provided me with countless positive experiences, would be an understatement. I truly want you to have similar experiences with Cubase. It can happen for you if you practice each day, take breaks when overwhelmed, learn from your mistakes, and revel in your accomplishments. The music you make can enrich not only your life but also the lives of others. It can provide you with a creative outlet, additional income, and a way to make your living, and it has the potential to change the world. When all is said and done, it will leave a legacy of your time on earth. Music has that power. But like so many other of life's experiences, it is better when shared with others.

With all that in mind, roll up your sleeves, take a deep breath, and open your mind and heart to the opportunities Cubase has to offer you.

Acknowledgments

I'd like to thank Karl Steinberg and Manfred Rürup for having the vision and courage to create such revolutionary products.

Thanks to Bill Gibson and everyone at Hal Leonard for bringing me into this project. Thanks also to copy editor Joanna Dalin Sexton for making the book readable. Together, they all made it a joy to create this book and bring the information to you.

Thanks to Alan Macpherson, Brian McGovern, Greg Ondo, Lacy Privette, and Robert Sermeño at Steinberg North America, along with Melanie Becker and Andreas Stelling at Steinberg Media Technologies GmbH. Every author should be lucky enough to have the support of such wonderful people.

I would like to thank my parents—my "executive producers"—Connie Jo M. Hepworth-Woolston and the late Dr. Loel T. Hepworth, for recognizing the autodidact in me and providing an environment in which I could flourish.

This book is dedicated to my wonderful extended family, The Tudballs, and our fearless leaders, E. Arthur and Connie Jo Tudball. I still marvel at our groovy troop of disparate personalities and am continually enriched by the presence of all of you in my life.

Setup, Installation, and Configuration

If you've purchased this book, I will assume that you have a computer and have purchased a copy of Cubase 7 or Cubase Artist 7 (herein, all will be referred to as Cubase). That's great, but there are other items that are required to take full advantage of what Cubase has to offer. Then, when you have all of those items, you'll need to know how to hook each of them up and how to configure your computer to get your components working properly. In this first chapter, you will learn about:

- How to use this book with your level of Cubase.
- Minimum system requirements for Cubase.
- Running Cubase in 32-bit or 64-bit mode.
- Installing Cubase on your computer.
- Using the eLicenser Control Center and USB-eLicenser.
- The importance and process of creating a MySteinberg account.
- The differences between Cubase on Mac OS X and Windows.

USING THIS BOOK WITH DIFFERENT LEVELS OF CUBASE

For several years now, Steinberg (the company that creates Cubase) has used the "good, better, best" approach to making different levels of Cubase. You'll notice I said *levels*, not *versions*. That was on purpose. You see, the version of software usually denotes how up to date an application is: the higher the version number, the more current the software. However, software also comes in different levels that offer a "features versus price" balance. For example, with the release of Cubase 7, there are two levels: Cubase Artist 7 and the fully featured Cubase 7. (There may also be a third level called Cubase 7 Elements, which was not yet announced at the writing of this book.) Each level has different features for a different cost. While you can use this book with any level of Cubase, it was written with the full Cubase 7 level in mind. That is to say, I'll be covering features and operations in Cubase that may not exist in lesser levels.)

However, one of the most magical advantages of software is how easily it can be upgraded. Not only can you upgrade to a new version at a reduced cost (from Cubase 6 or 6.5 to Cubase 7), but you can also upgrade from a lower level to a higher one (from Cubase 7 Artist to Cubase 7). If you have a lesser level of Cubase and you find a feature of Cubase that would enhance your productivity, you can simply upgrade to a higher, more fully featured level. Steinberg offers those upgrades at http://www.steinberg.net. You can also find a feature-by-feature comparison of all the Cubase levels on their website.

So please bear in mind that I won't be indicating what features come in which level of Cubase. It would behoove you to visit the Steinberg website and familiarize yourself with the features of your level of Cubase. That way, you won't spend time learning about features your level doesn't currently have.

DOES CUBASE RUN BETTER ON A MAC OR PC?

Thirty years after the birth of MS-DOS (Microsoft Disk Operating System) and almost thirty years after the birth of the Macintosh, the debate over which platform is better rages on. Fortunately, Cubase is cross-platform; it runs on both Mac OS X and Microsoft Windows. Both the Mac and Windows versions are included on the installation DVD, or on the downloadable upgrade installer for upgrade purchasers. In fact, there are only miniscule differences between the operations of Cubase from one platform to the other. So miniscule, in fact, that many users (me included) have to remind themselves which platform they're currently using. For the most part, it really comes down to what you like better or what type of computer you currently use. With Cubase, you have freedom of choice.

However, sometimes that decision is made for us when we find a VST plug-in (either a virtual instrument or effect) that only runs on one platform. The vast majority of plug-ins are cross-platform. But I occasionally find an indispensable or exciting plug-in that only runs on Mac OS X or Microsoft Windows. If I want to avail myself of using that plug-in, I'd better use the platform upon which it runs.

I've used the following criteria to help my clients choose a platform: find the application (program) you want to use, determine which platform it runs on, and then find out if any third-party plug-ins you want to use are available on that platform. By using those criteria, you will quickly determine whether a Mac or Windows PC will better serve your computing needs. If you're like me and already own an Intel-based Mac, you can always use Apple's free Boot Camp software (which is included in Mac OS X) to allow your Mac to boot, and run Cubase 7 with Microsoft Windows. All it takes is buying a copy of Windows. I've used Boot Camp for years, and I can verify it's a very reliable method of running Windows on a Mac.

RECOMMENDED MINIMUM SYSTEM REQUIREMENTS

Many new users will ask the question "How modern and powerful does my computer need to be to run Cubase?" Steinberg has listed their minimum system requirements on their website. It's a good idea to take a look and see if your computer meets that minimum requirement.

I will list Steinberg's requirements here so that I can explain why they're important. But first, I'll define each of these items.

Operating System

This is the software that makes the computer functional. Every computer (with very few exceptions) will come with an operating system (herein referred to as "OS") preinstalled. Macs will come with some version of OS X, while PCs will come with some version of Windows. As long as you've had your Mac- or Windows-compatible PC computer for a year or two, it will probably have a compatible OS.

CPU

This is an acronym for Central Processing Unit. You can think of the CPU as the "brain" of your computer. Many of today's modern CPUs are a multicore design. They do all the calculations and number crunching that allow Cubase to turn your computer into a recording studio. Each core is a CPU, so a multicore CPU is a "sandwich" of two or more CPU cores.

RAM Memory

This is the "workspace" into which the OS loads applications and documents. It's ultrafast, and you can never have too much RAM. (See "Deciding to Run Cubase in 32-Bit or 64-Bit Mode" later in this chapter.)

Hard Disk Space

This is where the OS, applications, and documents are stored for later recall. DAW (Digital Audio Workstation) applications such as Cubase will require more hard-disk space to carry out their primary function, which is making music. As with RAM memory, you can never have too much hard-disk space.

Display Resolution

This is how many rows of pixels (dots on a computer screen) your monitor can display. There are horizontal and vertical measurements. My personal favorite is a resolution of 1920 X 1200 (1920 rows across by 1200 rows top to bottom). The higher the resolution, the more "stuff" you'll be able to see on the display. Conversely, low resolutions can make it impossible to see the Cubase user interface in its entirety.

Audio Interface

While all computers will come with some sort of sound device, these are woefully inadequate for music production. Therefore, a high-performance audio interface is recommended. The audio interface is used to get sound into and out of your computer and Cubase. (See "Choosing an Audio Interface" in chapter 2.) Most, but not all, audio interfaces come with CoreAudio (Mac) or ASIO (PC, Audio Streaming Input-Output) drivers, or use a generic driver from within the OS.

DVD Dual-Layer Optical Drive

Cubase ships on a dual-layer DVD and therefore can only be installed from a compatible DVD drive. If your computer does not have onboard DVD drives, you'll need to attach an external (USB or FireWire) DVD drive to install Cubase. Alternatively, you can use a DVD drive–equipped computer to create an ISO image of the DVD, copy that image to a flash drive or other USB storage device, and then connect that device to the computer upon which you wish to install Cubase.

USB Port

Universal Serial Bus, or USB, ports are ubiquitous on all modern computers. Cubase uses a copy-protection device called the USB-eLicenser that must be connected to the computer's USB port before Cubase will launch.

Internet Connection

Once you have Cubase installed, you'll need to activate the product via the Internet. I would also strongly advise you to register your copy of Cubase at http://www.steinberg.net. Registration requires that you create a MySteinberg account and is highly recommended for a number of reasons, not the least of which is getting your Cubase license replaced should your USB-eLicenser ever become damaged or lost.

Now that you know what all of these specifications are, here are the basic minimum system requirements for both platforms that Cubase runs on:

MAC
- Mac OS X version 10.7 (Lion) or higher.
- A dual-core CPU or higher (for example, an Intel Core 2 Duo, i5, i7, or higher).
- 2 GB (gigabytes) of RAM memory.
- 8 GB of free hard-disk space.
- Display (computer monitor) capable of 1280 X 800 or higher.

- CoreAudio-compatible audio interface.
- DVD-ROM dual-layer-compatible drive for installation; CD-R or DVD+/-R for audio-CD burning or archiving.
- One open USB port for USB-eLicenser.
- Internet connection required for product activation.

PC
- Windows 7, Windows 8, or higher; 32-bit or 64-bit.
- A dual-core CPU or higher (for example, an Intel Core 2 Duo, i5, i7, or higher or AMD multi-core processor).
- 2 GB (gigabytes) of RAM memory.
- 8 GB of free hard-disk space.
- Display (computer monitor) capable of 1280 X 800 or higher.
- Windows-compatible audio interface, but ASIO compatibility highly recommended.
- DVD-ROM dual-layer-compatible drive for installation; CD-R or DVD+/-R for audio-CD burning or archiving.
- One open USB port for USB-eLicenser.
- Internet connection required for product activation.

DECIDING TO RUN CUBASE IN 32-BIT OR 64-BIT MODE

Before you can install Cubase, you'll need to know about the memory-addressing modes of 32-bit and 64-bit. Cubase can run in either mode. The mode you choose will have nothing to do with the sound of Cubase but rather how much memory it can use. Simply put, the amount of RAM memory a computer and/or application (such as Cubase) can address is determined by three things:

- The amount of RAM installed in the computer.
- The 32-bit or 64-bit architecture of the OS.
- The 32-bit or 64-bit architecture of the application.

Are you confused yet? Well, you're not alone. You see, for a long time, RAM memory was exorbitantly expensive. (I remember, back in 1987, paying $584 for 16 MB [yes, megabytes] of RAM!) Therefore, computers didn't come with much, and OSs and applications were small enough that they didn't require much. But today, 2 GB of RAM is barely enough to load your OS, let alone run high-performance recording software such as Cubase. Having an abundant amount of RAM is critical, but only if your OS and applications can utilize, or "see," your computer's installed RAM in its entirety.

To illustrate this as simply as possible, I'll use the example of a computer with 3 GB of RAM. In this scenario, using a 64-bit OS or application would be of no benefit. That's because a 32-bit architecture can only utilize 3 (or sometimes 3.5 to 4) GB of RAM. However, if the computer had 4 or 8 GB of RAM or more, then using both a 64-bit OS and application would have distinct advantages: the user would be able to load more applications and load more data into those applications, and the OS wouldn't be using the page file as much. (Paging occurs when the amount of physical RAM memory becomes too low during the course of performing tasks on a computer. In that case, the OS must offload some of that data back onto the hard disk to clear some RAM space in which to work. The paging process can seriously impede your workflow, because the hard disk is about one thousand times slower than the RAM.)

32-Bit or 64-Bit Mode for Mac Users

Making the decision to run in 32-bit or 64-bit mode is simpler for Mac users. First, since Cubase 7 requires that you use OS X 10.7 (Lion) or higher, your OS is already 64-bit compatible. Plus, unlike the Windows version, Cubase for Mac installs in both 32-bit and 64-bit versions. (See "Enabling 64-Bit Mode on a Mac" later in this chapter.)

Next, you'll need to determine how much RAM your Mac has. Click on the Apple (logo) menu in the upper left-hand corner of your display, and select About This Mac.

Chances are very good that the OS version will be 10.7.X or 10.8.X. So what you really want to determine is the amount of installed RAM memory. In Figure 1.1, you can see that this Mac has 8 GB of RAM. Therefore, it would be beneficial to run Cubase in 64-bit mode.

Figure 1.1. The About This Mac display.

But before I show you how, there are some extenuating circumstances that may require you to keep Cubase in its default 32-bit mode:

32-BIT-ONLY FEATURES

As I write this book, there are still a handful of features and operations that cannot be performed while running in 64-bit mode. Current information regarding 64-bit compatibility can be found at http://www.steinberg.net.

PLUG-IN COMPATIBILITY

Some 32-bit plug-ins simply cannot work in 64-bit mode. Steinberg uses a technology called the VST Bridge to maintain 32-bit compatibility of plug-ins even when running Cubase in 64-bit mode. However, my experience has been that not all third-party plug-ins behave properly in 64-bit mode.

As time marches on, the list of operations dependent upon 32-bit or 64-bit mode will diminish. The third-party plug-in developers have and will offer updates to their software that add 64-bit architecture, thereby bypassing the need for VST Bridge. But for now, you will need to do a little research to deduce which mode is better for you.

32-Bit or 64-Bit Mode for Windows PC Users

Determining which mode to install and use on a Windows PC is a little more challenging. First of all, you'll need to determine if your version of Windows is 32-bit or 64-bit. Second, you must know how much RAM your PC has. Fortunately, those are easy tasks.

For Windows 7 users, click on your Start button in the lower left-hand corner of your display, then click on Computer. In the window that appears, click on System Properties in the Taskbar. For Windows 8 users, drag your mouse to the lower left-hand corner of your display and click the Start icon. When the Start screen appears (containing the tiles), right-click anywhere that doesn't contain a tile. A Toolbar will appear on the bottom of the display, which contains the All apps icon on its far right. Click that icon, then scroll to the right until you find the Windows System category, in which you'll find the Computer icon. Right-click on Computer, then click the Properties icon that appears in the Toolbar at the bottom of the display.

Whether you're using Windows 7 or Windows 8, the System Properties window will appear.

Figure 1.2. The System Properties window.

Notice the Installed memory (RAM) and System type. If the System type is 64-bit, then you can install Cubase as a 64-bit application. However, if the Installed memory (RAM) is 4 GB or lower, then the benefits of 64-bit will be limited. Only if your computer has more than 4 GB of RAM can you fully realize the benefits of using 64-bit mode.

When it comes to installing Cubase for Windows, you can choose either the 32- or 64-bit version. However, I strongly recommend that you install both versions. Yes, it will take a very small amount of hard disk space to do so. However, as with the Mac platform, there are some circumstances that must be considered:

32-BIT-ONLY FEATURES

As I write this book, there are still a handful of features and operations that cannot be performed while running in 64-bit mode. Current information regarding 64-bit compatibility can be found at http://www.steinberg.net.

PLUG-IN COMPATIBILITY

Some 32-bit plug-ins simply cannot work in 64-bit mode. Steinberg uses a technology called the VST Bridge to maintain 32-bit compatibility of plug-ins even when running Cubase in 64-bit mode. However, my experience has been that not all third-party plug-ins behave properly in 64-bit mode.

That's why I would recommend installing both versions. That way, you can switch between 32-bit and 64-bit modes simply by launching the appropriate version. For example, if you need to use specific 32-bit-only plug-ins, just launch the 32-bit version. When you need to load a big project that requires more RAM, launch the 64-bit version. You can run the 32-bit mode of Cubase even if your version of Windows is 64-bit.

As time marches on, the list of operations dependent upon 32-bit or 64-bit mode will diminish. The third-party plug-in developers have and will offer updates to their software that adds 64-bit architecture, thereby bypassing the need for VST Bridge. But for now, you will need to do a little research to deduce which mode is better for you.

INSTALLING CUBASE ON YOUR COMPUTER

The process of installing Cubase on your computer is virtually identical when it comes to the Mac and PC versions. However, there are a few differences I will reveal. Installation is a very simple process, and the Cubase installer will prompt you through most steps. Therefore, I will not take you through the entire process, but rather some of the important steps that might require a bit more forethought.

To start the installation process, you'll need to insert your Cubase installation DVD into your optical drive. (For users upgrading from previous versions of Cubase who have downloaded the installer, double-click the file that was downloaded.) When you insert the disc, it will appear on your desktop (Mac) or on the Computer page. (Windows 7 users, click on the Start button, then click on Computer. Windows 8 users, drag your mouse to the lower left-hand corner of the display and click Start, then right-click on any blank section of the Start screen to expose the Toolbar at the bottom, then click the All apps icon on the right-hand side. Scroll to the Windows System settings on the far right side, and click the Computer icon.)

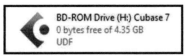

BD-ROM Drive (H:) Cubase 7
0 bytes free of 4.35 GB
UDF

Figure 1.3. The Cubase Install DVD icon.

Double-click on that icon. Within the next window, you will find the Start Center icon. Double-click that icon to launch the Start Center.

Figure 1.4. The Start Center Welcome screen.

The Start Center Welcome screen will appear, prompting you to click on a flag to choose the preferred language. After you click on a flag, the Installation screen will appear.

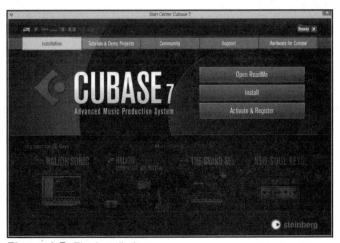

Figure 1.5. The Installation screen.

At the upper left-hand side of the screen, you will find the Installation tab. To the right of the large Cubase 7 icon and logo, you will find three large red text buttons: Open ReadMe, Install, and Activate & Register. (The other installers at the bottom offer trial versions of the full HALion Sonic, HALion Symphonic Orchestra, The Grand SE3, and several other very useful sound libraries and instruments. You may install these optional trial programs; however, none of them are required for using this book.) I would recommend clicking on the Open ReadMe button. (You will be prompted about installing Acrobat Reader if it is not currently on your computer.) Within the ReadMe file is very detailed information about the installation process. If you need further installation details, refer to this ReadMe file.

Click on the Install button to launch the Cubase installer. The next screen that appears takes a little explanation because it's a new feature.

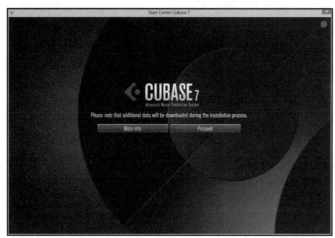

Figure 1.6. The additional data download window.

When you click the Proceed button, the installer will automatically download and install the most current version of Cubase 7. (Prerelease and beta releases will need to be downloaded and installed manually should you choose to try them.) This feature will require that your computer is connected to the Internet. However, if you'd rather install the version on your DVD (or downloaded installer), be sure your computer is disconnected from the Internet prior to installation. Go ahead and click the Proceed button to continue.

From here, the installation process will prompt you through a very straightforward set of steps. But PC users will be presented with this window:

Figure 1.7. 32-bit or 64-bit-mode installer (Windows only).

This is the screen that allows 64-bit Microsoft Windows users to choose which mode(s) to install. (If your Windows version is 32-bit, you will not see this screen.) As I stated previously, I prefer to install both modes, which requires two separate installation procedures: one for the 32-bit mode version and another for the 64-bit version. (See "32-Bit or 64-Bit Mode for Windows PC Users" earlier in this chapter.)

Note: During the process, you may notice the installation of a program called the eLicenser Control Center. This is software that runs the USB-eLicenser (see "Using the USB-eLicenser" later in this chapter) and is required to run Cubase on your computer. Please allow the entire installation of that program.

After the installation process completes, there are still some tasks you must perform before you can start using Cubase. To that end, please continue with this chapter.

ENABLING 64-BIT MODE ON A MAC

When you install Cubase, it is configured for 32-bit mode by default. So if you want to run Cubase in 64-bit mode, you must alter its configuration. It's a fairly simple thing to do. From the Finder, click on the Go menu and select Applications. A window will appear with a list of all the applications installed on the computer. Single-click on the Cubase icon, then click on the File menu and select Get Info.

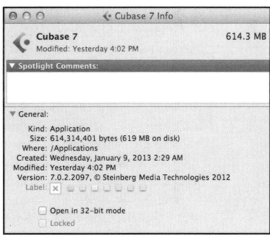

In the General area (which you may have to expand by clicking on the triangle next to "General"), you'll see the "Open in 32-bit mode" checkbox. Uncheck that box to enable Cubase to launch in 64-bit mode, or make sure the box is checked to launch in 32-bit mode, then close the window and launch Cubase normally.

Figure 1.8. The Cubase 7 Info window.

USING THE USB-ELICENSER

If you purchased Cubase for the first time, then the USB-eLicenser was in the box. If you've purchased an upgrade from a previous or lower version of Cubase, then you probably have a USB-eLicenser and know what it's all about. But for those who haven't worked with hardware copy protection before, let me help you understand what it is and how to use it.

Note: Cubase and Cubase Artist use the USB-eLicenser, while some other Steinberg-branded software uses a Soft-eLicenser that installs a software license on your computer.

Figure 1.9. The USB-eLicenser.

At first glance, the USB-eLicenser is easily mistaken for a USB flash drive or "thumb drive." Instead of containing computer documents such as photos and word-processor files, the USB-eLicenser contains the license for Cubase. That license must be downloaded and installed on the USB-eLicenser before you can start using Cubase. (See "Entering Your Activation Code" below.)

The USB-eLicenser is also known as a "dongle." Dongles have been around since the early days of high-performance software. It is a copy-protection device. Without the USB-eLicenser connected to a USB port of your computer, Cubase will not run. Think of it as the keys to your car; if you don't have the key, you won't be able to start the car. Suffice it to say, the USB-eLicenser is a very important component in your Cubase-equipped studio.

Instead of having a protracted discussion of the pros and cons of software copy protection, let me say this: of all the copy-protection schemes (serial number, challenge/response, etc.), I like the USB-eLicenser the best. (Or perhaps I should say I dislike it the least?) It allows me to install Cubase on all of my computers. I regularly use Cubase on nine different Macs and PCs. All I have to do is plug the USB-eLicenser into the computer I'll be using, and away I go. Other schemes allow installation on only two computers. In my case, that's a difficult proposition. The biggest advantage to the USB-eLicenser is that it protects the future development of Cubase and the other Steinberg products upon which I rely. Sure it's a drag, but so is learning a whole new program just because rampant piracy caused the demise of your trusted software. So not only does the USB-eLicenser protect Steinberg; it also protects your investment in the software, and possibly your livelihood.

Every copy-protection scheme has idiosyncrasies, and the USB-eLicenser is no exception. With that in mind, let's talk about them so that you can avoid disaster. You must realize that it's a piece of hardware. Therefore, it can be forgotten, damaged, or lost. Any one of those possibilities will prevent you from launching Cubase and working on your music. That's why I strongly recommend registering your USB-eLicenser. Registration is the only way for Steinberg to verify that you are a registered user and therefore eligible for a replacement USB-eLicenser should yours become damaged or lost.

Entering Your Activation Code

After you've installed Cubase or Cubase Artist, you'll need to download the license onto the USB-eLicenser. Or in the case of some other Steinberg products, you'll need to download the Soft-eLicenser. Either way, you'll need to enter the activation code.

Note: Retail levels of Cubase and Cubase Artist ship with a USB-eLicenser with a twenty-five-day license. That allows you to start using Cubase right away and also gives you time to get to an Internet-connected computer. After the twenty-fifth day, you will need to download a license, as outlined in these instructions.

The activation code is a thirty-two-digit string of alphanumeric characters that can be found on a single sheet of paper contained in the Cubase box, or was sent to you in an e-mail if you're upgrading. Either way, it's the activation code that allows you to download your Cubase license.

First, you must make sure you have the USB-eLicenser connected to a USB port of your computer. Next, run the eLicenser Control Center software.

Note: The license download process requires an Internet connection. If the computer with which you'll be using Cubase is not connected to the Internet, you'll need to install the eLicenser Control Center software onto a computer that has an Internet connection. Then you can connect the USB-eLicenser to that computer and download the license to it.

Mac users: From the Finder, choose the Go menu and select Applications. On the window that appears, double-click eLicenser Control Center.

Windows 7 users: Click the Start button in the lower left-hand corner of the Windows desktop, click All Programs, and then click on the eLicenser folder and select eLicenser Control Center.

Windows 8 users: Drag your mouse to the lower left-hand corner of your display and click Start, then right-click on the Start screen background and click the All apps icon on the right side of the Toolbar that appears at the bottom of the display. Find the eLicenser category, and click on eLicenser Control Center.

Figure 1.10. The eLicenser Control Center interface.

Have your thirty-two-digit code ready, and click on the Enter Activation Code button in the upper left-hand corner of the interface.

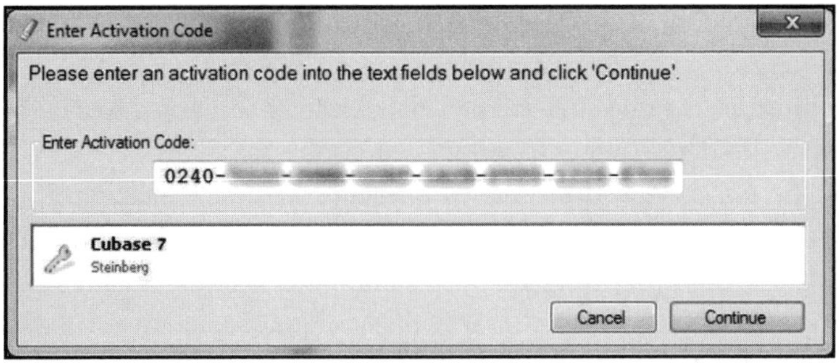

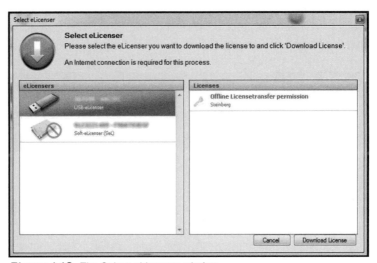

Figure 1.11. The Activation Code window.

Enter the thirty-two-digit code in the window. Every Steinberg code I've seen begins with "0240," but be very careful to enter the code precisely. Otherwise the license download will fail. When you enter the very last digit, the license type will appear in the bottom of the window. Click the Continue button to move on to the Select eLicenser window.

Figure 1.12. The Select eLicenser window.

Most users will see both a USB-eLicenser and a Soft-eLicenser in this window. (If you don't see the former, make sure the USB-eLicenser is connected to the USB port of the computer and that the eLicenser Control Center software was installed properly. You may also need to remove and reattach the USB-eLicenser or reboot your computer.) Click on the USB-eLicenser on the left-hand side of the window (represented by a blue USB-eLicenser icon), and then click on Download License. (If you have multiple USB-eLicensers, make sure to choose the one you wish the license to be downloaded to.) The License Download window will appear.

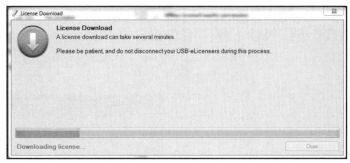

Figure 1.13. The License Download window.

The directions say that the download can require several minutes. In my experience, it takes less than a minute. Nevertheless, follow the instructions on the window to be patient, and don't remove the USB-eLicenser.

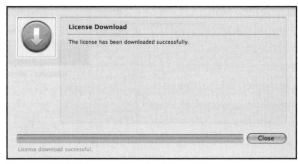

Figure 1.14. License Download Complete.

After the license download is complete, you will receive a confirmation screen. You can now launch and start using Cubase. If you received an error message during the download, please try again, and make sure your computer is connected to the Internet.

ADDING CUBASE TO THE "DOCK" (MAC)

The "Dock" is located at the very bottom of your screen. It provides a very convenient way to launch Cubase quickly. However, you must add Cubase to the Dock manually.

From the Finder, click on the Go menu and select Applications. Locate the Cubase icon, click and drag the icon to your preferred position on the Dock, and then release the mouse button.

Now you can launch Cubase by clicking on its icon in the Dock.

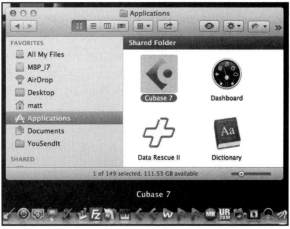

Figure 1.15. Adding Cubase to the Dock.

"PINNING" CUBASE TO THE TASKBAR AND START MENU (WINDOWS 7)

The Taskbar and Start menu are located in the lower left-hand corner of your screen. They provide a convenient way to launch Cubase quickly. However, you must add, or "pin,"

Cubase to the Dock manually. Plus, if you've installed both 32-bit and 64-bit versions of Cubase, you'll need to pin both versions.

From the Windows desktop, click on the Start button and then click on All Programs. You are going to pin the 32-bit version of Cubase by first clicking on the Steinberg Cubase folder and then right-clicking on the Cubase icon.

Click on Pin to Taskbar, and then click on Pin to Start Menu. (The submenu should remain open during the operations.)

Now pin the 64-bit version by clicking on the Steinberg Cubase 64-bit folder and then right-clicking on the Cubase icon. Click on the "Pin" commands described in the previous paragraph. When you're done, both 32-bit and 64-bit icons will be added to both the Taskbar and the Start menu.

Figure 1.16. The submenu with Pin commands.

If you installed both the 32-bit and 64-bit versions, I would recommend changing their names in the Start menu. Click on the Start button to reveal the Start menu. You'll notice that the 32-bit version is named "Cubase," while the 64-bit version is named "Cubase (2)." Right-click on either icon, and select Properties from the submenu. The Properties window will appear. Click on the General tab, wherein you'll see the Cubase Shortcut icon. To the right of the icon is a field into which you can enter the desired name. I would recommend something like "Cubase 32-bit" and "Cubase 64-bit," respectively. That way, you'll know which version of Cubase you'll be launching when you click on either icon.

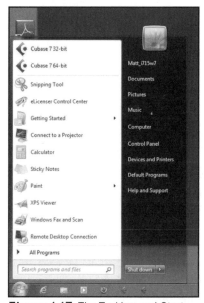

The icons in the Taskbar do not have names, and they look identical. For this reason, you'll have to remember which version is on the left and which version is on the right.

Figure 1.17. The Taskbar and Start menus with Cubase pinned within.

"PINNING" CUBASE TO THE TASKBAR AND START SCREEN (WINDOWS 8)

The Start screen is a new feature of Windows 8. It allows you to place all of your favorite Windows features and apps onto one screen, which makes them easier to find and launch. However, the installation of an app (such as Cubase) does not necessarily add the program to the Start screen. I would recommend adding Cubase (both 32- and 64-bit versions if you installed both) to both the Start screen and the Taskbar. (See "'Pinning' Cubase to the Taskbar and Start Menu (Windows 7)" above for instructions on changing the program names in the Taskbar.)

Drag your mouse to the lower left-hand corner of the display and click the Start icon, then right-click on the Start screen background and click the All apps icon at the right of the Toolbar at the bottom of the display. Then locate the Cubase 7 app(s). The 32-bit version will be located in the Steinberg Cubase 7 32bit category, and the 64-bit version will be located in the Steinberg Cubase 7 64bit category.

Right-click on the Cubase 7 app icon, and the Toolbar will appear at the bottom of the display. Located on the Toolbar are icons for Pin to Start and Pin to Taskbar.

Figure 1.18. The Cubase 7 64bit category and icon.

Figure 1.19. The Pin to Start and Pin to Taskbar icons.

Click each icon to complete the process. (Repeat the process with the 32-bit version, if necessary.) When you're done, you can drag your mouse to the lower left-hand corner of your display and click the Start icon, or type the Windows key on your computer keyboard to show the Start screen.

Now you can type the Windows key on your computer keyboard and click the desired Cubase 7 32-bit and 64-bit icons, depending upon which version you wish to launch.

Figure 1.20. Cubase apps (32- and 64-bit versions) added to Start screen.

CREATING A MYSTEINBERG ACCOUNT

As I mentioned previously in this chapter, creating a MySteinberg account and registering your software is very important. Steinberg has made this process fairly simple. First, the computer from which you're registering must be connected to the Internet. Next, from the Installation tab of the Start Center, click the Activate & Register button. (See Figure 1.5.) Or if you've already put away your installation DVD, you can also launch Cubase, and then close the Project Assistant window when it appears. The Registration Reminder window will appear.

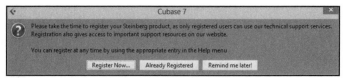

Figure 1.21. The Registration Reminder window.

On the window, you can choose from Register Now, Already Registered, and Remind me later! (Notice also that you can also register at any time by clicking on the Steinberg Hub menu and selecting Register Now.) Due to the importance of registering, I would recommend you take a few minutes and do so now. Using any method I've described will take you to the MySteinberg page at http://www.steinberg.net. There you will find more information about downloading a license and the registration process.

Entering Your eLicenser Serial Number

During the registration process, you'll be asked to enter the serial number of either your USB-eLicenser or, in the case of some other Steinberg products, your Soft-eLicenser. There are a couple of little tricks I've learned that can help you streamline this process.

First, you need to know that the twelve- or thirteen-digit USB-eLicenser serial numbers are case sensitive. Make sure you always use capital letters when entering the serial number. However, there's an easier way to copy the serial number and register your USB-eLicenser at MySteinberg. Launch the eLicenser Control Center app, then click on the Registration menu and choose your eLicenser that contains the Cubase 7 license. To the right of the USB-eLicenser are two options for Register at MySteinberg (which will start the registration process), or you can select Copy Serial Number if you've already started the registration process.

Second, Soft-eLicenser serial numbers are up to twenty digits long. You can use the same procedure for registering a Soft-eLicenser as for registering a USB-eLicenser. Simply launch the eLicenser Control Center app, then click on the Registration menu and choose your Soft-eLicenser from the menu. To the right of the Soft-eLicenser are two options for

Register at MySteinberg (which will start the registration process), or you can select Copy Serial Number if you've already started the registration process.

UPGRADING FROM CUBASE ARTIST TO CUBASE

One of the greatest things Steinberg has added to Cubase 7 is the speed with which you can upgrade from Cubase Artist to Cubase. During the Cubase Artist installation process, all of the software necessary to run full Cubase was already installed. Therefore, all you'd need to do is purchase an upgrade code at the shop at http://www.steinberg.net. Using that code will allow you to download the Cubase 7 upgrade via the eLicenser Control Center. That means you don't have to wait for the upgrade while it's being shipped to you. Plus if you find a feature of Cubase that would be beneficial for your music production, you can upgrade from Cubase Artist at any time, day or night.

ALMOST READY TO LAUNCH

Since you've completed the installation, activation, and registration processes, I'm sure you're excited to launch Cubase and start your music production. You could certainly do so at this time. However, in the next chapter, I'll be offering some critical information about other hardware, such as audio interfaces, microphones, and MIDI devices. Plus there will be really important information about how to use this book to its full potential and how to set up your studio for proper monitoring. Reading the next chapter will help you get started with Cubase the right way—the first time.

Hardware and Studio Configuration

2

A modern recording studio can be defined as a physical structure full of recording equipment. It can also be defined as a city bus while you have your laptop open and are mixing music on your way home from work. But regardless of whether your studio is brick and mortar or simply a laptop running Cubase, the process of recording still relies heavily on hardware. In the last chapter, I talked about a very important piece of hardware: the computer upon which you will run Cubase. But it doesn't end there. There are a myriad of hardware devices that are required for the recording process. You will be using some combination of microphones, keyboards, turntables, cables, and monitor speakers—most likely, all of the above. So this chapter is dedicated to choosing the right hardware for your purposes and configuring it to work with Cubase. In this chapter, you will learn about:

- Choosing an audio interface.
- Choosing microphones.
- Adding a MIDI controller or keyboard.
- Adding the right hardware for your music-production needs.
- PC versus Mac modifier keys.
- Configuring your studio space.
- Proper monitoring of audio recordings.

CHOOSING AN AUDIO INTERFACE

One of the most critical components in a DAW-based recording studio is the audio interface. It is the audio device through which you capture and monitor the recordings you're making. Most new DAW users make the easy mistake of trying to use their computers' built-in audio interfaces. Without going into a protracted discussion of why, the bottom line is that these are woefully inadequate for music production. Not only is the audio quality dubious, but also I've never seen a computer with high-quality XLR microphone preamps and phantom power. Suffice it to say, trying to use your computer's built-in audio interface will present you with challenges that are easily and inexpensively overcome by getting a high-quality audio interface.

There are a wide variety of different audio interfaces that you can use with Cubase. In fact, Steinberg is greatly responsible for the proliferation of high-performance audio interfaces. Steinberg created a technology called ASIO, which is an acronym for Audio Streaming Input/Output. It is a driver model that most audio-interface manufacturers adopted, due to its robust design and the fact that Steinberg made the ASIO technology license free. Therefore, all audio-interface manufacturers could create ASIO-compatible hardware without having to pay Steinberg for the technology. The outcome has been a veritable cornucopia of high-quality, highly specialized audio interfaces from which to choose.

With that variety comes the challenge of choosing the right one. But I can help you decide by introducing you to my method of choosing an interface. I recommend that you use my S.F.P. criteria, for they can quickly narrow the selection and help you choose the best audio interface for your purposes.

The S.F.P. Criteria

S.F.P. is an acronym for sound, features, and price, and should be used in that order (sound being the most important point and price being the least). The criteria are very useful no matter what audio commodity you're buying. I've used them to purchase everything from cables to audio interfaces, even for instruments. Once you've used them, you'll see how they can help you choose the right device. But in this case, let's use them to choose the right audio interface for you.

SOUND

Finding the audio interface with the right sound is usually the most challenging of the criteria to determine. How an interface sounds could be defined either by sound quality or sound character. I feel it should define both. The quality and variety of mic preamps (microphone preamplifiers) and AD/DA (analog to digital/digital to analog) converters has never been higher. Put simply, it's difficult to find a bad-sounding third-party audio interface these days. Therefore, it's better to base your sound criteria on character rather than quality.

The most popular audio interfaces on the market today have their own mic preamps. Having the preamps onboard allows you to plug microphones directly into the audio interface without the need for additional hardware such as a mixer or separate mic preamp. Therefore, having built-in mic preamps not only saves you money but also makes recording more convenient and less noisy.

Since audio interfaces are digital, you will have to make sure that the one you choose has appropriately high-performance digital specifications. Look for an interface that is at least 24-bit and has a sample frequency of at least 44.1 kHz. The amplitude of sound is measured in digital bits, while the frequencies of sound are measured by the sample frequency. In either case, the higher the numbers, the better chance you have of capturing the essence of the sound you're recording.

Some of you might be hoping for me to reveal the best-sounding audio interface with the best-sounding mic preamps. However, the subjective nature of how each of us perceives sound makes that determination impossible. In other words, I could no more accurately determine which mic preamp sounds best than I could which bass guitar sounds best, which country album sounds best, and which seventeenth-century composer wrote the best-sounding baroque music. I could certainly answer those questions (Status; Johnny Cash: At Folsom Prison; J. S. Bach), but I'm making those judgments based only on what I hear with my ears. Since I don't have your ears, I cannot predict what you would define as the best-sounding anything, let alone an audio interface.

The easy answer to this question is the same as the answer to most recording questions: use your ears. Sit down with an audio interface, and really listen to the recording and the playback of your music. Use microphones you're familiar with, and listen in your studio through your speakers. Then, and only then, can you truly determine the audio interface with the best sound character and sound quality. For example, I went to my local music store, and they let me borrow five popular audio interfaces. (Yes, a significant yet refundable down payment was required.) I spent the evening recording and the morning listening to each one. Which interface did I feel sounded the best?

Figure 2.1. The Steinberg MR816CSX audio interface.

I found the Steinberg MR816CSX to be the best-sounding audio interface of the bunch. It has very unique-sounding D-Pre (Darlington) mic preamps. They're not the flattest-sounding preamps you'll ever hear (flat rarely sounds good), but they have an extraordinary sonic character. That being said, recording and listening to a variety of audio interfaces will help you determine which one sounds best to you.

FEATURES

After you've found a great-sounding audio interface, you'll need to determine if it has the features you'll need. The list of features on a modern audio interface varies widely. However, I'll tell you about the three most critical features to consider.

The first is number of discrete input channels. The number of input channels will determine how many discrete tracks you can record simultaneously. For example, a Steinberg UR22 interface has two inputs.

That will allow you to record one stereo track (such as the output of a synthesizer) or up to two mono inputs (such as a mic and guitar) simultaneously. When I'm working

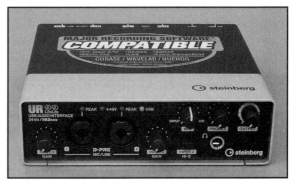

Figure 2.2. The Steinberg UR22 audio interface.

on my solo projects, I rarely need to record with more than one or two inputs.

But there are situations that require more than two inputs to be recorded simultaneously. For example, a drum set would normally require at least three inputs (kick drum, left overhead, and right overhead) and usually many more to capture each drum instrument on its own discrete track. A five-piece drum set normally requires kick, snare, hi-hat, tom 1, tom 2, floor tom, overhead left, and overhead right. That's a total of eight inputs all recorded simultaneously. If that's the case, you'll need to find an interface that features eight discrete inputs. The Steinberg MR816CSX is such an interface.

The next feature is compatibility. If you find a great-sounding interface such as the Apogee Duet and you use a Windows PC, you should be aware that the Duet (like most Apogee interfaces) are Mac only.

Make sure the audio interface you're considering is compatible with your computer platform.

The last feature to consider is connectivity. In other words, how will the interface connect to your computer, and how will the devices you wish to record connect to the interface? I'll start with the first part of that equation. Audio interfaces connect to a computer by one of four

Figure 2.3. The Apogee Duet audio interface.

methods: USB, FireWire, Thunderbolt, or PCI. The first two allow you to easily move the device from one computer to another and are by far the most popular types of computer connectivity. (Apple's Thunderbolt technology is very promising, albeit not widespread as of the writing of this book.) The last method of PCI (or PCI-X, or PCIe) uses a card slot inside of the computer, which can be higher performance at the cost of portability. Just make sure that the interface that you're considering can connect to your computer.

Now I'll consider audio connectivity—that is, being able to connect all of the devices you plan to record.

For example, if you're capturing digital data from a DAT (Digital Audio Tape) recorder, you'll need an interface with S/PDIF (Sony/Philips Digital Interface Format) or AES/ EBU (Audio Engineering Society/European Broadcasting Union) input ports. Or if you're using a mic preamp (such as the PreSonus DigiMax D8) with an ADAT optical interface

Figure 2.4. S/PDIF and ADAT ports on the Steinberg MR816CSX.

(a.k.a. lightpipe) connection, make sure the interface you're considering also has an ADAT optical interface.

PRICE

Price is the easiest of the criteria with which to choose an audio interface: if you can't afford it, it won't help you make any music. That might sound harsh, but it's the truth. Fortunately, we live in an age where quality and functionality goes up, while at the same time, cost comes down. Today's modern audio interfaces can cost $100 or less. Of course, some of the more potent interfaces can run several hundred dollars. But by using the S.F.P. criteria, you will be able to find a great-sounding interface that serves you well at a price you can afford.

ADDITIONAL HARDWARE REQUIREMENTS

An audio interface is just one piece of hardware you'll need. There are others, so I'd like to go over a few. Bear in mind that you may not need all of the following items. For example, if you're not recording "real" instruments (such as acoustic guitars, vocals, or trumpets), then you won't need microphones. However, there are some items that are absolutely necessary for music production.

Microphones

If you plan to capture sound from acoustic devices such as vocals and guitars, then you will certainly need a number of microphones. The importance of high-quality microphones cannot be overstated. Microphones are the "ears" of your recordings. In fact, many of the "British invasion" records (such as those by the Beatles and the Who) still hold up to today's audio standards simply because the microphones used during the recording processes were exceptionally good. A great microphone recorded on average equipment will always sound better than an average microphone recorded on great equipment. The rule is: unless your budget is extremely limited, never, ever, ever skimp on microphones.

It's also important to consider the instrument you're recording before choosing which microphone to record it with. For example, I'm a big fan of the Audio Technica AT4033/CL side address microphone. In fact, I own eight of them. It's a very affordable, wonderful-sounding general-purpose microphone when recording vocals, acoustic guitars, brass, strings, woodwinds, and more. However, it wouldn't be my first choice for snare drum, bass drum, or a guitar-amp speaker edge, nor would I use it for live-performance vocal recording. For those applications, you'd be better served by choosing a microphone specially designed for those purposes.

Another important recommendation is this: unless you simply can't afford a recording microphone, don't try to record vocals with a live-performance microphone such as a Shure SM58 or other handheld model. While they sound good on the stage and are of rugged design, they are ill suited for vocal capture in a recording studio.

Getting a good pop filter will also help you keep the unavoidable "plosives" in the consonants of words such as power and popular from overloading the microphone. Steadman makes some truly innovative metal designs that tame the plosives without coloring the sound.

I would recommend reading Hal Leonard Recording Method—Book One: Microphones and Mixers for a thoughtful tutorial on choosing recording microphones.

Studio Monitors

Studio monitor speakers are another critical component to your modern recording studio. Unlike consumer-grade speakers, studio monitors are designed to accurately reproduce an average- or "flat"-sounding recording. The idea is that if you can make a good-sounding mix on average speakers, the mix will sound even better when played on consumer speakers.

Many new DAW users will be tempted to mix with headphones or consumer speakers they already own. Doing so is an understandable yet profound mistake! Many unwitting users will waste hours mixing and remixing their music, because while it sounds great on their consumer speakers, it sounds terrible on their car stereo or MP3 player. To spare you from this fate, spend some time at your local music store listening to different studio monitors. Take a combination of your own music along with some of your favorite CDs. That way, you'll be able to judge the studio monitors by listening to music you're familiar with. Try and do it during the day and not on a weekend; otherwise the salespeople will be busy and your ears will be competing with some guy playing the opening riff to "Crazy Train" over and over and over…

Headphones

While you cannot accurately mix on them, headphones are critical when recording acoustic instruments, vocals, or anything that requires a microphone. The rule is that a musician must be able to hear a mix of his or her performance along with the previously recorded tracks. However, if the mix is being played back through speakers, the microphones will record that sound along with the desired sound. This phenomenon is known as a "feedback loop." Not only will it negatively impact the recording, but it will also result in obnoxious squealing and howling if the volume becomes too loud. Either way, your tracks will be ruined.

Instead, the musicians must wear headphones. They'll be able to hear the mix and their instruments without the sound being looped back into the microphone. I would recommend getting a pair of closed-back headphones. Open-back designs might leak sound back into the microphone and could also be prone to high-pitched squealing feedback. Try and get headphones with large diaphragms. They produce richer bass and are easier for a musician to use in a "one-off" configuration (one cuff on the ear, the other cuff off).

Another consideration during the mixing process is determining how the mix will sound on consumer headphones. It's a good idea to take those earbuds that came with your iPhone (or other "i" device) and listen to your mix through those. They are certainly not the pinnacles of headphone fidelity, but they will allow you to hear your music as it will be heard by the public who use those ubiquitous small, white earbuds.

MIDI Controller and/or MIDI Interface

If you're planning to use MIDI or VST (virtual) Instrument tracks, you'll need a MIDI controller with which to enter the data. If you have a keyboard-equipped synthesizer, you're all set. Such a synthesizer would have either MIDI ports or a built-in USB MIDI interface. But if cost and/or portability are important, you may want to consider a dedicated controller design with an onboard USB port. Dedicated controllers have no sound of their own, relying instead on the sounds generated by Cubase or instrument plug-ins. They plug directly into your computer's USB port, so no dedicated MIDI interface will be required. Since they lack their own internal sound-generation hardware, controllers are more affordable, and they come in a wide variety of keyboard and pad-style designs. I carry a small twenty-five-note controller in my "go" bag, so that I can record MIDI tracks when I'm on the road. A visit to your local music store will reveal numerous MIDI controllers in every configuration and price range. Checking out the offerings from Alesis, Arturia, and Nektar would be a good place to start.

However, if your keyboard or controller does not have its own USB port, you might need to invest in a dedicated MIDI interface. Before you do, determine if your audio interface has MIDI ports (in, out). If it does, you can use those to establish MIDI communication between Cubase and your external MIDI controller. Otherwise, you'll need a USB-to-

MIDI interface: basically, a converter with a USB port on one end and MIDI ports on the other. If you have multiple MIDI devices without their own USB ports, the MIDI interface you choose should be of a multiport design. Such interfaces would have only one USB port but two, four, six, or more MIDI ports, and spare you from purchasing a separate interface for every MIDI device.

KEEPING UP TO DATE

The speed at which music technology evolves is staggering. Add to that the rapid pace of operating system and hardware development, and you have a recipe for crashes and operational weirdness. To minimize the chances of getting detoured by such an event, I strongly recommend that you keep all of your software and hardware up to date. If your computer is connected to the Internet, both Macs and Windows PCs will update themselves with your approval. However, programs such as Cubase and eLicenser Control Center will require a manual update process. Visit both http://www.steinberg.net and http://www.elicenser.net for the most up-to-date program versions.

Your other computer hardware (including but not limited to audio and MIDI interfaces) comes with driver software that connects the devices to the operating system and Cubase. Those drivers are usually found on an installer disc that came in the box. However, I strongly recommend that you not install those drivers without checking the manufacturer's website for the most current drivers. You see, the disc in the box got shipped, stored, stocked, and possibly even reshipped before you received it. Therefore, it will probably contain obsolete drivers. Out-of-date drivers are notorious for causing a myriad of computer problems. For that reason, visit the website of your audio and MIDI interfaces regularly, and make sure you download and install the most current drivers. (This practice is prudent for all computer hardware, including printers, scanners, cameras, mice, smart phones, etc.)

WINDOWS, MACS, MICE, AND MODIFIERS

Cubase is cross-platform, meaning that it runs on both Windows and Mac operating systems. That's great for you, but it makes it more challenging when writing or reading this book because of the differences between mice and keyboards. I've come up with a simple way to streamline the deceptions of operations that are mouse- or keyboard-centric.

Using and Enabling Right-Click on a Mac

There are a lot of functions in Cubase that are accessed by right-clicking your mouse. That's an easy proposition for Windows users, because their mice have two buttons: one for left and one for right. However, Apple hardware only has one mouse button, which makes right-clicking a little harder. By default, Mac users will need to hold the Control key on their keyboards and then click on something to reveal the right-click submenu. However, you can enable your Apple-branded mouse or (MacBook, MacBook Pro, MacBook Air) trackpad to use right-click. Those settings are located in the System Preferences under the Apple logo menu in the upper left-hand corner of your screen. Click on Mouse and/ or Trackpad in the Hardware row, and enable the secondary click options for right-click. That way, when you read "right-click" in this book, you'll be able to access the right-click submenus with your mouse instead of having to Control-click.

Over the past few years, Apple has been including little videos in the Mouse and Trackpad control panels that show you the "gestures." While you're configuring your secondary click options, have a peak at the videos, for they will help instruct you on how to use gestures. (You may need to consult the online help for your Mac for further details.)

Key Commands and Modifier Keys

Key commands (a.k.a. keyboard shortcuts) can make short work of commonly used software operations. Instead of relying on using your mouse to select a menu, drag down the list, select an operation, and finally click on OK, a key command allows you to execute the operation simply by typing a key (or series of keys) on your computer keyboard. I'm a firm believer in key commands, and this book will show you how to use them.

However, a standard computer keyboard wouldn't offer many key commands without the invention of modifier keys. Those are the keys that work in combination with the standard keys to expand the number of key combinations.

A Windows PC has the following modifier keys:

Shift
Control (Ctrl)
Alternate (Alt)

An Apple Macintosh has the following modifier keys:

Shift
Control (Ctrl)
Option
Command (⌘)

You can see that both platforms share the Shift key, so that modifier is interchangeable. The Control (Ctrl) key is also found on both platforms; however, it is not interchangeable. Most cross-platform applications (such as Cubase) interchange the Windows Control key with the Mac Command key. I know that can be confusing. To that end, let me show you how I'll be indicating the modifier keys.

The Copy operation on a Windows PC is: Control + C. That is to say, to execute a copy, press and hold the Control key and then type the "C" key on your computer keyboard.

(Note: the "+" in the key command indicates a combination of modifier and key, not actually typing the "+" key.)

The Copy operation on an Apple Macintosh is: Command + C. That is to say, to execute a copy, press and hold the Command key, and then type the "C" key on your computer keyboard. (See the note about the "+" indicator in the previous paragraph.)

Now let me show you how the Copy operation will be indicated in this book:

Ctrl/Command + C

Notice that the Windows modifier (Ctrl) comes first, while the Mac modifier (Command) comes second, separated by a "/." That is the way it shall be throughout this book. However, in the case where unique modifiers are used with the interchangeable Shift key, the key command will appear as:

Shift + Ctrl/Command + L

That is to say, pressing and holding both the Shift and the related PC/Mac modifier key, then typing the "L" key, will execute the operation. In this case, it's the Lock operation.

"F" or Function Keys

Some of the most commonly used Cubase key commands are located on the function keys of your computer keyboard. The function keys appear above the number keys of your QWERTY keyboard. They're usually labeled—F1 through F12, or in some cases there will be up to F19 or more. If you're using Windows, it's most likely that you can just type the key to access the key command. For example, typing F3 will make the Cubase MixConsole visible, F4 will display VST Connections, and F11 will display the VST Instruments rack. Easy, right?

FUNCTION KEYS ON A MAC

Well, it's not quite as easy on a Mac, at least not yet. You see, the Mac OS reserves the Function buttons for everyday Mac operations. For example, typing F3, F4, and F11 (depending on the vintage of your Mac keyboard) will activate Exposé, Dashboard, and volume Mute respectively. Therefore, you'll need to know how to access the function keys when you see them throughout this book.

There are two ways make the Mac function keys into the actual function keys. One method is to locate the "fn" button on your Mac keyboard. Holding the fn key and then typing a function key will allow you to access the prescribed Cubase key commands.

Figure 2.5. The "fn" key on a Mac keyboard.

This method might work best for you if you're a casual Cubase user or rely on the Mac commands during your daily computer use. However, if you are using Cubase a lot (and I sincerely hope you are), I would recommend changing the function key behavior from within the Mac OS. Click on the Apple menu, and select System Preferences. Then locate the hardware row, and click on Keyboard.

Make sure the Keyboard tab is selected at the top of the window. When you enable the "Use all F1, F2, etc. keys as standard function keys" option, then most of the function keys will operate as function keys rather than Mac functions. That way you won't have to hold the fn key to access the Cubase key commands assigned to the function keys. However, there is one other setting you should disable. Click on the Keyboard Shortcuts tab at the top of the window.

Click on Mission Control on the left side of the window, then uncheck the right-hand boxes for Mission Control, Application windows, Show Desktop, and Show Dashboard. Close the window when finished.

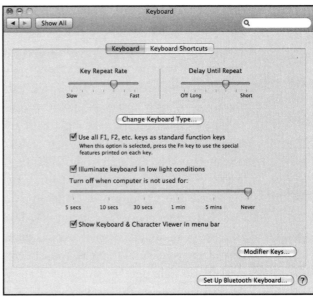

Figure 2.6. The Keyboard Preferences window.

YOUR STUDIO SETUP

The setup of your studio equipment is paramount to your workflow. Not only can it speed up your rate of production, but it can also critically affect what you're hearing. And since music is about being able to communicate with sound, you'll really need to

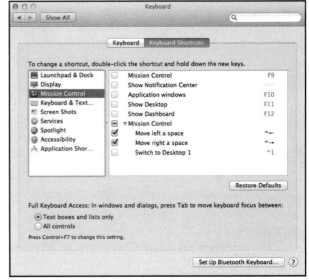

Figure 2.7. The Keyboard Shortcuts Preferences window.

hear what's going on in your recordings, mixes, and mastering. To that end, let me offer some advice on how to arrange your equipment and why.

Arranging Your Studio Monitors

There is a very simple and effective method for arranging your stereo studio monitors. (Note: This method is for stereo monitors. Surround-sound configurations are much different.) By using the triangle method I'm about to show you, you'll be able to get the most accurate representation of your mix. Failure to use this method will make it more difficult or even impossible to really hear what's going on.

Imagine an equilateral triangle with one point at the center of your head and the other two points touching the center of each studio monitor. Believe it or not, this represents 98 percent of the calculations you'll have to make for proper studio-monitor setup.

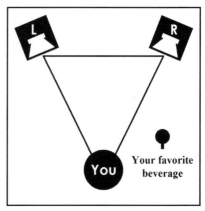

Figure 2.8. Overhead view of the triangle method.

The diagram above (that admittedly resembles a grade-school geometry lesson) depicts an overhead view of the equilateral triangle. You can see the left speaker and right speaker and your head. Basically, the distance between the speakers should be the same as the distance between the left speaker and your left ear, and the right speaker and your right ear. You should also consider angling the speaker toward your head a few degrees. That degree is exaggerated in Figure 2.8, but avoid pointing the studio monitors flush toward the back of the room.

The height of the speakers should ideally be equal to the height of your ears when sitting (I'm assuming you're not one of those "stand while mixing" types) in front of the speakers. However, I've found that situation more difficult to achieve. Every studio I've ever been in has, due to practicality, put its studio monitors higher than ear height. Then, tilting the monitors toward the engineer's head completes the optimal speaker configuration. This is a perfectly acceptable way to arrange your studio monitors. If you have a desk that raises the height of your monitors above your ears, consider getting some Auralex MoPADs (http://www.auralex.com). They not only allow you to tilt the speakers toward your head but also help isolate the speakers from the desk.

Woe to the Ears of a Musician

In an episode of Star Trek: The Next Generation, Counselor Troi was driven mad by a song placed in her subconscious. She could hear it, but others could not. This situation is identical to a condition known as tinnitus. We've all experienced tinnitus at one time or another, usually after attending a loud concert or other event involving higher than average sound-pressure levels. The ears ring for a period of time, after which it disappears.

But imagine if that ringing in your ears were permanent. You'd hear it from the time you woke up to the time you tried to go to sleep. It would drive you mad too. Well, if you damage your hearing due to excessive exposure to loud music, you won't just have a diminished frequency response, you'll also have tinnitus. You won't be able to stop it; earplugs and hearing aids won't help; there is no therapy, no magic pill, and no cure. Once you have it, it's a life sentence.

The only way to keep from suffering the tortures of tinnitus is to reduce the volume and limit your exposure to loud music. I know we're all guilty of wanting to "crank it up" when we feel the need. But if you exercise some caution, you'll be able to not only enjoy music throughout your life but also cherish the sound of raindrops, a good night's sleep, and the gentle stirrings of your grandchildren.

To that end, be aware that the optimal average volume level when mixing music should not exceed 85 dB (decibels). I strongly recommend obtaining an SPL (Sound Pressure Level) meter with a slow or RMS (Root Mean Squared) response setting. If you have an iPhone, iPad, or iPod Touch, you can also download the Decibel Meter Pro 2 for $0.99 from the App Store. It may not be as accurate as a dedicated SPL meter. But I've tried the two side by side, and the Decibel Meter Pro 2 is extremely similar in response to my rather expensive SPL meter. More information can be found at http://www.performanceaudio. com.

Keeping Your Equipment Handy and Close

Every so often, I visit clients' studios and am amazed by how far apart they have their components arranged. For example, the computer running Cubase is at one end of the room, while the MIDI controller is on the opposite side. From an aesthetic standpoint, it might look great. However, if the person doing the recording were also the keyboardist, he or she would have to run back and forth across the room several times (or in my keyboard skill–deficient case, several hundred times) during the recording process. That situation would be frustrating and distracting for the user and uncomplementary for the production workflow.

Instead, I would recommend you keep your instruments and other equipment as close together as possible. I like to keep my gear at arm's length. That way, I can have everything at my fingertips, and I'm not needlessly running around the room while I'm working. I also prefer to not lose a magical musical moment because I'm wrangling gear from all corners of the room.

MOVING OUT OF THE BASEMENT

Speaking of the corners of a room, I've laid the foundation of your new relationship with Cubase. Now it's time to move out of the basement and start adding the framework by launching Cubase for the first time.

Launching Cubase for the First Time

Launching a deep program like Cubase can be both exciting and a little scary. Hopefully you've read the previous chapters, for if you have, excitement will more quickly allay any fears. Also, starting with this chapter, be on the lookout for things called "Cubasics." Cubasics are fundamental operations, settings, and procedures that must become part of your operational relationship with Cubase. The sooner you memorize and implement the Cubasics, the faster you will become proficient with the program.

Before proceeding, you will need to make sure that you've installed Cubase and the eLicenser Control Center software, installed the drivers for your audio interface and MIDI interface (if necessary), connected your audio and MIDI interfaces to your computer, and connected the USB-eLicenser to a USB port of your computer. Then you can continue on to this chapter, in which you will learn about:

- Configuring your audio and MIDI interfaces.
- The Wi-Fi and network activity factor.
- Eliminating a common source of hum and buzz.
- The Project Assistant window.
- Using proper media management.
- Setting up Auto Save.

GO FOR LAUNCH

In chapter 1, you learned how to add the Cubase program to your Start Menu or Taskbar (Windows PC) or your Dock (Mac). Go ahead and launch Cubase by clicking on one of those icons. The first thing you'll see is the Cubase splash screen.

Figure 3.1. The Cubase splash screen.

There are two items to pay attention to on the splash screen. The first is the version number of Cubase you currently have installed, along with the current memory address mode (See "Deciding to Run Cubase in 32-Bit or 64-Bit Mode" in chapter 1). While you needn't do it every time, do periodically compare the version number to that of the most current version on the Steinberg website. (See "Keeping Up to Date" in chapter 2.)

The second is the progress display. As Cubase initializes its core program components, hardware devices, and plug-ins (including third-party plug-ins, if you have any) they will appear in the progress display. It also tests the plug-ins to make sure they're Cubase compatible.

When the initialization process is complete, the splash screen will disappear, and you'll see the Steinberg Hub window, which contains the news and tutorials section and the Project Assistant. However, I won't be going over these items yet. Before you can proceed, you'll need to configure your MIDI and audio interfaces. So at this time, click the Cancel button in the lower right-hand corner of the Steinberg Hub window. If you see the registration reminders, take a moment to register. (See "Creating a MySteinberg Account" in chapter 1.) Now locate the Devices menu.

CONFIGURING YOUR MIDI INTERFACE

Click on the Devices menu, and select Device Setup at the bottom. You will then see the Device Setup window. If this is the first time you've opened the Device Setup window, then the first selection in the Devices column will be MIDI Port Setup. If it is not, click on it to select it. There are slight differences between the MIDI Port Setup on Windows and the Mac, so I will show both.

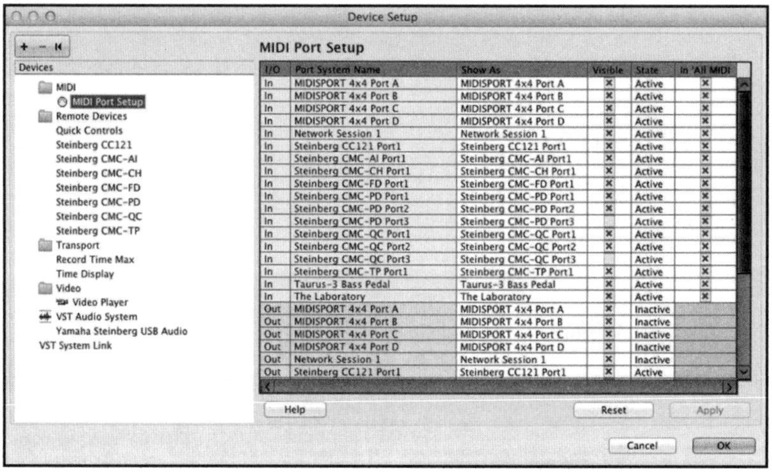

Figure 3.2. The Device Setup/MIDI Port Setup window (Mac).

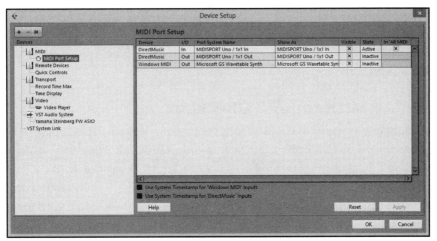

Figure 3.3. The Device Setup/MIDI Port Setup window (Windows).

The Device Setup window is divided into a left column labeled Devices and a right column that will display the settings for the selected device. In this case, the right column displays the settings for any and all MIDI interfaces you currently have connected to the computer. (Note: If the hardware is not currently connected, it will be absent from the right column. For the device to appear in the MIDI Port Setup window, you must quit Cubase, connect the hardware, and then restart Cubase.)

The MIDI Port Setup Settings

The Devices column will display the settings for each connected interface. For Mac users, Figure 3.2 shows the settings of the many MIDI interfaces I have connected to my Mac. Don't be startled if you don't see as many MIDI interfaces in your MIDI Port Setup window. The In port settings have a yellow background, while the Out port settings are blue. For Windows users, Figure 3.3 shows only one connected interface along with the default Windows MIDI Out port for the Microsoft GS Wavetable Synth. The background colorations are identical: yellow for In ports and blue for Out ports.

There won't be a need to learn about all of the MIDI Port Setup settings, but you should make sure that all of your interfaces appear in this window and that they all have their visible checkboxes enabled.

Renaming the MIDI Ports

The Port System Name and Show As fields contain the same name. However, if you'd like to rename the ports, you can double-click in the Show As field and type in a new name. This is useful for truncating a verbose name or for identifying an external MIDI device connected to a port or interface. For example, in Figure 3.3, the name of the USB MIDI interface In port is "MIDISPORT UNO 1x1 In." I would be tempted to rename it "UNO IN."

Another suggestion would be to identify the port by the device to which it is connected rather than by the name of the interface. For example, if the UNO interface were connected to a Yamaha Motif synthesizer, I would probably change the Show As port names to "Motif IN" and "Motif OUT."

The In "All MIDI Inputs" Checkbox

This in an important setting and is located at the far right of the Settings column. However, it may be difficult to find, because the default column width only allows for "In 'All MIDI'" to be displayed. Regardless of that idiosyncrasy, the setting is enabled on every In port by default. That allows you to record on a MIDI or Instrument track from any In port so that you don't necessarily have to change the Input setting of each track. You'll learn more about this later, but just make sure all of your In ports have In "All MIDI Inputs" enabled.

Device Field (Windows Only)

The Device field in Figure 3.3 is unique to the Windows version of Cubase. There are two different types of MIDI devices in Windows: DirectMusic and Windows MIDI. DirectMusic devices are used by third-party MIDI hardware developers, and will most likely be used by your MIDI interface. Windows MIDI devices are used to interface with components within the Windows operating system. For example, Figure 3.3 shows one Windows MIDI device to which is connected the Microsoft GS Wavetable Synth. This is a GS-compatible virtual synthesizer found in the Windows operating system. Without sounding too cruel, it's nothing to write home about. It can be used if you need to make GS-compatible SMF (Standard MIDI Files), but with the breadth of the Cubase sound palette, I doubt you'll ever need to use the Microsoft GS Wavetable Synth. To that end, I usually uncheck its visible box so that it doesn't create confusion.

System Timestamp Settings (Windows Only)

The System Timestamp settings are a little hard to explain. The timing, or synchronization, of MIDI devices can be controlled either by Cubase or Windows (System). By default, Cubase controls the timing; therefore, the System Timestamp checkboxes are disabled. However, if you need to have Windows control the timing, you'll need to enable the setting for the desired device (Windows MIDI and/or DirectMusic). Weirdly, every Windows-based PC will require either Cubase or Windows to control the timing.

But how do you know which timing method is best? There's only one way to find out, and that is by recording some MIDI information to the Cubase Click (Metronome) and then listening to the playback timing. If you find that the playback is ahead of the Click (as if you played way ahead of the beat, but you didn't), then you'll need to change the current System Timestamp setting. In other words, if the timing was noticeably off with System Timestamp disabled, you'll need to enable it, or vice versa.

If you don't know about the System Timestamp settings, the MIDI timing problem will be impossible to deduce. I've had customers spend hours or days trying to figure out why their MIDI tracks sound as if they were recorded in an alternate universe that exists several hundred milliseconds in the future. "I'll record quarter-notes on the beat of the metronome, but during playback, they're ahead of the beat," many a befuddled client has exclaimed. Hopefully by knowing about System Timestamp and how to change it, you'll save yourself the time and hassle.

CONFIGURING YOUR AUDIO INTERFACE

Configuring the audio interface is very similar to configuring the MIDI interface. If you've already closed (or never opened) the Device Setup window, you can click on the Devices menu and select Device Setup.

On the left-hand side of the window (the Devices column), click on VST Audio System. On the right-hand side, find and click on the ASIO Driver drop-down selector. A list will appear, from which you can select your audio interface. (Other interfaces, including the default Windows or Mac audio drivers, will appear in the list.) When you've selected your interface, a dialog box will appear, asking you if you want to Switch or Keep the ASIO driver. Clicking on Switch will return you to the VST Audio System window.

Figure 3.4. The VST Audio System window.

Changing Advanced Options

Usually the defaults (which you can always restore by clicking on Set to Defaults) will provide you with the proper Advanced Options settings. However, make sure that Multi Processing is enabled. That will allow Cubase to access all of the processors and cores of your computer's CPU. Also make sure that ASIO-Guard is enabled. ASIO-Guard is a high-performance audio buffering scheme that can help prevent audible pops, clicks, and other anomalies when working in Cubase. On a Windows computer, you'll also have the option to Activate Steinberg Audio Power Scheme. I would highly recommend enabling that option, because it will provide you with higher audio performance. Basically, Cubase will run your CPU to its rated performance and then restore the Windows Power Scheme after you quit Cubase. (Due to the nature of the OS, Mac users won't have to select a power scheme.)

Interface-Specific Settings

Clicking on whatever appears directly underneath VST Audio System will allow you to further configure your audio interface. The reason I'm being so nonspecific in my directions is that your interface will determine the text; therefore, what's listed on your window will be different than mine.

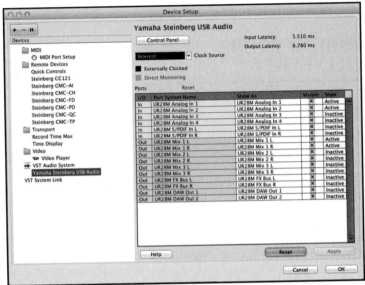

Figure 3.5. Interface-specific settings window.

You'll notice that the text in Figure 3.5 says Yamaha Steinberg USB Audio directly beneath the VST Audio settings. That's because I have a Steinberg UR28M audio interface, which uses the Yamaha Steinberg USB Audio driver. Your text, unless you happen to also use a UR-series interface, will say something different. For example, if you're using an RME audio interface, then something like RME Fireface 800 will be listed. Whatever the case may be, make sure to click on the name of your interface to change the following settings.

The In and Out port settings are very similar to the MIDI Port settings: yellow backgrounds are Ins, while blue backgrounds are Outs. The number of In and Out ports are determined by the physical connectors on your audio interface. For example, if your audio interface has sixteen inputs (like a Steinberg MR816CSX), then you'll see sixteen In ports and sixteen Out ports. In the case of my UR28M (in Figure 3.5), there are six inputs and ten outputs. (Another way to look at that would be three left inputs, three right inputs, five left outputs, and five right outputs.) Make sure that the visible checkboxes are enabled for any and all ports.

Renaming the Audio Ports

If you'd like to rename the audio ports, you can double-click in the Show As field and type in a new name. This is useful for truncating a verbose name or for identifying a specific audio device (such as a microphone or drum machine) that is usually connected to an audio interface input. For example, in Figure 3.5, the name of the first two inputs are "UR28M Analog In 1" and "UR28M Analog In 2." I'd be tempted to change the names to "IN 1" and "IN 2." Or if I primarily recorded in stereo, then "IN Left" and "IN Right" would be appropriate. Finally, if I usually had my vocal mic plugged into the first input and my acoustic guitar pickup plugged into the second input, I could rename the ports "MIC" and "GTR." You could certainly just use the default port names, but being able to identify them more specifically is a nice feature.

Control Panel Settings (Including Latency)

Clicking on the Control Panel button will reveal another window. However, the appearance of the window and the settings themselves will be specific to your audio interface. Therefore, I cannot describe all the settings you might find on your control panel, save one: buffer size. The buffer size is what controls your audio interface latency. Latency is how long it takes for your computer to receive an audio signal at the interface In port and then send it to the interface Out port. Or in the case of virtual instruments, the buffer size determines how long it will take for MIDI information to be received, converted into audio by a virtual synthesizer, and then sent to the audio Out port. The faster your computer is, the lower the latency. However, there are many factors that can impact proper buffer size, including number of audio tracks, number of virtual instruments, number of notes being played on those virtual instruments, and number and type of effects processors (particularly reverb). Since all of those variables will impact the latency, the proper buffer size will be similarly variable.

The most common sign of a buffer set too low is popping and crackling in the audio playback. When the buffers are too low, the computer doesn't have enough room to sufficiently process the audio being produced by Cubase. If you hear popping and crackling or if you notice the VST Performance meter going into the red (see "VST Performance Meters" in chapter 5), then you should increase the buffer size.

Conversely, a buffer set too high will result in longer latency times. In other words, you might hear some "lag" time between when you sing into the mic and you hear the sound in your headphones. Or in the case of MIDI tracks assigned to VST Instruments, you'll play a note on your MIDI controller, and the audio will come out of the speakers a few hundred milliseconds later (hence the term latency).

With all this in mind, the rule of thumb is to start your Cubase Projects with low buffer sizes. Then, as the number of Audio tracks, VST Instruments, and effects increase, so should the buffer sizes. A good rule of thumb is to start with buffer sizes between 128 and

384 samples, then increase the buffers to between 512 and 2,048 samples when you start mixing. Don't be afraid to make incremental adjustments throughout the development of each Cubase Project. Since the buffer size is systemic to Cubase, you can alter the size to fit the currently loaded project.

Resetting Your Audio System

Cubase, like any computer program, can crash or become inoperative. So can your audio interface. That's why there's a Reset button located at the bottom of the window. (See Figure 3.5.) Clicking the Reset button will interrupt the audio processing and restart the Cubase audio engine. If you notice that your audio interface has become unresponsive, you may want to click the Reset button. If that doesn't reestablish the audio system, you'll need to save your work and restart Cubase. In the case of USB, FireWire, or Thunderbolt audio interfaces, you may need to unplug them from the computer and their own power sources to fully reset them. Or if your audio interface is nonremovable (like a PCI or PCI Express card), you may need to shut down and unplug the computer for the audio interface to fully reset.

THE NEGATIVE IMPACT OF WI-FI AND ETHERNET CONTROLLERS

I've mentioned that low buffer settings can induce popping, crackling, stuttering, and other anomalies into your recordings and playback. These are problems that can appear on any computer running any DAW program. There are other factors that can seriously degrade your computer's music-production capabilities. One of the most common causes is network traffic on Wi-Fi (Wireless Internet) and even hardware Ethernet network controllers. Some computers will not exhibit audio anomalies during network activity. However, if you've increased your buffer size and are still getting the occasional pop or click, you may want to disable your network controllers. (Note: Some of you cross-platform users can attest that Windows exhibits far more network-induced audio problems than Mac OS. However, I've seen this phenomenon on both platforms. Better safe than sorry.)

Network activity can occur even when you're not actively surfing the Internet or accessing another computer or server. Parts of the Mac OS, Windows, and other applications occasionally create network traffic. When they do, they can also create pops, clicks, and stutters. Here's a good way to find out if your network controllers are causing such problems. Load a Cubase Project that contains Audio or VST Instrument tracks, and start playback. Then load a web browser and start surfing to some websites. (A good one to use is http://www.speedtest.net, because it measures the upload and download speeds of your ISP [Internet Service Provider] and will create a lot of network traffic in the process.) If you notice an increase in popping and clicking during the time a web page is loading, you should disable your network controllers. Here's how to do it:

Disabling Network Controllers in Windows 7

Click on your Start button, and then select Control Panel. Click on Network and Internet, and then click on Network and Sharing Center. On the left-hand side of the screen, click on Change adapter settings. Right-click on each and every connection, and select Disable. Usually one or more Local Area Connections or Wireless Network Connections are the culprits. Then return to Cubase to see if the pops and clicks are gone. When you're done making music and want to get the computer back on the Net, repeat the process, but click Enable.

Disabling Network Controllers in Windows 8

Drag your mouse to the lower left-hand corner of your display, and click the Start icon. Right-click on the Start window background, and click the All apps icon in the lower right-hand display of the Toolbar. Scroll across the screen to the Windows System category, and click the Control Panel icon. Click on Network and Internet, then Network and Sharing Center. In the upper left-hand corner of that window, you will see the text "Change adapter settings." Click on that text, and a new window will appear that displays all of your network adapters, such as Bluetooth, Local Area Connections (hardwired Ethernet), and Wi-Fi adapters. Right-click on each adapter icon, and select Disable from the mini-menu. That will disconnect your Windows-based computer from any and all networks. To enable your network adapters, repeat the process, but choose Enable from the mini-menu.

Disabling Network Controllers in Mac OS X

If you're connected to a network via your AirPort card, you can simply click on the Airport icon in the upper right-hand side of your Finder menu bar and select Turn AirPort Off. However, if you're connected through the Ethernet port, it's a little more work. Click on the Apple button in the upper left-hand corner, and select System Preferences. Click on Network, and then click on the Ethernet port on the left-hand side of the window. Click on the Configure IPv4: drop-down menu and make a note of the current setting, which is commonly set to Using DHCP. (You'll need to change that setting back to reconnect to the network when you're done using Cubase.) Choose Off from the menu. You may want to do the same thing with the AirPort, FireWire, and any other device that appears on the left. Then return to Cubase to see if the pops and clicks are gone. When you're done making music and want to get the computer back on the Net, repeat the process, but choose the setting (likely Using DHCP) you made note of before changing the setting to Off.

GETTING RID OF HUM AND BUZZ

Before I go further, let me preface by saying that this procedure may be dangerous and could result in electric shock. Hum and buzz in audio systems (including computers) are usually caused by ground (earth) loops. The ground (you know, the Earth's dirty crust we walk on and grow food in) is part of the electrical circuit. Electricity needs a path to ground to be safe. If spurious charges are created within an electrical circuit, they'll start looking for the point of least resistance into which they'll harmlessly disperse. That point is the ground. If there is no path to ground, it will flow to the next point of least resistance, which could very well be the human body—your human body. These spurious charges could be a tiny shock, or they could carry enough amperage to injure or even kill you. Therefore, before you use a ground lifter (as I will describe in the next paragraph), understand the dangers.

Using a Ground Lifter

That being said, ground loops are caused by having more than one path to ground. For example, if you plug a keyboard's audio outputs to your audio interface and there's suddenly an audible hum or buzz, chances are the keyboard has one path to ground and the computer has another path to ground. One or both devices would have to have a three-prong AC cable for this to occur. Using a ground lifter will remove the ground wire from a three-prong power cable.

Figure 3.6. A ground lifter.

Ground lifters are available at hardware stores or even in the household section of your local market. You can connect a ground lifter to the power cable of either the keyboard or the computer to see if a ground loop is the cause of the hum. You'll still have one path to ground, but make sure to remove the ground lifter when you disconnect the audio cables from your interface. Otherwise, you may be removing both the audio pathway and your safe path to ground.

Checking for ground loops is even easier on laptops, because they have their own batteries. You can simply unplug the AC adapter from the laptop, even when the computer is running, to see if the hum goes away. If it does, try the ground lifter on the laptop's AC adapter. But just like with a desktop computer, remove the ground lifter after you've disconnected the audio device from the audio interface to reestablish a safe path to ground.

Determining if Your Home or Studio Is Properly Wired

Using a ground lifter will serve no purpose if the AC outlet itself is not wired properly. Not only that, but improper electrical wiring can negatively impact the clarity of your audio pathway. I would recommend getting a wiring checker.

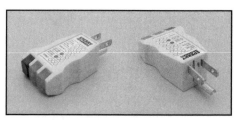

Figure 3.7. A wiring checker.

While you're at the hardware store purchasing some ground lifters, grab a wiring checker. All you have to do is plug it into an electrical outlet to see if the sockets are wired properly. Dealing with all sorts of weird noises after moving my home studio to a new house, I went around and checked the wiring. My house was obviously wired on a Friday at about 4:30 p.m. when everyone wanted to go home for the day, including the electricians. Wires were reversed, and ground wires were rarely even connected. So not only did I have audio problems, there was also a significant risk of electrocution. If you determine that you have improperly wired plugs and you don't know your way around a fuse box, then hire a competent, bonded, and insured electrician to do it for you. Then, when he or she is finished, don't hesitate to double-check his or her work with your wiring checker (again, better safe than sorry).

Use High-Quality Cables

If you've purchased Cubase, a great audio interface, and recording microphones, why would you ever want to connect them with cheap cables? Here's the rule: you may never hear the highest-quality component in your studio, but you'll always hear the lowest-quality component. More often than not, crappy cables cause bad audio, and you will hear them as they degrade or ruin your recordings. Do yourself a favor, and invest in some good cables with ample shielding. Your local music store salesperson can lead you to the good stuff.

THE STEINBERG HUB AND PROJECT ASSISTANT

The Steinberg Hub usually appears immediately after you launch Cubase. However, you had to close the window to facilitate the setup of the audio and MIDI interfaces. To reopen the Project Assistant, click on the File menu and select New Project.

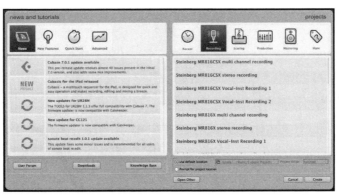

Figure 3.8. The Steinberg Hub.

Definition of a Cubase Project

Before you dive into the Steinberg Hub and the Project Assistant within, let me describe what a Cubase Project is. A project is simply the document you'll be using in Cubase. But why isn't it called a song or a tune or a composition? Because those names wouldn't work for sound-effects designers, special-event recordings, or any of the other unique purposes Cubase can facilitate. It's the same reason a word processor doesn't refer to its documents as novels, poems, or lesson plans. Project is simply more generic. So whenever you're about to create music (or any other sound-related undertaking) with Cubase, it will be called a project.

The Steinberg Hub

The Steinberg Hub is divided into left and right halves. On the left side is the news and tutorials section, wherein you will find current information about Cubase and Steinberg from steinberg.net. However, you must be connected to the Internet to get that content. You will also find videos of new features, the Quick Start guide, and more advanced features. Buttons located at the bottom will quickly take you to the online user forum, downloads, and knowledge base. Take a moment to browse through these very useful features.

The Project Assistant

The Project Assistant is located on the right side of the Steinberg Hub and comes with a wide variety of Cubase templates. Templates are projects with preassembled tracks and other settings that can make it easier to create a project. For example, at the top of the Project Assistant (see Figure 3.8) are six tabs: Recent, Recording, Scoring, Production, Mastering, and More. The latter is where you can store your own custom templates. It's a good idea to look at some of the templates that come with Cubase. But for now, click on the More tab and single-click on the Empty template.

The reason you're going to start with the Empty template is so you can understand the types of tracks as you add them to your project. It will also allow you to more easily see the Project window in which you'll be spending a lot of time. Now before you're tempted to click the Create button, it is critical that you understand media management.

Cubasic No. I: Using Proper Media Management

If you learn only one thing while reading this book, I hope you commit to using proper media management. If you don't, you're setting yourself up for a lot of unnecessary work and hassle. Cubase, like all DAW software, creates a large number of files on your computer. Every time you hit the Record button on an Audio track, it creates a new audio file on your hard disk that is separate from the Cubase Project file. Unless you define the Project Folder in which to store those audio files, they'll be stored at unpredictable locations.

They might also be stored in one central folder, which would make it impossible to determine which audio files belong to which projects. This can make it impossible to accurately archive a project when it's completed. For example, I recently visited a very prolific composer who needed me to archive some of his work onto a separate hard drive. (Archiving, or backing up your projects, is of paramount importance, and I'll be discussing this in chapter 16.) But he stored all of his projects in one folder. Finding the Project files was easy enough (there were about one hundred), but there were over two hundred thousand audio files! Can you imagine trying to figure out which of the files went with which project? Even the naming of the audio files didn't help. Of the two hundred thousand–plus audio files, 68,776 had the word vocal in the file name. He was in for a long and expensive night.

Fortunately, Cubase has a way to reassemble the Cubase Project and its audio files into a new Project Folder. However, doing so is labor intensive, and it will only get in the way of your workflow. If you use proper media management, you'll never have to go through this hassle or pay me by the hour to do it for you.

(Note: The procedure I'm about to show may seem very involved the first time you do it. However, after a little practice, you'll be able to do it in less than five seconds. Five seconds now can save you many hours later.)

THE TWO MEDIA-MANAGEMENT OPTIONS
Cubase offers two different options for media management: Default location and Prompt for project location. Both of those options are located in the Steinberg Hub at the bottom of the Project Assistant.

Figure 3.9. The two media-management options.

You won't be using the Default location option because I really want to illustrate how media management works. However, if you already have a grasp of media management and wish to use that Default location option, make sure you set the Default location and create a newly named Project Folder for this and every project. (See Figure 3.9.)

You are going to use the Prompt for project location option. Click on the Radio button to the left of Prompt for project location. You'll notice that the Create button turns into a Continue button. Go ahead and click Continue.

THE SET PROJECT FOLDER WINDOW

The next window to appear will differ slightly between the Windows and Mac versions. However, the function is the same: to choose the location for the Project Folder on your computer. I will show you both, but I'll also be showing two common places for your Project Folder. So make sure you read both the Windows and Mac instructions that follow.

The first popular location is your Music folder inside your User folder. In the case of Figure 3.10, it's located at my user name (blurred out for privacy purposes) and then in the My Music folder. To set a Project Folder here, I would recommend clicking the New Folder button and creating a folder called "Cubase Projects." (You'll only have to do that this one time. Then every other project you create can be stored in the Cubase Projects folder.) Inside that folder, create a folder called "My First Cubase Project," then click OK.

Figure 3.10. Set Project Folder/ Windows 8/User Music folder.

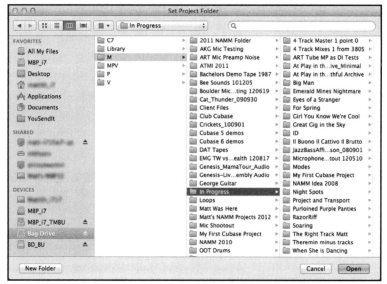

Figure 3.11. Set Project Folder/Mac OS X/External Hard Disk.

If you're a power user like me, you may have already added an additional hard disk to your computer, upon which to store your Cubase projects. In my case, it's an external eSATA hard disk attached to my MacBook Pro (which requires an ExpressCard3/4 eSATA card). I highly recommend using an additional hard disk for Cubase Project storage. You'll get more performance and more room, plus you won't lose your work if your system hard disk fails. To that end, I've selected (see Figure 3.11) my external hard disk (Bag Drive), then selected the M folder (short for music) and the In Progress folder (where I store my music rather than my clients' music). From there, click the New Folder button and title the new folder "My First Cubase Project." When finished, click the Open button.

SAVING THE PROJECT FILE INTO THE PROJECT FOLDER

After you've set the Project Folder, Cubase will display a blank project named "Untitled1." The window that is displayed is called the Project window. You'll learn more about that later. Right now, you need to complete the last step in accomplishing proper media management: saving the Project file into the Project Folder you just created. Click on the File menu, and select Save As.

The Save As window will differ slightly between Windows and Mac; however, the function is the same: to save the Project file into the Project Folder. You'll notice that, in either case, the Project Folder gets selected as the storage location automatically. This way, you'll never have to navigate to the location of the Project Folder (another benefit of using proper media management). All you have to do is type in the desired name of the Project file. That name should be the same name as the Project Folder. In this case, type "My First Project File R01." (More on the "R01" in a moment.) You'll also notice in Figure 3.12 that "Cubase Project File (.cpr)" is selected. While both Windows

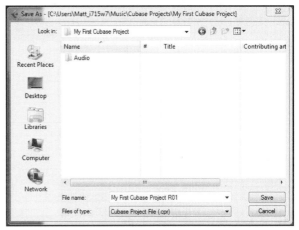

Figure 3.12. The Save As window/Windows.

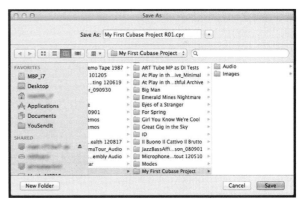

Figure 3.13. The Save As window/Mac OS X.

and Macs use file extensions, only the Windows version gives you the option to change them. So regardless of which version you use, don't worry about including ".cpr" in the file name, because it's done automatically. When you have the Project file named, click the Save button to return to the Project window.

Understanding the Benefits of Proper Media Management

The biggest advantages of proper media management are focus and portability. I'll talk about focus first. In Figures 3.12 and 3.13, you'll notice the Audio folder that Cubase automatically created when you made the Project Folder. From now on, when you're working on the "My First Cubase Project R01" project, the audio files will get stored in the corresponding Audio folder. In other words, Cubase focuses on that Audio folder and stores every audio file within it. In fact, as you get further along on a project, you'll notice other items automatically created by Cubase and stored in the Project Folder. These will include the Images folder (graphic depictions of the audio waveforms), Edits folder (processed audio files), Freeze folder (offline frozen audio files), Video folder (video files) and .bak (backup) files.

Cubase is focused on the Project Folder while you're working on the Project file. That means that every piece of media that was created by you or Cubase will be stored in the Project Folder. That makes your Cubase Project very portable. Portability is critical, but not limited, to the following situations:

- Moving a project from one hard disk to another.
- Backing up a project to another hard disk or DVD data disc.
- Moving a project between two or more computers.
- Sharing projects between different people with different computers.

In any case, when you use proper media management, all you have to do is move, back up, or share the Project Folder, because it contains all of the elements of the project.

Now just in case I haven't properly motivated you to use proper media management, I charge $600 per day, plus expenses and travel costs, and would love to fly to your studio to clean up your Cubase (or any other DAW) media problems. With an ominous-sounding voice comically drenched in reverb, I say unto you, "You've been warned!"

Using Matt's Project-Revision-Naming Method

In Figures 3.12 and 3.13, you'll notice that I added "R01" at the end of the Project file names. To me, that indicates the first version of a project. Then when I'm about to significantly add to or edit a project, I'll perform a Save As command with an incremental version number. For instance, R01 might have all the tracks created and named. R02 might include the drum tracking. R03 might include the bass guitar tracking, R04 the guitars, R05 the vocals, and so on. That way, I can always go back to a previous version (which I call "swimming upstream") if the need arises.

I use that same method when I'm mastering a project. In other words, "My First Cubase Project R10M07" would be the seventh version of mastering on the tenth version of the project or "mix." That way, I always know which version of a project I'm mastering, and I can return to that project if it needs any tweaking that was revealed in the mastering stage.

ENABLING AUTO SAVE

Have you ever worked really hard on a word-processor document, an e-mail, or another computer-related project, only to have it disappear due to a crash, a power failure, or accidentally hitting Don't Save before closing the program? It's happened to me, it's happened to you, and it happens to everyone who uses a computer. We all know we're supposed to occasionally save the file while we're working on it. However, we creative types tend to neglect that practice when the music is flowing. To help spare you from such an unfortunate occurrence, Cubase has an Auto Save feature that will execute the Save command for you at regular intervals.

Auto Save is located in the Cubase Preferences window. In Windows, go to the File menu and select Preferences. In Mac, go to the Cubase menu and select Preferences.

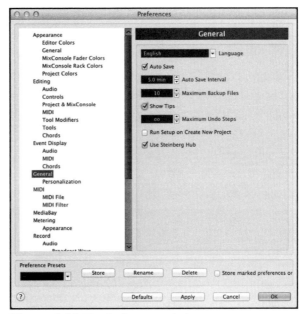

Figure 3.14. The Preferences window.

The Preferences window is divided into left and right halves. The left side contains the preferences, while the right side shows the settings for the selected preference. Click on the General preference, and then observe the settings on the right. I usually find that Auto Save is enabled on default. However, due to the importance of this preference, now is a great time to make sure that Auto Save is enabled. The Interval is definable. I usually set it to 5.0 seconds. However, if you're working with a large number of tracks or VST Instruments that use a lot of samples (such as Steinberg HALion 4, The Grand, or Native Instruments Kontakt), you'll notice that the process of saving takes longer. Therefore, you may want to set the Interval to 10.0 or 15.0 minutes.

Every time Cubase Auto Saves the project, it will make a backup file. As I mentioned previously, backup files have a .bak rather than a .cpr file extension and are saved in the Project Folder. The default Maximum Backup Files setting is 10, but you can set this as you see fit. When you've set the Preferences appropriately, you can click Apply and/or OK at the bottom of the Preferences window.

I/O, I/O, IT'S OFF TO WORK YOU'LL GO

You're very close to being able to start recording your first tracks. However, you still need to configure your hardware Ins and Outs. You'll see how that's done in the next chapter.

The Ins and Outs of Cubase...Literally

4

A computer is an input/output device. In other words, you put stuff in, and you get stuff out. For example, you put text into a word processor, and you get a printed page out of your printer. You input a search into Google, and you see the output of results. Or in the case of a compelling computer game, you put in every waking minute, and what you get out is another dateless night. I hope you're not currently deeply involved in any computer games, because we have a lot of music to get into and out of Cubase. In this chapter, you will learn about:

- Assigning MIDI inputs and outputs.
- Configuring your audio inputs and outputs.
- Creating a simple Control Room (Cubase only).
- When to record in mono, stereo, or multichannel.
- Setting the Metronome (Click).
- Recording some test tracks to confirm your software and hardware configuration.

CUBASIC NO. 2: ASSIGNING MIDI INPUTS AND OUTPUTS TO TRACKS

In chapter 3, you learned how to configure your MIDI interface. Now I'll show you how to assign those MIDI inputs and outputs to MIDI and Instrument tracks. Before proceeding, make sure you have your "My First Cubase Project" project loaded. What you should be seeing is a blank Project window.

Figure 4.1. A blank Project window.

You'll learn more about the Project window in the next chapter. For now, what you're looking at are the three columns of the Project window: Inspector, Track List, and Event Display. If you're only seeing two columns, it's because the Inspector is currently disabled. To enable the Inspector, click on the Window Layout button (second button from the left at the Toolbar, upper left-hand corner of the Project window), and make sure Inspector has a check next to it. To close the Window Layout screen, just click anywhere outside the Window Layout screen boundary.

Creating a MIDI Track

Now you'll need to add one MIDI track so that I can show you how the MIDI Inputs and Outputs work. Click on the Project menu, select Add Track, and then select MIDI. The Add MIDI Track dialog box will appear, but all you need to do is make sure the count is set to "1," and then hit Add Track in the lower right-hand corner.

Figure 4.2. One MIDI track added to project.

Notice that the MIDI track has been given the arbitrary name of MIDI XX, and since this is the first MIDI track that was added to the project, the name is MIDI 01.

Assigning MIDI Input, Output, and Channel

Now that you've added the track, you can assign its MIDI Input, Output, and Channel. Every MIDI or Instrument track has all three of those assignable parameters.

The Inspector has several sections in a vertical order. The topmost section is colorized (the default color is gray) and contains the name of the track. The MIDI assignments are located underneath the top section. If you can't see the settings listed in Figure 4.2 (the Track MIDI settings), you may need to click on the top section to reveal the settings.

Track MIDI Input

Near the center of the top section, you will find the Track MIDI Input setting. Currently it's assigned to All MIDI Inputs. That means that the MIDI track can receive and record MIDI information from any In port in the MIDI Port Setup window. (See "The MIDI Port Setup Settings" in chapter 3.) If you'd like to choose a specific In port, you can click on the All MIDI Inputs setting to reveal a list of all the available In ports. Make sure it's not set to Not Connected, or you won't be able to record MIDI information onto that track.

Another way to think about the Track MIDI Input is to ask the question "Where do I want the MIDI information to be received from?" It could be your USB MIDI keyboard, your pad controller, or a device connected to a MIDI interface port.

Track MIDI Output

Similarly to the Input setting, the Track MIDI Output setting will allow you to route the MIDI or Instrument track to the desired Out port destination. In Figure 4.2, it's assigned to Network Session 1. Clicking on that setting will reveal a list of all the available destinations.

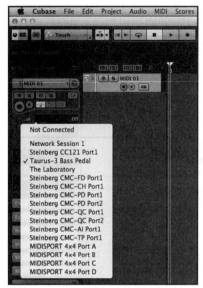

Figure 4.3. Track MIDI Output destinations.

In Figure 4.3, I've reassigned the destination of Track MIDI 01 from Network Session 1 to Taurus-3 Bass Pedal, which is an external synthesizer with its own USB port for MIDI. (I guess I'd better call the neighbors and prepare them for the onslaught of rumbling bass frequencies they'll experience when I play them.)

Another way to think about the Track MIDI Output is to ask the question "Where do I want the MIDI information to be sent to?" Again, it could be any device that appears in your MIDI Port Setup window (see "The MIDI Port Setup Settings" in chapter 3), or it could also be a VST Instrument inside Cubase. I'll discuss that possibility later.

Track MIDI Channel

Every MIDI device can receive on any one of sixteen MIDI channels. Some devices can receive MIDI information on multiple channels, including all sixteen simultaneously. Setting the Track MIDI channel allows you to assign the track to the desired device. If you refer back to Figure 4.2, you'll see that the channel of the MIDI 01 track is set to 1. Clicking on that setting will drop down a list of the sixteen MIDI channels, including a special Any setting at the top of the list that allows the MIDI channel of the event itself (that's recorded on the track) to determine the MIDI channelization. Chances are, you won't use that setting very often, if at all. But do make sure to set the MIDI channel to the same channel number as the MIDI device to which you'll be sending the MIDI information.

Note: There are sixteen MIDI channels that can travel through one MIDI port. This allows you to "daisy-chain" MIDI cables from one device to another. Setting the MIDI channel of both the track and the MIDI device to which the track transmits will establish proper MIDI communication. This is true of both hardware and software MIDI devices. While setting the MIDI channel is an important step, there are times when you won't have to assign the channel. This situation usually occurs when using VST Instruments or virtual instruments from within Cubase. When that situation arises later in this book, I'll let you know. I won't be able to discuss all the principles of MIDI. So if you'd like to learn more, I'd recommend reading Jeff Rona's The MIDI Companion from Hal Leonard.

MIDI Settings Are Made Track by Track

It's important to note that every MIDI or Instrument track has its own MIDI settings. That means that you'll need to verify the settings for every track. If you don't, erroneous settings can result in frustrating communication problems.

CUBASIC NO. 3:
CONFIGURING YOUR VST CONNECTIONS

The inputs and outputs of your audio hardware must be configured to the inputs and outputs of Cubase. These routings are known as VST Connections. To access the VST Connections window, click the Devices menu and select VST Connections, or type F4 on your computer keyboard. (For Mac users, see "'F' or Function Keys" in chapter 2.)

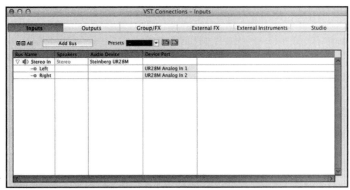

Figure 4.4. The VST Connections window/Inputs tab.

Assigning Audio Inputs to Cubase

Depending on which level of Cubase you're using, there will be between two and six tabs at the top of the VST Connections window. To configure the inputs, make sure you click on the Inputs tab. Then click on the Presets drop-down box and select the Stereo preset. (Note: You will only be configuring one stereo input at this time. In a later chapter, I'll discuss adding the additional audio inputs on your audio interface, if applicable.)

Now your VST Connections window will look very similar to Figure 4.4. In the Bus Name column, you'll see one bus named Stereo In. If you don't see the left and right ports directly beneath the Bus Name, click the little triangle to the left of Stereo In.

Now look across to the Audio Device column. If Not Connected is listed, click on it to reveal your audio interface. In my case, it's my Steinberg UR28M interface. Then in the Device Port column, if Not Connected is listed, click on it to reveal the input ports of your audio interface. In my case, the left bus is connected to UR28M Analog In 1, and the right bus is connected to UR28M Analog In 2. Basically, the left bus is assigned to the first input of my audio interface, and the right bus is assigned to the second input of my audio interface. Your interface may designate the first input as 1, left, or A, while the second input could be 2, right, or B. Every audio interface manufacturer has its own preference for input designation, but just get the first input to the left bus and the second input to the right bus.

RENAMING AN INPUT BUS

You can rename an input bus simply by single-clicking the current bus name, pausing for a second or two, and then single-clicking the name again. The current name will become highlighted, and you can type in the desired name. In the case of Figure 4.4, I could name it "UR 1/2 Ins," or something else that would remind me that this is the first pair of audio inputs. Renaming the input buses is especially useful when your audio interface has more than two inputs.

STORING AN INPUT PRESET

VST Connections are stored as part of each project. That means that different projects can have different VST Connection configurations. It's a very flexible system, but it can get a little unwieldy when you use multiple VST Connections between a number of different projects. Fortunately, there is a Store button to the right of the Presets drop-down box. When you click on Store, you'll be given a dialog box in which to name the preset. I would recommend storing the current preset as something like "My Default Inputs."

WHY A STEREO BUS INSTEAD OF TWO MONO BUSES?

While there are occasions when mono buses are advantageous, Cubase allows you to assign mono Audio tracks to either left or right input buses. Therefore, mono tracks can be addressed by either left or right buses. Conversely, stereo tracks must be addressed by stereo buses.

Assigning Audio Outputs to Cubase

The process for assigning outputs is almost identical to that of inputs. Click on the Outputs tab at the top of the VST Connections window.

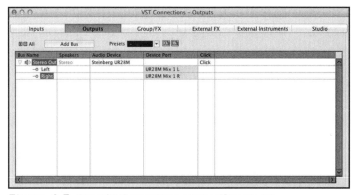

Figure 4.5. The VST Connections window/Outputs tab.

Click on the Presets drop-down box, and select the Stereo preset. You'll see one stereo output bus with left and right outputs. Make sure your audio interface is assigned in the

Audio Device column. You should also check the Device Port column to make sure the left and right outputs are assigned to the left and right buses.

The procedures for renaming output buses and presets are identical to those for renaming the inputs. Also be aware that different Cubase Projects can use different output configurations, so make sure you store the outputs as something like "My Default Outputs."

SPECIAL CONSIDERATIONS FOR THE CUBASE OUTPUTS SETTINGS

The output assignments accomplish two things: they direct the signal flow of Cubase to your audio interface hardware outputs, and they assign the Cubase MixConsole Output Channel Fader to the virtual output of Cubase. The latter is significant, because the Output Channel controls the volume level of your mixdowns, and therefore the overall volume of the MP3s and audio CDs you'll be creating. It's very important not to use the Output Channel Fader (on the MixConsole) of Cubase to control your monitor speaker volume, because it will impact the volume level of your mixdown. It's better to use the physical volume control on the audio interface or create a Control Room with which to adjust monitor level.

Creating a Simple Control Room (Cubase Only)

The Control Room is a fantastic feature of Cubase. It allows you to assign the inputs and outputs of your audio hardware to common destinations, such as monitor speakers, headphone mixes, and talkback microphones. The advantages of the Control Room become very significant when your audio interface has more than two inputs or two outputs. However, there is one specific advantage you'll enjoy by creating even the simplest of Control Rooms: independent volume controls for the mixdown and the studio monitor volume from within Cubase.

To configure your Control Room, click on the Studio tab at the top of the VST Connections window.

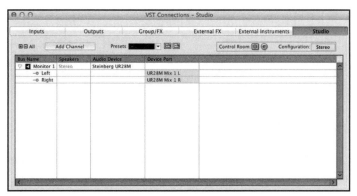

Figure 4.6. The VST Connections window/Studio tab.

ENABLING THE CONTROL ROOM

If this is the first time you've gone to the Studio tab, chances are good that the Control Room is turned off. Click on the Control Room Power button to the top and slightly left of center, and turn it on. You'll see a notification screen saying that the Control Room is indeed disabled and asking if you'd like to enable it. Click on Enable. You'll see a new bus added to the Bus Name column called Monitor 1, and it will have a left and right Output Channel. You might also have the Control Room Mixer displayed after turning on the Control Room power. If that's the case, close the Control Room Mixer for now. Your Studio tab should now look like Figure 4.6.

Monitor 1 is the destination for your studio monitors. If you have an audio interface with more than two outputs and you have more than one pair of studio monitors, you can create as many as four monitors and the Cubase Control Room will allow you to switch between all of them. But for now, all you need to do is connect the hardware outputs of your audio interface to the inputs of your monitor speakers (or in the case of passive studio monitors, the power amp to which they're connected.)

ASSIGNING THE AUDIO DEVICE AND DEVICE PORTS TO THE CONTROL ROOM

Assigning the Audio Device and Device Ports settings to the Monitor 1 bus is identical to the procedure for assigning outputs in the Outputs tab. All you need to do is assign your audio interface to the Audio Device column, and then assign the left bus to the left Device Port and the right bus to the right Device Port.

The procedures for renaming Control Room buses and presets are identical to those of the inputs and outputs. And just like inputs and outputs, different Cubase Projects can use different Control Room configurations. Therefore, make sure you store the Control Room preset as something like "My Control Room."

A FUNNY THING HAPPENED ON THE WAY TO THE CONTROL ROOM

By assigning your audio interface left and right ports to the Monitor 1 bus, you've also disconnected them from the Outputs tab. Click on the Outputs tab at the top of the VST Connections window to see what I'm talking about.

After taking the time to make the proper assignments in the Outputs tab, you may be a little miffed that the Control Room has automatically

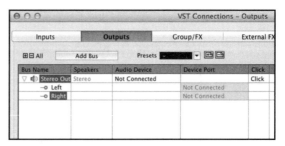

Figure 4.7. Outputs bus disconnected.

disconnected the Audio Device and Device Ports. However, this is normal. By doing so, the Cubase Output Channel Fader is now in full control of the mixdown volume only, while the Control Room volume (i.e., your studio monitors) can be adjusted without impacting the volume of the mixdown.

I should mention that it's not critical to use the Control Room. But I think after you've experienced even the most minor of its advantages, you'll enjoy using it for all of your monitoring needs.

ASSIGNING AUDIO INPUTS AND OUTPUTS TO AUDIO TRACKS

Now that you've made the proper input and output settings in the VST Connections window, you'll need to know how to assign them to Audio tracks. To that end, you'll need to add some Audio tracks to your project. Make sure you have your "My First Cubase Project" project loaded, then click on the Project menu and select Add Track, and then click on Audio. The Add Audio Track dialog box will appear, on which you can set the Count to "1" and the Configuration to Stereo. Click the Add Track button in the lower right-hand corner of the Add Audio Track dialog box. Now repeat the process, but this time, set the Track Configuration to Mono.

You'll find the two new Audio tracks added underneath the MIDI track you created earlier. The Audio tracks will have the default names of Audio 01 and Audio 02, respectively. You can now assign audio inputs to those tracks.

Figure 4.8. Audio tracks added to the Cubase Project.

Assigning Audio Inputs to Stereo and Mono Tracks

Stereo tracks can only be addressed from Stereo input buses, while Mono tracks can be addressed from either Mono or Stereo input buses. Look at Figure 4.8, and locate the Track Audio Input setting. Click on that setting, then take a close look at the following figure:

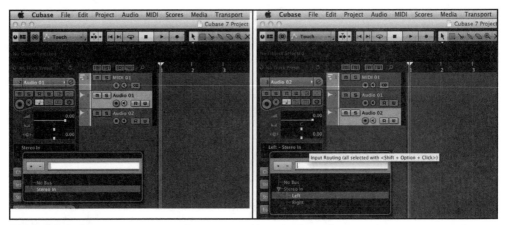

Figure 4.9. Track Audio Inputs on Stereo versus Mono Audio tracks.

Figure 4.9 is divided to show the different Track Audio Input settings for a Stereo Audio track (Audio 01) and a Mono Audio track (Audio 02). Notice that the Stereo Track Audio Input can only be assigned to Stereo In (as defined in the VST Connections Input tab). However, the Mono Track Audio Input can be assigned to either the Left or Right input of the Stereo In. This is why I usually create Stereo buses in the VST Connections Input tab. However, if you'd rather have Mono buses, don't let me stop you. In fact, Cubase will allow you to create Mono and Stereo buses that are assigned to the same Audio Device and Device Ports. (Cubase is indeed a flexible little minx.)

Assigning Tracks to Audio Outputs

If you refer back to Figure 4.8, you'll find the Track Audio Output settings. Most of the time, Audio tracks are assigned to the Stereo Out bus, as defined on the Outputs tab of the VST Connections window. That means that you won't have to worry about changing this setting unless you have a specific need to do so. Such occasions usually include assigning a number of Audio tracks to a Group Channel track or when routing Cubase tracks directly to independent audio interface hardware outputs. The latter is only necessary when interconnecting your audio interface to another audio device that has multiple inputs, such as a mixer or the audio interface of another computer. The bottom line is that unless you encounter such a specific need, leave the Track Audio Output set to the Stereo Out bus. (If you changed the name of the Stereo Out bus in the Output tab of the VST Connections window, make sure the Track Audio Output is set to that bus. Otherwise, you won't be able to hear the playback from the Audio track.)

Before proceeding, go ahead and save your Cubase Project by clicking on the File menu and selecting Save.

WHEN TO RECORD IN MONO, STEREO, OR MULTICHANNEL

When people start recording their first Audio tracks, there can be some confusion as to whether to record in mono or stereo. A lot of that confusion comes from hearing other seasoned audio engineers say things like "Stereo sounds better" or "Mono recordings are from the 1950s." Therefore, we should always record in stereo, right?

Well, the answer isn't quite that simple. The contemporary recording practices usually involve recording in one of three input configurations: mono, stereo, or multichannel. But how do you know which one is right for the recording you're about to make? I've found a way to easily determine the answer.

Count Your Sources

Sources, in this case, would be the origin of the audio device or signal you want to record. Some signals are mono, while others are stereo. Multichannel signals will require a mix of mono and/or stereo input configurations. All you need to do is count the sources to determine the proper input configuration. To help you further understand this concept, let's take a look at some examples.

COMMON MONO SOURCES

A single microphone is the most common mono source. A microphone (unless it's a specialized stereo microphone) has one output. One output equals one source. So when you're recording a vocalist, acoustic guitar, or trumpet with one microphone, the input configuration needs to be set to mono. Other mono sources might include a synthesizer with a single audio output or a bass guitar connected directly to the audio interface. Creating a mono Audio track would be required to accurately record any of these examples.

ARE VOCALS STEREO?

The human voice is not inherently stereo. The vocal cords, while they consist of a pair, can emit only one sound, or one source. Vocals only become stereo when they're recorded onto a mono track and then processed with some sort of stereo treatment, or when the recording takes place in an acoustically complementary environment with stereo or multiple microphones. In an acoustic environment—for example, the live performance of an opera—the sound of the performer's voice as it bounces around the opera house creates a stereo image. That image can be created in Cubase by using a reverb processor such as the REVerence. Other stereo treatments of mono Audio tracks include panning the track further to the left or right side of the Stereo Out. Each track has its own pan (short for panorama) control to place a track at a specific location within the stereo mix. The bottom line is that recording one vocalist through a closely placed microphone is not stereophonic, but you can use panning and effect treatments to give them a sense of stereo.

COMMON STEREO SOURCES

Most electronic musical instruments have stereo outputs. In other words, they have one output connection labeled Left (or L) and another output connection labeled Right (or R). These include synthesizers, drum machines, samplers, phonographs, and CD players. When capturing the sound from a device that has stereo outputs, you should create a stereo Audio track upon which to record.

But stereo recording is not limited to electronic devices. Many acoustic instruments are inherently stereo. For example, when you're sitting at a grand piano and you play some low notes, the sound will be louder in your left ear than your right. Playing middle C results in the sound being heard equally in both ears. Notes above middle C will be louder in the right ear than the left. And the higher the note, the more dramatically the sound will be sensed by your right ear. Therefore, to accurately record a grand piano, you should use at least two microphones in a stereo configuration—in other words, one mic pointed at the low strings and another pointed at the high strings. When you count the sources, you end up with two. Therefore, you should create and record on a stereo Audio track.

Many acoustic instruments are more accurately recorded with two microphones in a stereo configuration. That's because the sonic characteristics of the instrument are measurably different from the right and left "halves" of the instrument. These include, but are not limited to, acoustic guitar, harp, vibraphone, string quartet, or vocal choir. However, woodwinds such as clarinets and saxophones have more of a top-to-bottom arrangement, and while they are usually recorded with multiple microphones, they are generally not recorded in stereo. Rather, they are recorded as a multichannel source.

Figure 4.10. Recording a five-piece drum set with eleven microphones: kick (2); snare (2); toms 1, 2, and 3; hi-hat, ride; and overheads left and right.

COMMON MULTICHANNEL SOURCES

Perhaps the most demonstrative of multichannel examples is the recording of a drum set. In the early days of pop music, a drum set was recorded using only one microphone. However, the contemporary practice would be to put a microphone on every instrument that makes up a drum set and then record each microphone onto its own mono Audio track.

If you take a look at a five-piece drum set, it generally consists of a bass (or kick) drum, snare drum, two rack toms, one floor tom, one hi-hat cymbal, plus a multitude of other cymbals. To accurately record the essence of the entire drum set, you'd need at least eight microphones and an audio interface with eight discrete inputs, such as the Steinberg MR816CSX. (See "Choosing an Audio Interface" in chapter 2.) Then you'd create eight mono Audio tracks to capture each component of the drum set. Usually they'd be kick, snare, hi-hat, tom 1, tom 2, floor tom, overhead left, and overhead right. The overhead microphones are placed above the drum set to capture not only the ride, crash, and other cymbals, but also the ambient stereophonic image of the whole drum set.

Then, prior to or immediately after the recording, the drum tracks would be panned according to their placement in the stereo image of the listener. In other words, the hi-hat track would be panned toward the listener's right ear while the floor tom would be panned toward the listener's left ear. Usually the overhead microphones are recorded onto their own separate mono Audio track so that panning and EQ (tone controls) can be applied independently. When I record a five-piece drum set, I'll usually mic the snare drum with two microphones: one over the top head and one underneath the bottom head. The same is true of the bass drum: one on each side of the drum to capture the front and rear heads separately. Also, make sure to have some 3-In-One household oil for lubricating the bass drum pedal. Otherwise, you may be capturing the squeak of a poorly maintained bass drum pedal. (Listen to any of the early James Brown recordings such as "Get Up" or "I Feel Good," or Led Zeppelin recordings [especially "Bonzo's Montreux" from the Coda album], for examples of squeaky bass drum pedals.) Basically, the more microphones you record with, the more options you'll have during the mix.

The same is true for any large instrument or ensemble. For example, a large vocal ensemble such as the Mormon Tabernacle Choir would need a lot of microphones on each section (bass, tenor, alto, and soprano) to accurately record the performance. Care would also need to be exercised for capturing the pipe organ, piano, or any other accompanying instrumentation onto individual tracks. Then recording each microphone onto its own Audio track (mono or stereo, depending on the microphone placement) would allow for discrete volume, pan, EQ settings, and other treatments to be applied during the mix.

CUBASIC NO. 4: CONFIGURING AND RECORDING WITH THE CLICK OR METRONOME

For many years, music has been recorded while the performers listened to a metronome or click track in their headphones. This allowed for a noticeably tighter "feel" of the recording, because all the musicians were aware of the true tempo. Every DAW, including Cubase, has a Metronome with which you can accomplish the same tight feel.

Note: Cubase uses the terms Click, Clik, and Metronome interchangeably.

Not only are the recordings tighter, but the Metronome also establishes an accurate time base within Cubase. While there are many different time bases to choose from, the default of measures, bars, beats, and clocks is the most common and useful. That way, when the artist says, "Let's pick it up from measure 57," you'll know right where to go.

Reluctance to Use the Metronome

The members of a pop music–style band (rock, jazz, country, etc.) are very comfortable playing their instruments together at the same time, just like they would during a performance. But their "vibe" can be seriously disrupted when going into the studio. Basically, the drums are usually laid down first, then rhythm instruments, then soloists, and finally vocals. So when each musician has to conform to a click track, it can be intimidating and frustrating. This discomfort might lead you and/or the musicians you're recording to forego the click track. I would strongly dissuade you from not using the Click. Once you or the musicians get comfortable with it, it can make the difference between an average recording and a polished one.

Configuring the Metronome

Click on the Transport menu, and select Metronome Setup.

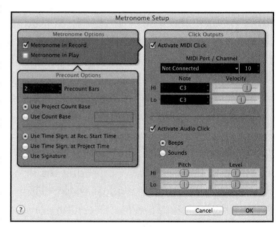

Figure 4.11. The Metronome Setup window.

I would recommend the settings you see in Figure 4.11 if they're not configured this way by default. In the Metronome options, you can choose whether you hear the Click during record, playback, or both. Personally, I'd rather not hear the Click during playback unless I'm monitoring tracks for timing. The Precount Bars allow you to define how many bars of Click you'll hear before recording engages. Start with 2, but after you get used to the Precount, you may want to set it to 1. The MIDI Click will not be necessary, so you can disable it. However, since the settings are defaulted to MIDI Port is Not Connected, it wouldn't be heard anyway. Make sure Activate Audio Click is enabled and set to Beeps. The Click Pitch and Level can be customized with the controls located underneath the Beeps setting. When you've made the desired settings, click the OK button to close the Metronome Setup window.

Metronome and Precount On/Off

You can turn the Metronome and Precount on and off by clicking on the Transport menu.

A checkmark next to each item will indicate whether the option is on or off. You'll also notice that typing "C" on your computer keyboard can toggle the Metronome On/Off. The same can be accomplished with the Click button in the Transport Panel. (See "Project Tempo and Time Signature" in chapter 5.)

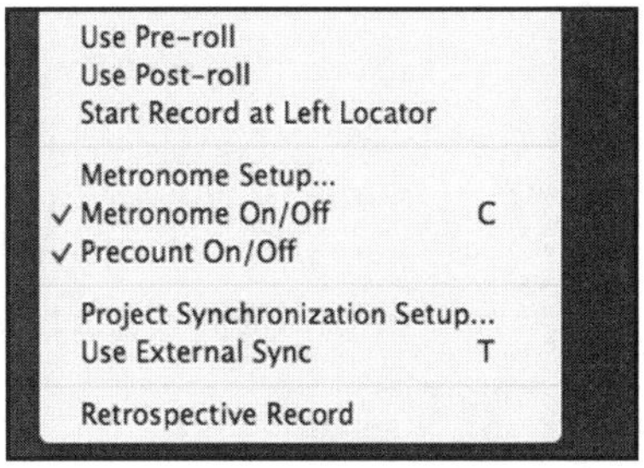

Routing the Click Output

The method for defining where the Click will be sent will be handled in one of two ways. The method you choose will depend upon whether you use the Stereo Out bus in the VST Connections Outputs tab for monitoring or if you use the Control Room. (See "Assigning Audio Outputs to Cubase" and "Creating a Simple Control Room (Cubase Only)" earlier in this chapter.)

Figure 4.12. Metronome and Precount On/Off.

STEREO OUT METHOD

If you refer back to Figure 4.5, you'll notice a Click column on the right-hand side of the Outputs window. Make sure you click on the Click field directly across from the Audio Device setting. That will route the Metronome to your Stereo Out bus.

CONTROL ROOM METHOD (CUBASE ONLY)

This method is only applicable if you've configured even the most modest Control Room configuration in the Studio tab of the VST Connections window. Click on the Devices menu, and select Control Room Mixer.

Finding the Click button on the Control Room Mixer can be a little daunting. Notice in Figure 4.13 that there are many more settings at the bottom of the Control Room Mixer than you're probably seeing right now. So what you'll need to do is make sure you click the Control Room and Mixer tabs at the top and bottom of the Control Room Mixer. Then locate the Control Room Power button just above the Mixer tab and click anywhere near (but not on) that button. The Control Room settings will rise gently from the bottom of the Control Room Mixer to reveal many additional settings, including the Click button. (Gray is off, magenta is on.) If the Click is off, just single-click it. That will allow you to hear the Click through your studio monitors, as defined in the Studio tab of the VST Connections window. (See "Creating a Simple Control Room (Cubase Only)" earlier in this chapter.)

Figure 4.13. The Control Room Mixer.

Note: If you're using a more elaborately configured Control Room with multiple cue mixes and headphones, you will need to enable the Click for those outputs as well.

RECORDING SOME TEST TRACKS

Now that you have your MIDI and audio inputs and outputs configured, it's time to verify their operation by recording some test tracks. Make sure you have your "My First Cubase Project" project loaded and that it contains one MIDI track, a mono Audio track, and a stereo Audio track. If you've been following along through this chapter, you should have all three tracks created already.

Recording a MIDI Test Track

To make this process as easy as possible, you're going to use a built-in VST Instrument as your sound-generating source. That will spare you from having to configure an external

synthesizer or prematurely go over Instrument tracks. Selecting a track will usually record enable the track. However, if the Record Enable button is gray on the MIDI track, click on it so that it turns red.

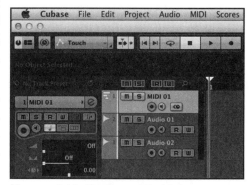

You'll notice in Figure 4.14 that there is a Record Enable button both on the track and in the Inspector. They are one and the same, so if one is red and enabled, both buttons will have record enabled.

Figure 4.14. The Record Enable button.

If you were to play some notes on your MIDI controller now, you wouldn't hear anything. That's because you need to create a virtual or VST Instrument to which the MIDI track will have its output assigned. You will, however, see the vertical MIDI Activity Indicator just to the right of the track lighting up to show you that the track is receiving MIDI information. The harder you play the note, the higher the MIDI Activity Indicator will jump.

CREATING A VST INSTRUMENT

Click on the Devices menu and select VST Instruments, or type F11. The VST Instruments "rack" will appear.

I call the VST Instrument window a "rack" because it reminds me of a nineteen-inch equipment rack into which all sorts of synthesizer modules can be mounted. We essentially do exactly that when we load a VST Instrument into one of the empty numbered slots. We just don't need cables, screws, or a physical rack to do it. To load a VST Instrument, locate the first slot and click on the black area that contains the dim text "no

Figure 4.15. An empty VST Instruments rack.

instrument." A drop-down menu will appear and display all of the VST Instruments you can choose from.

The menu will display the virtual instruments you have installed on your computer, but not the individual sounds. You'll work that out in a moment. For now, click on the Synth category and then click on HALion Sonic SE. (Note: Don't be confused by the number of VST Instruments you see in the menu. Depending on how many third-party plug-ins you have installed, your menu could include more or fewer than are listed in Figure 4.16.) You will then see a dialog box asking if you'd like to create a MIDI track assigned to HALion Sonic SE. While this is great time-saving feature, hit the Cancel button for now. The HALion Sonic SE control panel will appear.

I'll spend more time on HALion Sonic SE (hereby referred to as HSSE) later in this book. For now, HSSE is a special-edition version of Steinberg's very powerful HALion Sonic Synthesizer Workstation. This SE version has a generous palette of sounds from the HALion Sonic Library. One of those sounds (First Contact) has already been loaded into Program slot 1 by default. HSSE has sixteen Program slots, and the slot number is usually the same as the slot MIDI Channel. However, that number can be altered at the top of the control panel. Just leave it set to "1" for now.

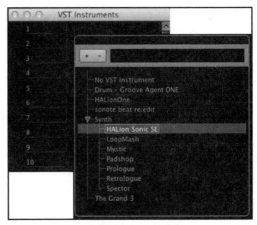

Figure 4.16. VST Instrument choices.

Figure 4.17. The upper-left quarter of the HALion Sonic SE control panel.

SETTING MIDI TRACK
INPUT, OUTPUT, AND CHANNEL

If you were to play some notes on your MIDI controller, you still wouldn't hear the First Contact sound. That's because you need to assign your MIDI track to HSSE on MIDI Channel 1. Go to the Inspector of MIDI track 1 and set the Track Input, Output, and Channel as they appear in Figure 4.18.

Once you've made those settings, you can play some notes on your MIDI controller, and you'll hear the First Contact sound. It's a synth sweep with an arpeggio layer that follows the tempo of Cubase. While it would be fun to play around with this sound, we do need to get on with the process of recording.

Figure 4.18. MIDI track settings for slot 1 of HSSE and Transport controls

USING THE TRANSPORT CONTROLS
FOR RECORDING AND PLAYBACK

The easiest way to quickly bring the cursor back to measure 1 is to click the Go to Previous Marker button at the far left of the Transport Panel. Since you shouldn't have any markers in this project, it should bring the cursor back to measure 1. Then click the Record button in the Transport Panel, and you'll hear the Metronome for the two Precount bars I previously defined in the Metronome Setup window. After the Precount, the recording will commence and the Cursor will scroll across the display indicating the current position. A horizontal event will be drawn from left to right and will be equal to the track height. This is the event that will contain the MIDI information that you're recording and will soon be playing back. You won't need to worry about what you're playing on your MIDI keyboard. (You're not going to win any Grammys…yet.) Just play some notes to record the performance onto the MIDI track. When you're finished recording, click the Stop button, then the Go to Previous Marker button, and then click the Play button to review your recording.

Figure 4.19. A recorded MIDI event on the MIDI track.

If you didn't hear the playback, review the procedures for setting both MIDI and audio inputs and outputs. Also make sure that your audio interface is turned up and your studio monitors are powered up and that their volumes are turned up too.

Recording an Audio Test Track

Now it's time to test your audio inputs and outputs by recording an Audio track. You can use anything you want as long as it makes sound. This could be a synthesizer, vocal microphone, acoustic guitar—whatever you prefer.

CONNECTING THE INSTRUMENT OR MICROPHONE

A cable (or, for a stereo source, you'll need two) will be required to connect the instrument or microphone to the input of your audio interface. Go ahead and make that connection. If the instrument (such as a synthesizer or acoustic guitar pickup) has a volume control, make sure it's turned all the way up. If it's a condenser microphone you'll be recording from, make sure that you enable the phantom power (+48 V) on your audio interface. (Condenser microphones require phantom power to charge the microphone capsule. Consult the owners' manuals of both the microphone and your audio interface to see if you need, and how to enable, phantom power.)

SETTING AN INPUT LEVEL

Your audio interface will have some sort of facility to adjust the input sensitivity or gain of its inputs. You'll usually find a knob or slider marked Gain, Level, or Volume. Setting an appropriate input level is critical for capturing the best recording possible. Fortunately, it's really easy to set. Your audio interface will probably have a peak light for every input. While you or the musician is playing or singing the loudest volume he or she will perform during the recording, turn the input gain control up until the peak light glows. Then turn the gain down until the peak light disappears. The rule is: always set the input gain as high as possible without peaking.

SETTING AUDIO TRACK RECORD
ENABLE, INPUT, AND MONITOR

You made two Audio tracks in your project; one is mono and the other is stereo. Click on the Record Enable according to the number of sources required for the instrument or microphone(s) you connected to your audio interface. The example in Figure 4.20 is an acoustic guitar pickup that is a mono source; therefore, the mono track is record enabled.

Figure 4.20. Audio track Record Enable, Input, and Monitor settings.

I double-clicked the name of the track ("Audio 02") and renamed it "Q-stick." (That's the silly way I label acoustic guitar tracks.) I highly recommend changing the names of your tracks, especially Audio tracks, prior to recording. Otherwise you'll end up with "Audio 01" through "Audio 40" and not know what any of the tracks have recorded on them.

Click on the Track Audio input, and choose the desired input. For example, I plugged the acoustic guitar directly into the right input of my audio interface. Since it's mono, I set the Track Audio input to Right (that is to say, the right bus of my Stereo In bus as defined in the Input tab of the VST Connections window).

You might need to click the Monitor button to be able to hear the instrument or microphone prior to or during the recording. I'll go over monitoring in more detail in chapter 8. But for now, see if your audio interface has a "mix" control to balance the input and the playback. If it does, set it somewhere in the middle. (Every audio interface will provide you with the ability to monitor, but there are several methods, depending on make and model. You may also need to consult the owner's manual of your audio interface to learn how it facilitates monitoring.)

RECORDING THE AUDIO TRACK

Review Figure 4.18 for the location of the Transport controls. Then you can refer to "Using the Transport Controls for Recording and Playback" (earlier in this chapter) to learn how to record and review your track; only this time you'll be recording audio, and an Audio event will appear in the Event window.

Figure 4.21. A recorded Audio event on the Audio track.

Press the Play button to review your recording. (If you can't hear the Audio track, try disabling the Monitor button.) Now you'll hear the MIDI track (if you recorded one) and the Audio track simultaneously. If your Audio event doesn't display a waveform of the recording or you can't hear the playback, review this chapter and verify your settings.

ANTICIPATING THE POSSIBILITIES

If everything was configured properly, you just made your first recording with Cubase! You should be feeling empowered and ready to forge on. I hope you are, because you can create a lot of music with the simple operations you've learned so far. However, there's a lot more to Cubase, and I hope you're ready to learn more.

DVD Option No. 1

If you'd like to hear what I came up with for my "My First Cubase Project" project, you will find that project inside of its Project Folder on the DVD that came with this book. You might be interested to hear how your inspiration differed from mine. I added another Audio track, upon which I recorded a bass guitar. (Be kind in your critique of my project, for I have been writing this book and not practicing my guitar or bass skills.)

The Project Window and Transport Panel

5

The Project window is where you'll be spending most of your time while working in Cubase. Think of it as the driver seat of a new automobile, for that is the place in which you spend the most time in your car. Since this car is new, you'll have to learn how to start the engine, where the operational controls are, how to tune to your favorite radio station, and how to set the climate controls. (You'll notice how I put music before comfort; I do have my priorities straight, you know.) Cubase is the same way, except you've already learned how to "start the car" by launching Cubase. Now you'll need to learn where all the operational controls and features are. In this chapter, you will learn about:

- The three columns of the Project window.
- The Time Ruler.
- The Left and Right Locators.
- How to set the Window Layout options.
- The Inspector, the Toolbar and the Status, Info, and Overview Lines
- The Transport Panel and the numeric keypad.

THE PROJECT WINDOW

Before I can talk about the Project window, you'll need to start a new project. Up to this point, you've been using "My First Cubase Project." If you still have it loaded, close that project so that you can focus on a new, empty project. You'll also need to know how to add tracks to a project, so make sure to review those steps in chapter 4. Basically, you can create tracks by clicking the Project menu and selecting Add Track, or by right-clicking in the Track column. (See Figure 5.1.)

Click on the File menu, and select New Project. Then follow the procedures described in "The Steinberg Hub and Project Assistant" in chapter 3 to create a new project named

"Project and Transport." You should now see an empty Project window, as shown in Figure 5.1.

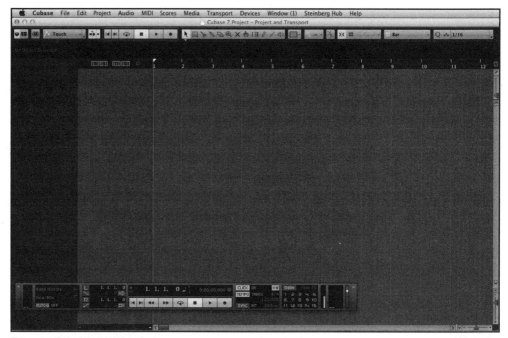

Figure 5.1. An empty project.

The Project window is comprised of several columns and rows similar to a spreadsheet. (The rows are referred to as lines, which I will discuss shortly.) Make sure that you can see all three columns, including the Inspector. If you can only see two columns, click the Window Layout button (second button from the left on the Toolbar) and make sure that Inspector has a checkmark next to it. (To close the Window Layout, click anywhere outside of the window.) Now I'll talk about the three main columns of the Project window.

Inspector

The first column is called the Inspector. The Inspector contains all of the settings for each individual track. Those settings are located within sections that appear within the Inspector. The sections found within the Inspector will vary depending on the type of track you have selected. In other words, an Audio track will have an Inserts section, while a MIDI track will have a MIDI Inserts section. The former will have an Equalizers section, while the latter will not. Other specialized tracks (such as Markers and Tempo) will have unique sections that won't appear for any other track. For now, let's talk about the sections for MIDI and Audio tracks. Go ahead and click on the Project menu, select Add Track, and then click on MIDI Track. The Add MIDI Track dialog box will appear, wherein you will set the Count to 1, then click the Add Track button. Repeat the process, but this time add one mono or stereo Audio track.

MIDI TRACK INSPECTOR SECTIONS

Make sure that you have the MIDI track selected to reveal the MIDI sections, as shown in Figure 5.2.

The top section will be easy to spot, because it has the same name and color as the MIDI track. In this example, it's MIDI 01. If you cannot see the settings within the top section, click on the section to reveal the settings that appear in Figure 5.2. The top section contains the most common settings for a MIDI track, including Track Controls, Volume, Pan, Input & Output (see "Cubasic No. 2: Assigning MIDI Inputs and Outputs to Tracks" in chapter 4), and so on. Underneath those settings, you will see the remaining sections: Chord Track, Expression Map, Note Expression, MIDI Modifiers, MIDI Inserts, MIDI Fader, Notepad, and Quick Controls. Click on any section to reveal the settings. When you do, the top section will become hidden, and the selection section will be revealed. (You can also Ctrl/Command-click to reveal or hide multiple section settings, or Alt/Option-click to reveal or hide all of the sections.) For now, click on the top section so that the Inspector appears as it does in Figure 5.2.

Figure 5.2. The MIDI track sections.

Figure 5.3. The Audio track sections.

AUDIO TRACK INSPECTOR SECTIONS

Now make sure you have the Audio track selected to reveal the Audio sections, as shown in Figure 5.3.

The settings that appear in the top section of an Audio track are very similar to those of a MIDI track, especially the Track controls such as Record Enable, Monitor, Input, and Output. However, there are some new sections you haven't seen before, including Inserts, Equalizers, Sends, and Channel. Click on any section to reveal the corresponding settings. The Chord Track, Notepad, and Quick Control sections are common to both MIDI and Audio tracks. The behaviors of revealing and hiding Audio track sections are identical to those of MIDI tracks.

INSTRUMENT TRACK INSPECTOR SECTIONS

You haven't worked with an Instrument track yet. However, due to the popularity of virtual instruments, I think you'll use it more often than its cousin, the MIDI track. An Instrument track starts with MIDI data and ends with audio data. It's basically a MIDI track and an Audio track with a virtual synthesizer in between. A virtual instrument sandwich, if you will. (Great, now I'm hungry.) Therefore, you'll find many of the same sections used by both MIDI and Audio tracks. Go ahead and click on the Project menu, select Add Track, and then select Instrument. The Add Instrument Track dialog box will appear. Locate and click on the Add Track button without making any other selections within the dialog box; save the Count of 1. You will now see a third track added to your Track column, as it appears in Figure 5.4.

You will find MIDI sections such as Expression Map and Note Expression along with Audio sections such as Inserts and Equalizers. The top section is identical to a MIDI track. The behaviors of revealing and hiding Instrument track sections are identical to those of MIDI and Audio tracks.

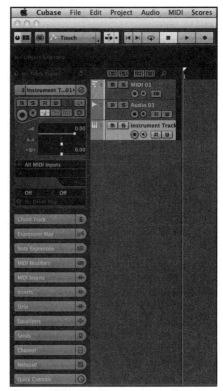

Figure 5.4. The Instrument Track sections.

Track Column

To the right of the Inspector, you will find the Track Column. (See Figure 5.1) You've already added three tracks to this project: one MIDI, one Audio, and one Instrument. Clicking on a track will reveal its sections and settings in the Inspector.

CHANGING THE TRACK NAME

The track itself has a name that you can change by double-clicking on the default name and typing the desired name, followed by typing the Enter key on your computer keyboard. I strongly recommend naming each track immediately after its creation. If you don't, you'll end up with a bunch of tracks with default names, such as "MIDI 01" through "MIDI 40." If you don't name the track, you'll have to listen to each one to determine what it contains, and that will certainly slow your workflow. Simple names are the best, such as "Lead Vocal 1" or "Drum Overhead Left." However, if your names get longer than about fourteen characters, the Track Name field will be contracted. But you can hover your mouse over the Track name to have the entire name crawl (like the text at the bottom of a cable news broadcast) from right to left.

ALTERING TRACK HEIGHT

When you hover your mouse over a track (upper or lower) boundary, the pointer will turn into an icon resembling two horizontal parallel lines with one arrow pointing up and one pointing down. Now click and drag the lower boundary of a track to increase the track height, as in the Instrument track in Figure 5.5.

Figure 5.5. Altering the track height.

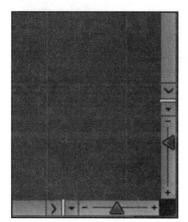

Figure 5.6. Track Zoom controls.

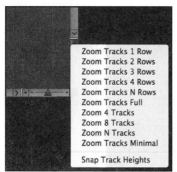

Figure 5.7. Track Zoom Presets menu open.

You can also hold Ctrl/Command to adjust the height of all tracks simultaneously. Or holding Shift + Alt/Option will adjust the height of all tracks below the track you've selected to adjust.

There are also controls for adjusting the height of all tracks simultaneously. In the lower right-hand corner of the Project window, you will find the Zoom controls, as seen in Figure 5.6.

Moving the vertical Zoom slider up or down will adjust the height of all tracks. Clicking on the Zoom In or Zoom Out will alter track height in steps. There is also the Track Zoom Presets button. Clicking on that button will reveal the Track Zoom Presets menu, as seen in Figure 5.7.

The Track presets allow you to quickly conform all the tracks to predefined heights. For example, clicking on Zoom 8 Tracks will quickly adjust the height so that eight tracks will be visible in the Project window.

When you increase the track height, you'll be able to see more Track Controls. The Track Controls will vary by the track type. Increase the height of all three tracks so that they appear like Figure 5.8.

TRACK CONTROLS FOR INDIVIDUAL TRACKS

Track Controls are the little buttons that appear on the tracks themselves. There are many different Track Controls, and they'll vary depending on track type. However, there are several commonly used Track Controls I'd like to describe. To identify which Track Control I'll be describing, simply hover your mouse pointer over each one and pause until the name appears under the mouse pointer. (Note: Multiple Track Controls can be used simultaneously across multiple tracks.)

Figure 5.8. The most commonly used Track Controls.

Mute disables the playback so that you don't hear the material recorded on the track.

Solo allows you to hear only the track that is soloed.

Record Enable will allow new material to be recorded the next time you hit the Record button on the Transport Panel. (See "The Transport Panel" later in this chapter.)

Monitor allows you to hear the track as it's being recorded. Monitor is used mostly on Audio tracks, and its behavior depends greatly on your monitoring strategy. (See "Choosing a Monitoring Strategy" in chapter 8.)

Edit Channel Settings will open the Track Channel Setting control panel.

Read enable will set the track to play back automation data.

Write enable will set the track to record automation data.

Track Type Icon is not a Track Control but does indicate the track type. The icons are identical to the icons in the Add Track command.

TRACK CONTROLS FOR ALL TRACKS

At the top of the Track Column, you will find four Track Controls that affect all tracks simultaneously. These are great when you want to disable all active Mutes or Solos, or disable all reading and/or writing of automation data.

Event Display Column

The Event Display contains visual representations of all the data you record or enter into your Cubase Project. The events may be MIDI or audio data, but can also be automation or MIDI controls data. When you start recording, the types of data and their representation in the Event Display will become more obvious.

THE RULER

The Ruler represents the timeline of your project and is shown in Figure 5.9.

Figure 5.9. The Ruler, Ruler options, and Waveform Zoom slider.

The Ruler depicts the temporal measurement of the data in the Event Display, with earlier events to the left and later events to the right. The default time unit is Bars + Beats, which is the most musical of representations. You can click on the Ruler Options button (far right of the Ruler) and select a different unit of measurement, such as Timecode or Seconds.

WAVEFORM ZOOM

When editing audio data, it can be difficult to see the quiet passages. The Waveform Zoom slider (represented by a vertical slider at the far right-hand side of Figure 5.9) allows you to adjust the height, not of the Audio track, but of the waveform display of the events. It has no effect on nonaudio data. The default slider position is at its lowest position. Moving the slider up will increase the waveform height. While it will make your waveforms look louder, no volume or gain adjustments are occurring.

EVENT ZOOM CONTROLS

As with the Event Zoom options, there are multiple ways of zooming the Event Display. My favorite way is a little difficult to describe. But once you've used it, you'll wish every software program zoomed the same way. Click on the Ruler and hold your mouse button. Then push your mouse upward to zoom out, or pull it down to zoom in. Once the preferred zoom level has been achieved, release your mouse button.

You can also increment or decrement the zoom by typing "G" to zoom out or "H" to zoom in. Plus, there are Zoom controls located in the lower right-hand corner of the Project window, as shown in Figure 5.10.

Figure 5.10. The Event Zoom controls.

Most Event Zoom controls work similarly to their Track Zoom counterparts but alter the scale of the timeline rather than the track height. However, the Zoom presets are a bit different, as you'll see in Figure 5.11.

The Event Zoom presets are always depicted in minutes, seconds, or ms (milliseconds), regardless of the Ruler units setting. I like to think of them as "Show me X amount of time in the Event Display." For example, choosing ~1 minute will zoom the display to a one-minute region. A setting of ~30 seconds will zoom the display to a thirty-second region, and so on. (Note: You can also perform an Event Zoom in the Overview Line, which I will discuss later in this chapter.

THE CURSOR

The Cursor indicates the current temporal position within the project. For example, click on measure 2 within the Ruler of your Cubase Project. The Cursor will move to the position of measure 2, as in Figure 5.12.

Moving the Cursor allows you to select a temporal location where you can start recording or playback. It's similar to fast-forwarding or rewinding, except that it instantly locates the Cursor

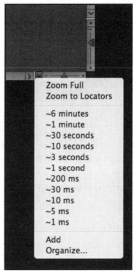

Figure 5.11. The Event Zoom presets.

to the position you choose on the Ruler. The precision with which the Cursor (and, as you'll learn later, Locators and Events) is placed on the Ruler is determined by the Snap.

CUBASIC NO. 5: SNAP

Snap will allow for precision placement of the Cursor, Locators, and Events. (The latter two you will learn about a little later.) Snap is normally enabled by default, which

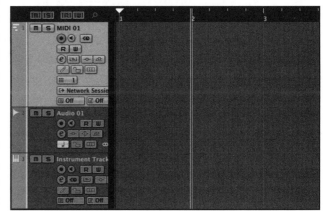

Figure 5.12. The Cursor with Snap on.

means that when you placed the Cursor at measure 2, it magnetically snapped to the measure. There may be times when more or less precision is required. Such situations would require a modification of the Snap settings or disabling Snap altogether. Those settings are located at the top of the Cubase Project window, as shown in Figure 5.13.

Figure 5.13. The Snap settings.

The Snap button looks like >:< and reminds me of an emoticon. You can turn the Snap on and off completely by clicking the Snap On/Off button or by typing "J" on your computer keyboard. To alter the precision of the Snap when it's on, click on the Grid Type button. The default setting is Bar, which means that Snap will place the Cursor or other items to the nearest bar. But a Grid Type of Beat will allow the Snap to place items on the nearest quarter-note beat within a bar. Or for further precision, the setting of Use Quantize will conform the Snap to the currently selected Quantize Preset. The default of 1/16 will set the precision to sixteenth-notes. (Note: The Grid Type and Quantize Preset settings will have no effect when the Snap is off.)

CUBASIC NO. 6: AUTO-SCROLL

Auto-Scroll constantly updates the event display and the Cursor position during recording, playback, and editing. I find myself leaving Auto-Scroll on practically all the time, because I like to see the events during recording and playback. During editing, however, Auto-Scroll can unexpectedly move the display, leaving you wondering where your data went. Steinberg added a new behavior to the Auto-Scroll that makes it possible to edit events while leaving Auto-Scroll on. The Auto-Scroll button can be located near the upper left-hand corner of the Project window, as seen in Figure 5.14.

Figure 5.14. Auto-Scroll buttons.

Finding these little buttons takes some work. They're the sixth and seventh buttons from the left on the Cubase Toolbar. Both Auto-Scroll and Suspend Auto-Scroll when Editing buttons are enabled by default. You can disable Auto-Scroll either by clicking the button or by typing "F" on your computer keyboard. I would recommend leaving Suspend Auto-Scroll when Editing enabled at all times. If you turn it off, Auto-Scroll can unceremoniously reposition the Event Display and Cursor while you're trying to edit something and cause a lot of consternation. Prior to Cubase 5, there was no Suspend feature, which required you to either stop playback or turn off Auto-Scroll (formerly Follow, hence the key command of "F") if you wanted to edit and continue playback at the same time.

CUBASIC NO. 7: THE LEFT AND RIGHT LOCATORS

At first, the Locators can be a little challenging to understand and work with. But they are equally useful and necessary, and learning to use them will be critical for a variety of operations. When you start recording in a new Cubase Project, chances are you won't be continuously recording from the very beginning of a track to the very end. Throughout history, composers have compartmentalized their work so that they could focus on each section, each instrument, and every note. Focusing is exactly what the Locators do: restrict the attention of both the user and the program to a specific region of the Event Display.

The Left and Right Locators are found on the Ruler. However, by default they might both be located at bar 1. That makes them a little hard to see, as shown in Figure 5.15.

The Locators appear as small triangle shapes in the Ruler. When they're back to back, as they are in Figure 5.14, they make one bigger triangle and are impossible to differentiate from one another. They won't be of much use to you until you move them.

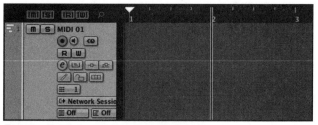

Figure 5.15. Locators both at bar 1.

Positioning the Locators

Before you start moving the Locators, make sure that your Snap is on and that the Grid Type is set to Bar. Next, there are a multitude of methods for moving the Locators. I find myself using all of the methods during the course of a project, except one:

DRAGGING

While it is possible and seemingly logical to click and drag each Locator to the desired position, I would dissuade you from using this method. Personally, I find it to be cumbersome. However, if dragging the Locators works for you, don't let me stop you.

CLICKING

This is by far my favorite method. It involves clicking on the Ruler while holding a modifier key on your computer keyboard. To position the Left Locator, type and hold Ctrl/Option and then click on the Ruler. To position the Right Locator, type and hold Alt/Command and then click on the Ruler.

USING THE KEYPAD

By keypad, I'm talking about the numeric keypad that is located on the right-hand side of a full-sized computer keyboard. Having a keypad is critical for transport control of Cubase. (You'll learn more about the Transport Panel and the keypad in the next section.) If you are using a laptop or have an abbreviated keyboard without a keypad (such as the Apple Wireless Keyboard), I would strongly recommend that you get a USB or Bluetooth (if your computer has Bluetooth capabilities) keypad.

Start by moving the Cursor to the desired position by clicking on the Ruler. Then type Ctrl/Command + 1 (the "1" on the keypad) to place the Left Locator at the Cursor position. Repeat the process for the Right Locator, but this time type Ctrl/Command + 2. (The use of the keypad "1" and "2" keys will become apparent in the next section.) I find the keypad method a little slower than the clicking method. But it's very useful if your cursor happens to be positioned where you'd like to place a Locator.

PROPER LOCATOR POSITIONING

It's important to note that the Left Locator must always be placed to the left of the Right Locator, and the Right Locator always placed to the right of the Left Locator. If I've succeeded in confusing you with this directional dichotomy, let me illustrate what I'm talking about with Figures 5.16 and 5.17. In both cases, the Locators are placed at bars 2 and 4.

Figure 5.16. Proper Locator positioning.

It's easy to see when the Locators are placed properly, because there will be a blue region displayed in the Ruler between the Locators.

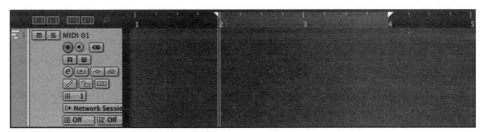

Figure 5.17. Reversed Locator positioning.

When the Locator positions are reversed, two things will happen. First, the region on the Ruler will be red, indicating reversed Locator positioning. Second, certain operations (such as Audio Export and Mixdown) will be impossible. Therefore, it's very important to keep the Left Locator on the left and the Right Locator on the right.

TOOLBAR, STATUS, INFO, AND OVERVIEW LINES

Now that I've gone over the three columns of the Project window, it's time to discuss the rows that make up the Toolbar, Status, Info, and Overview Lines. You can think of them as the vertical rows of a spreadsheet. They're all made visible or hidden with the Window Layout settings. See Figure 5.18 for the location of the Window Layout button, and click on it.

Figure 5.18. The Window Layout settings.

When you reveal the Window Layout settings, the Project window will become covered in opaque blue. This is a behavior you will see during some Cubase operations, and is normal. It basically means there's a screen visible that may need your attention before proceeding. In the case of the Window Layout, make sure that the Inspector is still checked, along with the Status, Info, and Overview Lines. You'll see a few vertical rows appear across the top of the Project window. When you're finished enabling all the lines, click away from the Window Layout setting, and the window will close.

Since there's nothing in the Project and Transport Project yet, I'm going to load a project that has some material already recorded in it. That project, along with all the lines, is depicted in Figure 5.19.

Figure 5.19. The Toolbar, Status, Info, and Overview Lines.

Each of these lines depicts different data, and all but the Toolbar can be configured on a project-by-project basis.

Toolbar

The Toolbar is visible at all times. It's the Cubase equivalent of a handyman's tool belt. Basically, it's where you keep the tools. Take a look at some of the buttons on the Toolbar. You've already used ones such as the basic transport controls, Auto-Scroll, and Snap settings.

Status Line

The Status Line contains the basic Project settings such as Record Format and Project Frame Rate. It also contains the Record Time Max indicator that displays how much recording time you have left on your hard disk. In Figure 5.19, it reads 217 hours and 42 minutes. (I guess I need to get recording!) Clicking on the reading will open a separate Record Time Max display that can be repositioned on your computer monitor (or second monitor) anywhere you'd like.

PROJECT SETUP

The other settings displayed in the Status Line are part of the Project Setup. Clicking on anything other than the Record Time Max indicator will open the Project Setup window, as show in Figure 5.20. The Project Setup window can also be accessed from the Project menu or by typing Shift + S.

The Project Setup window is divided into six sections from top to bottom. Pay particular attention to the four settings in the fifth section, because they are the settings displayed in the Status Line. Unless you have the specific need to use different values, I would recommend using the settings as they appear in Figure 5.20.

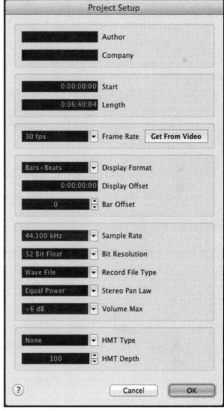

Figure 5.20. The Project Setup window.

Info Line

When you click on an event in the Event Display, the Info Line will display very detailed information about the event. For example, the event selected in Figure 5.19 is an Audio event. In the Info Line, you can see the File Name and Description, along with very detailed timing information, such as Start, End, Length, and Offset. Clicking on any field will allow you to edit the text and/or timing values.

Overview Line

The Overview Line has two basic functions. First, it provides a very small-scale display of the Event Display and can give you an idea of where you are in the project. Second, you can click and drag across the Overview Line to perform an Event Zoom.

THE TRANSPORT PANEL

In the previous chapter, you used the Transport controls in the Toolbar for Play, Stop, and Return to Zero. But there are a great many more Transport controls, all of which appear in the Transport Panel. The Transport Panel is an independent floating window that is visible by default. If you cannot see it in your Project window, click the Transport menu and select Transport Panel, or type F2 on your computer keyboard. The appearance of the Transport Panel may vary from that of Figure 5.21, but the controls I will be discussing are visible by default.

Figure 5.21. The Transport Panel.

Primary and Secondary Time Displays

These are the two large numeric windows above the Transport controls such as Play and Stop. By default, the Primary and Secondary Time Displays are set to Bars + Beats, and Seconds, respectively. They provide a constant readout of the Cursor position at all times. You can click on a digit in either readout to enter a value to locate to. You can also hover your pointer slightly above any value and click to increment, or slightly below any value and click to decrement.

To the right of the digital readouts is a small icon (usually looking like a quarter-note for Bars + Beats, or a clock face for Seconds) showing the current format. Clicking that icon will allow you to change the format. For example, if you're working on a project that is based on timecode, you could click on the Secondary Time Display Format icon and choose Timecode. At the division of the readouts is the Exchange Time Formats button that will exchange the placement of the Time Displays.

Main Transport Controls

The main Transport controls are pretty self-explanatory. However, there may be some functions with which you're not familiar. I'll cover all those bases by referring to Figure 5.22, and going from left to right.

Figure 5.22. The main Transport controls.

GO TO PREVIOUS MARKER/ZERO

Since you haven't inserted any Markers into your Project and Transport Project, this button will return the Cursor to the very beginning of the project. This is also known as RTZ, or Return to Zero, but Cubase refers to it as Zero. If your project does have Markers, clicking this button will move the Cursor backward, stopping at every Marker.

GO TO NEXT MARKER/PROJECT END

This button works the same as the Go to Previous Marker/Zero button, except that it moves the Cursor forward in time. Clicking the button will move the Cursor to the end of the project or forward, stopping at every Marker, if present.

REWIND

You can click or click and hold on the Rewind button to move the Cursor backward in time. The speed of the rewind is determined by the current Event Zoom setting. In other words, the more zoomed out the Event Display, the faster the rewind will proceed.

FORWARD

The Forward button functions identically to the Rewind button, but moves the Cursor forward rather than backward in time.

CYCLE

Cycle is a Cubase mode wherein the Cursor plays (or records) repeatedly through a predetermined time range. That range is determined by the placement of the Left and Right Locators; the Left Locator is the start of the Cycle, and the Right Locator is the end of the Cycle. The Cycle button enables or disables the Cycle mode. When enabled, the button will be purple, but it will be gray when disabled.

STOP

The Stop button has two behaviors, depending on whether playback is engaged or not. During playback, clicking Stop will discontinue playback, and the Cursor will remain at the current location. However, if playback is already disengaged, clicking the Stop button will locate the Cursor to the previous playback location. For example, if you start playback at measure 10 and press Stop when the Cursor reaches measure 15, the Cursor will remain at measure 15. Pressing Stop again will move the Cursor back to measure 10. This is very useful for playing back or recording a section several times without using Cycle mode with the Left and Right Locators. (Whenever I'm recording, I'm always using the Locators.)

PLAY (START)

Weirdly, the Play button is sometimes referred to in Cubase as "Start." Either way, pressing the Play button will start playback. During playback, the Play button will be green, but if playback is stopped, it will be gray.

RECORD

Clicking the Record button will start the recording process for any and all tracks that are record enabled. Recording can occur either from a stopped position or during playback. The former will result in the Precount (if enabled) occurring before recording proceeds. The Record button itself is gray with a red dot in the center, but it will be completely red during recording.

CUBASIC NO. 8: TRANSPORT AND THE KEYPAD

As I previously mentioned, having a keypad when you're using Cubase is critical. That's because the Transport controls are tied to the keypad as key commands. Have a look at Figure 5.23 to see what I mean.

The Transport controls are usually the most frequently used Cubase buttons. Basically, you'll be hitting buttons such as Play, Stop, and Record a lot. And if you rely on the Transport Panel for all of these commands, you'll need to grab your mouse and move the pointer to each button every time. That makes using Cubase much more laborious than it needs to be. You will find using the

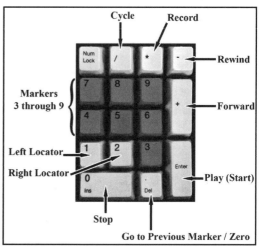

Figure 5.23. The keypad and associated Transport controls.

keypad a much faster way of accessing your Transport controls. The concept is what I call the "mouseless recording workflow," and you'll be using that workflow when you start recording in chapter 7. On the disc that accompanies this book, you will find a PDF folder that contains a file named "Keypad and Transport.pdf." It is a printable version of Figure 5.23 and shows the keypad and its associated Transport controls. Please print that PDF, and place it where you can easily see it.

The Spacebar

The Spacebar is the largest key on your computer keyboard: It is a Transport control, even though it's not located on the keypad. It operates as a Play/Stop toggle. In other words, if Cubase is stopped, typing the Spacebar will start playback. Type Spacebar during playback, and Cubase will stop.

The Left and Right Locators on the Keypad

The Locators are not found in the Main Transport controls of the Transport Panel. They appear to the left of the Main Transport and are labeled "L" and "R." But as with the Transport controls, moving the Cursor to the Left or Right Locator positions is much faster with the keypad. Simply type "1" or "2" to move the Cursor to the Left and Right Locators, respectively.

Yes, We Have No Keypads

I also previously mentioned that many laptops and some keyboards (such as the Apple Wireless Keyboard) don't have keypads. On laptops, the keypad is sometimes located on the keyboard and can be accessed by holding the "fn" (function) key on the keyboard and then typing the key. The keypad keys are usually listed on the keyboard in the same color as the fn key. For example, if the fn letters are blue, look for similarly colored numbers on the keyboard.

While the fn method works, it's not…well…fun. It requires that you use both hands to type one keypad key. To that end, let's explore some other options.

ADDING A KEYBOARD OR KEYPAD

The answer might be as simple as adding a full-sized keyboard that has a keypad. USB keyboards are very inexpensive. Or if you're space limited, you could look for a USB or Bluetooth keypad. (Your computer would need to be Bluetooth equipped for the latter to be a viable option.) However, make sure that you can return the keypad to the store, just in case it's incompatible. You see, I've seen some keypads that don't type the right keys. In other words, typing the keypad "1" instead types the "1" on the top row of keyboard keys. When that happens, you're not moving the Left Locator; you're accessing the Toolbar pointer. Test the keypad thoroughly with Cubase before tossing your receipt in the recycle basket.

THE STEINBERG CC121

Steinberg makes a USB controller for Cubase (and Nuendo) called the CC121.

It not only provides the Transport controls, but also adds lightning-fast control of other Cubase parameters such as Fader, Pan, Track Controls, EQ, shuttle/jog, and Control Room volume. Plus, you can hover your pointer over any control on Cubase and adjust it by turning the CC121 AI (Advanced Integration) knob. The CC121 is made of metal and a real joy to use. Steinberg also makes a series of Cubase, Nuendo, and WaveLab controllers called the CMC-series, including the TP or Transport Controller. However, if the hardware options are out of your price range, Steinberg created the Cubase iC app.

Figure 5.24. The Steinberg CC121 Cubase/ Nuendo controller.

THE CUBASE IC AND IC PRO APP
FOR IPHONES, IPOD TOUCH, AND IPAD

Who can argue with free? (Well, I've met many who can, but I digress . . .) For some of the Apple products listed above, Steinberg made the free Cubase iC app, which is available from the Apple App Store. For users who need more power and have newer models of the iPhone, iPod Touch, and iPad, there's also the Cubase iC Pro that provides much more power (such as mixing and cue mix control) for a nominal cost.

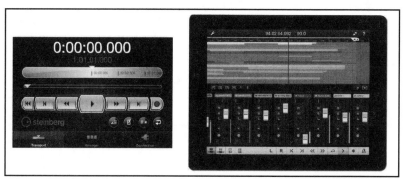

Figure 5.25. The Cubase iC (left) and iC Pro (right) control panels.

Cubase iC and iC Pro require your Apple device and computer to be connected to a router with Wi-Fi. Your computer doesn't have to connect via a Wi-Fi connection, but it must be connected to the router to which the device running Cubase iC is connected. Both apps require the installation of the Steinberg SKI Remote extension onto your computer. See more details at http://www.steinberg.net/ski.

SAITARA SOFTWARE FOR IPHONE, IPOD TOUCH, AND IPAD
While their apps aren't free, Saitara Software makes some really killer apps that control Cubase Transport, Faders, Pan, EQ, and a myriad of others. Most of their apps are under $10, so they're very affordable. The connection requirements are identical to those of Cubase iC. However, they work faster when your computer creates its own Wi-Fi network to which the Apple device connects. You can get more information and check out their AC-7 family of apps at http://www.saitarasoftware.com.

PROJECT TEMPO AND TIME SIGNATURE

Cubase has two different modes that control the tempo of a project: fixed tempo or variable via the Tempo track. Either method can be adjusted at any time. However, you should be aware that altering the tempo of a project that contains Audio tracks will have some seemingly strange results. You see, altering the Project tempo will have no effect on the tempo of Audio tracks. MIDI and Instrument tracks will follow tempo changes, but Audio tracks will play back at the tempo at which they were recorded. There are methods for adjusting the tempo of audio data, but it usually results in audible artifacts. Therefore, make sure you're happy with your tempo settings prior to recording your first Audio track. (Note: While the Élastique Pro algorithms that come with Cubase do allow your Audio tracks to change tempo with the Cubase tempo settings, the results never sound as good as tracks recorded at their original tempos.)

Located to the right of the Transport buttons on the Transport Panel are the tempo and time signature settings, as seen in Figure 5.26.

Figure 5.26. Tempo and time signature settings.

Tempo Fixed

By default, Cubase has its Tempo mode set to Track with an establishing tempo of 120 BPM (beats per minute). However, many pop songs maintain the same tempo throughout the entire composition. That tempo probably won't be 120 BPM. For this reason, you can click on the Tempo button to switch from Track mode to Fixed. Then you can double-click on the Tempo value and enter the desired BPM amount. For now, since you're still working on some of the basics, set the mode to Fixed. That way you can quickly change the Tempo while you're working with MIDI or Instrument tracks.

Tempo Track

I've already discussed the three most common tracks: MIDI, Instrument, and Audio. But there's also a track known as the Tempo track. This track exists in every Cubase Project even if you haven't purposely added it. The Tempo track can be displayed within the Track column, or by clicking on the Project menu and selecting Tempo track, or by typing Ctrl/Command + T.

Time Signature

The Tempo track also contains time signature changes. Since the Tempo track is on by default, it contains an establishing time signature of 4/4. But since you'll be using the Tempo Fixed mode, the default value of 4/4 will appear in the time signature setting in the Transport Panel. If you prefer to change the value, double-click on the current time signature setting and enter the desired value. Make sure to separate the integers with the "/" (forward slash) key.

VST PERFORMANCE METERS

Cubase offers two meters that constantly monitor the performance of your computer. These meters can be used to identify performance issues that can appear as audible anomalies such as pops, clicks, static, and dropouts. There is an Average Performance Load meter and a Disk Cache Load meter, and these are located at the far left of the Transport Panel, as shown in Figure 5.27.

Each is a ladder-style meter, but they display different performance aspects.

Figure 5.27. The Average Performance Load and Disk Cache Load meters in the Transport Panel.

ASIO Meter

The Average Performance Load meter displays the average amount of computer processing power that Cubase is using to create your project. The need for power increases when you add more Audio tracks, VST Instruments, EQ, effects, and other plug-ins to a project. It will also increase if you import a video file onto a Video track. As you add more power-hungry components to a project, the meter will climb higher. Think of it like the tachometer on your car: the higher the meter, the more power you're using…and there's a limit.

The limit is reached when the red overload indicator appears at the top of the meter. When it appears, you'll start to hear the pops, clicks, and other anomalies. Just like with a car—if you red-line the tachometer, you won't be moving any faster (at least, not in the current gear). But with the Average Performance Load meter, the overload indicator tells you when the amount of processing power you're demanding has exceeded the design specification of your computer. There are ways to lower the demand, such as lowering the ASIO buffer size. (See "Setting the Lowest Possible Buffer Size" and "Keeping Your Latency Expectations Realistic" in chapter 8). However, if you've taken all the possible steps to conserve processing power, the ultimate solution would be to purchase a computer with a faster CPU or multiple processor cores.

Disk Cache Load Meter

The Disk Cache Load meter is similar to the Average Performance Load meter, except that instead of monitoring processing power, it measures disk throughput. Think of it as a highway with multiple lanes: the more lanes, the more cars or "traffic" can move along the highway without causing a traffic jam. (You Californians know what I'm talking about.) The faster your hard drive, the more throughput it is capable of. It allows you to record and play back more and more Audio tracks. (Note: Today's hard drives are so fast that you may only see the Disk Cache Load meter when working on projects with high Audio track counts.) And as with the Average Performance Load meter, audible anomalies will appear when the Disk Cache Load overload light comes on (or, to perpetuate the metaphor, people start honking in a traffic jam).

There are ways to increase disk throughput, such as defragmenting the drive. However, if you're encountering the overload indicator frequently, it might be time for a faster hard drive. I recommend the Western Digital Caviar Black series of hard drives, or if you have the means, an SSD (Solid State Drive) will give you the highest performance money can currently buy.

VST Performance Window

The ASIO and Disk Cache Load meters on the Transport Panel are quite small. Therefore, Cubase has another way to view the meters in the VST Performance window that can be accessed by clicking on the Devices menu and selecting VST Performance or typing F12.

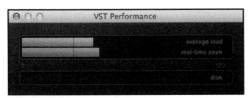

Figure 5.28. The VST Performance window.

This is a floating window that can be placed anywhere on your computer monitor(s). The meters are identical to those found in the Transport Panel with the addition of a Real-time Peak meter. It's similar to the Average Load meter except that it keeps track of the momentary bursts of power required usually by virtual instruments. Rather than being oriented vertically as in the Transport Panel, these meters are oriented horizontally and are much bigger for easier and more accurate analysis.

MOVING ON TO MIDI

While MIDI itself hasn't changed much in the decades since its invention, the way we use it in Cubase has changed dramatically. With that in mind, I'll be presenting the concepts of MIDI and VST (virtual) Instruments in the next chapter.

A Primer on MIDI and Virtual Instruments

6

MIDI (Musical Instrument Digital Interface) has been around since 1983. It is a computer-based protocol and language that interconnects all sorts of electronic musical instruments, including computers and music software. It helped revolutionize the home and project recording studio. With MIDI, musicians and composers could finally record, edit, process, and mix music without the need to book time in a recording studio. You can do the same thing with Cubase, plus the powerful virtual instruments give Cubase a built-in palette of sounds to choose from. In this chapter, you will learn about:

- The basics of MIDI.
- The most commonly used MIDI data.
- How sound is generated by hardware and virtual instruments.
- The concepts of monotimbral and multitimbral synthesizers.

THE BASICS OF MIDI

The MIDI Specification has been modified and refined over the years. But for the most part, the basic concepts remain unaltered. So even though MIDI has been around for almost thirty years, it is by no means an obsolete format. However, the concepts of MIDI are still a little difficult for beginners. To that end, I want to describe to you what MIDI is. The easiest way to start is to tell you what MIDI isn't.

MIDI Is Not Sound

The biggest misconception about MIDI is that it is sound. While it is true that you can record MIDI data onto MIDI and Instrument tracks, the sound itself is not captured. What is captured are the actions of the performer. What do I mean by "actions"? Well, let me illustrate by having you look at your computer keyboard. When you're writing an e-mail, the program is capturing the keystrokes from your keyboard. In other words, when you type the letter "B," the computer records that key being pressed. It does not record the sound the letter makes, nor would it record a word beginning with that letter, such as beekeeper. The only data captured by the computer is that of the "B" key as you type it.

Now take a look at your MIDI keyboard. When you're recording a MIDI track in Cubase and you press a "B" key on your MIDI keyboard, the sound itself is not captured. Instead, Cubase records the key being pressed. But unlike an e-mail or word processor program, Cubase captures other data, such as how hard the note was played, how long the key was held, if it was pressed on while the key was down, and a myriad of other actions that can come from a MIDI keyboard (for example, the sustain pedal being pressed, the pitch-bend and modulation wheels being adjusted, patch buttons being switched, and so on). Because MIDI can transmit and receive a great deal of nuance, the data stream of a MIDI keyboard (or any MIDI controller) is much denser than a QWERTY computer keyboard.

MIDI Is Actions

The creators of MIDI were some of the brightest minds in the music technology business. By designing the MIDI Specification, they provided musicians with the means to capture every action they could perform on a musical instrument. Notes are not the only actions that occur when a musician plays a musical instrument. For example, imagine a trombone player playing and sustaining a B. (Let's hope he can circular breathe.) After the note is played, there are a lot of things the player can do to accentuate the performance, such as adding vibrato, glissando, more volume, less volume, and growl. All of those nuances are added by performing some physical action on the instrument or by altering the way the air enters the horn.

THE MOST COMMONLY USED MIDI DATA

Now that you know that MIDI Data is comprised of actions, take a look at the most commonly used types of MIDI data.

Notes

As I've discussed, pressing notes on your MIDI keyboard will produce MIDI notes. Notes are depicted in MIDI by their note names and octave positions as well as by MIDI note number. For example, middle C can be depicted as C3 (sometimes C4, depending on the brand of synth or software) and note number 60.

Duration

As far as the MIDI Specification, there are note ons and note offs. The note offs determine when a note is released. However, musical notes are depicted by their duration. (Quarter-note, half-note, etc.) So even though the data that's being recorded when a note is released is being recorded as a note off, Cubase (like most music software) will represent this as duration.

Velocity

The speed at which the key is being depressed equates to how hard the note is played. Velocity is a measurement of that speed. When a key is pressed slowly, it's played lightly, like a pianissimo. When a key is pressed quickly, it's played hard, like a forte.

Aftertouch

While you're playing and holding a note, some synths and controllers record the pressure you apply to the key. This is known as aftertouch and usually adds vibrato or brightness to a sound, depending on what the synthesizer programmer had in mind. However, I've seen a lot of newer MIDI controllers that are not aftertouch compatible. You'll need to read the owner's manual to find out if your controller can transmit aftertouch.

Pitch Bend

Many synthesizers and MIDI controllers have one or two wheels on the left side of the chassis. One of these is the pitch bend wheel, which can simulate a trombone slide or a "whammy bar" on a guitar.

Continuous Controllers

The MIDI Specification includes 128 separate MIDI control numbers. Some of those control numbers are dedicated, such as the sustain pedal (CC No. 4), modulation wheel (CC No. 1), and volume (CC No. 7). So if you're using any of those non-note controls to add nuance to your MIDI recording, they're being recorded as continuous controllers.

Patch Select

These are the numbers assigned to the different sounds in your MIDI synth or sound-generating device. Early synths only came with thirty-two or sixty-four patches (a.k.a. sounds, instruments, programs, etc.), so the MIDI Specification allowed for 128 patch select numbers. But as technology grew, so did the number of patches a synthesizer could hold. It's not uncommon to see thousands of patches in a modern synthesizer. So the MIDI

Specification was modified to change two unassigned continuous controllers (CC No. 0 and CC No. 32, a.k.a. MSB [Most Significant Byte] and LSB [Least Significant Byte]) to Bank Select controllers.

Beyond the Basics of MIDI

There is other MIDI data, such as system exclusive and MIDI clock. In an effort to keep MIDI accessible to you, I won't go over them in this book. If you do want to learn more about MIDI, I would recommend Hal Leonard's The MIDI Companion Book.

WHEN MIDI BECOMES SOUND

When all of the actions have been recorded on a MIDI track, there will come a time when a sound is generated. Another way to look at it would be the somewhat silly behavior of someone (not me, of course) playing "air guitar." The sound of the guitar will not be heard until you hand the mime a real guitar. (If the mime is playing air guitar inside an imaginary box, please maintain the illusion by first opening the imaginary door.) Then and only then will the sound be perceptible by others.

In the same way, you have to make a connection between the MIDI data (actions) and a device that can generate a sound. Early in my electronic music career, I made the mistake of assuming that MIDI was sound. I recorded a bass line on a MIDI track using my Sequential Circuits Prophet-5 synthesizer. When I played it back, I could hear the recording. Then I took my computer to a friend's house to have him listen to my musical idea. When I pressed Play, no sound came out. I was baffled. I could see the MIDI data on the track, the time counter was running, and the Cursor was streaming from left to right. Everything should have worked, except I didn't realize it was my Prophet-5 making the sound, not the computer. If I had brought along my synth and keyboard speaker, we'd have both been able to hear the sound. It is the instrument that generates the sound, not the MIDI data.

It also means that you'll need to have the audio outputs of each and every MIDI device plugged into some sort of mixer and/or speakers. Personally, I use multi-input audio interfaces (Steinberg MR816CSX) so that I can connect all of my MIDI synths simultaneously to my studio monitors. This is important because you do eventually have to convert MIDI tracks to Audio tracks before you can mix your projects down to MP3 or audio CD. More on that later.

The Invention of Multitimbral Synthesizers

Back in the 1980s, most synthesizers were monotimbral, meaning that they could only produce one sound at a time. Therefore, a composer needed an arsenal of synthesizers, samplers, sound modules, and drum machines to simultaneously generate the sounds for his or her MIDI tracks. For example, if I were working on a song that had five MIDI tracks, such as drums, piano, bass, saxophone, and marimba, I would have needed four synthesizers and one drum machine. Bear in mind that my prized Prophet-5 synthesizer could only play one sound at a time. I would have needed three more to hear all my MIDI tracks simultaneously. But at almost $4,000 each, one Prophet-5 was all that I could afford. Then Sequential Circuits came out with a synthesizer called the SixTrak. It was one of the first multitimbral instruments on the market. As the term implies, a multitimbral synth can play back multiple sounds. In the case of the SixTrak, it provided me with simultaneous MIDI playback of up to six different sounds. In that configuration, each sound could only consist of one MIDI note. But since I was crafty, I used one note for the bass, one for the sax, and four for the marimba; the piano notes (up to five) came from my Prophet-5; and the drums came from my Roland TR-505 drum machine.

Most of the synthesizers on the market since 1990 are multitimbral, so having only one synthesizer won't limit you to using only one sound or require a large investment in multiple synths. However, time and technology have introduced us to the wonderful world of virtual instruments. (Note: Virtual instruments can be either monotimbral or multitimbral.)

The Invention of Virtual Instruments

The term virtual instrument can be a little deceiving. It's commonly misunderstood as the approximation of a real instrument (such as a piano or flute) coming from a synthesizer or sampler. What it actually describes is a synthesizer being generated inside of a computer. Earlier I told you that the computer doesn't make the sound of the MIDI track. However, with the invention of virtual instruments, you can use your computer as your recording studio and your synthesizers. In fact, today's modern computers can create virtual instruments that are more powerful and capable than a hardware or "real" synth.

In 1996, Steinberg created VST, or Virtual Studio Technology. With it came the capability of computers to generate hardware devices (such as signal processors and equalizers) in software. Later on, VST Instruments were added to the VST Specification. VST Instruments are synthesizers and samplers created "virtually" in the computer. Virtual instruments are capable of generating very sophisticated sounds when played from a MIDI keyboard and can cost hundreds or thousands less than their hardware counterparts. But how is this possible? How can a computer generate such magnificent sounds?

The answer is easier than you might think. That's because digital hardware synthesizers are very similar to computers. They both have screens, a keyboard, CPUs, memory, storage, and an audio output. It's just that hardware synths are very specialized computers that don't surf the web, run accounting software, or send e-mails. While they do offer a wide range of musically useful functions, their primary purpose is to create sounds. By using virtual instruments, your computer can not only create sounds and record audio, but also run programs with which to surf the web and balance your budget. (Quick! Call Congress! Maybe they don't know about computers.)

CUBASE AND VST INSTRUMENTS

Cubase 7 comes with twenty-eight hundred virtual instrument sounds comprised from five high-quality VST Instruments. While they all sound wonderful in their own right, you will be working with the most popular: HALion Sonic SE.

Recording MIDI and Instrument Tracks

7

I was debating upon which recording chapter should come first: Audio, or MIDI and Instrument tracks. I decided to follow my personal workflow. My musical endeavors always start with me sitting at my computer with Cubase and a MIDI keyboard. Even if I'm planning to replace some of the MIDI tracks with "real" instruments, I record a lot of the early tracks as MIDI or Instruments tracks. This allows me to listen to my ideas in context before I hire musicians or spend a lot of time creating Audio tracks that I may not use. It also allows me to map out the song form to see if all the sections flow together correctly.

However, I would strongly suggest that you read this chapter even if you plan to work with Audio tracks exclusively. I'm going to be introducing many of the Cubase recording fundamentals in this chapter. Therefore, it would behoove you to have a grasp of them. In this chapter, you will learn about:

- The relationship of MIDI and Instrument tracks.
- When to use MIDI tracks instead of Instrument tracks.
- Using the Browser with Instrument tracks.
- Recording your first Instrument tracks.
- The basics of editing MIDI data.
- Achieving the "mouseless recording workflow."
- The concept of multitrack recording.
- Using the VST Instrument "rack."
- Using external sound devices with MIDI tracks.

THE RELATIONSHIP OF MIDI AND INSTRUMENT TRACKS

As I mentioned earlier, Instrument tracks are a combination of MIDI data that a virtual instrument converts to audio data. I sometimes say that Instrument tracks have a MIDI front end and an audio back end. With Instrument tracks, you won't need to hook up and configure your MIDI synthesizers and/or sound modules; you'll just need to launch Cubase with your MIDI controller and audio interface connected to your computer. (You will, or course, need your studio monitors on or headphones plugged into your audio interface.) That makes it much easier for you to start learning about recording MIDI data.

The Advantages of Instrument Tracks

Instrument tracks make it a lot easier to teach you about MIDI. Before the invention of virtual instruments, I'd have to make a lot of assumptions about what kind of synthesizers you owned and what sorts of sounds they could produce. With VST Instruments, you and I can be using the exact same sounds. So can the others you collaborate with either around town or around the world.

Another big advantage is the speed with which you can start recording. In a moment, you'll learn about the Browser (a.k.a. Sound Browser) and how to quickly audition and assign sounds to Instrument tracks.

While the cost advantage of virtual instruments is an important distinction, I find that the biggest advantage is how Cubase retains the instruments, tracks, sounds, and settings within the Project file. That means you can open your Cubase Project on any Cubase-equipped computer, and the project will sound identical to the computer upon which it was recorded, presuming that both computers have Cubase and the same virtual instruments installed upon them. Prior to virtual instruments, I'd have to make sure I had all the right sounds and all the right settings loaded into my hardware synths. If I didn't, the bass track might be playing a xylophone. Or the drum tracks might be playing piano sounds. While this made for instant avant-garde compositions, the results were usually less than predictable.

The Advantages of MIDI Tracks

If you plan on using the sounds in your hardware instruments (such as your synthesizer, sampler, sound module, or drum machine), you'll need to use MIDI tracks. MIDI tracks can be assigned to the MIDI out port on your MIDI interface to transmit data to the MIDI input of external MIDI devices.

You can also use MIDI tracks with virtual instruments via the VST Instruments rack. This method gives you the advantages of virtual instruments. It also allows you to use multitimbral virtual instruments and route more virtual audio outputs to your Cubase mixer. That gives you the ability to mix and process the sounds more discretely.

RECORDING YOUR FIRST INSTRUMENT TRACK

Before you proceed, you're going to create a new project using the empty template. (Review the procedure in "The Project Assistant" in chapter 3.) When you name the Project Folder and the Project file, use the name "The Right Track X," where X is your name. On the

DVD that accompanies this book, you will find a project named "The Right Track Matt," with several iterations of the examples I'll be using in the following chapters.

I should also mention that chances are slim that you'll be recording a masterpiece. Like any beginner, you're going to be making a lot of mistakes along the way, so don't turn into a perfectionist, at least not yet. The idea is to throw caution to the wind and get recording!

Adding an Instrument Track

Add an Instrument track either by clicking on the Project menu, selecting Add Track, and then clicking Instrument; or by right-clicking in the Track column and selecting Add Instrument Track. The Add Instrument Track dialog box will appear and resemble either Figure 7.1 or Figure 7.2.

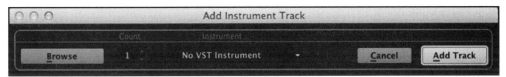

Figure 7.1. The Add Instrument Track dialog box with Browser closed.

If your Add Instrument Track dialog box looks like the one in Figure 7.1, it means that your Browser is closed. Click on the Browse button to open the Browser.

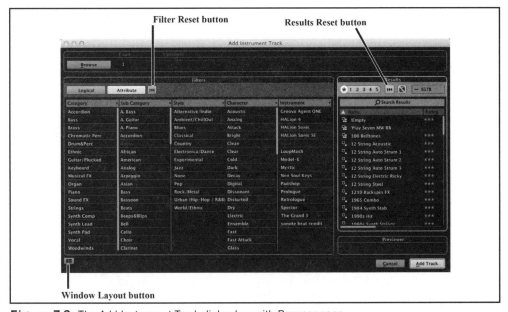

Figure 7.2. The Add Instrument Track dialog box with Browser open.

Now your Add Instrument Track dialog box should look more like the one in Figure 7.2. However, let's make sure that you and I are looking at the exact same thing. First, click on the Attribute button. Next, remove any previous selections by clicking on both the Filters reset and Results reset buttons. Finally, click on the Window Layout button and make sure that only the Filters and Previewer are checked, leaving the Location Tree unchecked.

Auditioning and Choosing Sounds

Refer to Figure 7.2, and notice that the Browser is divided into a Filters section and a Results section. When in Attribute mode (Attribute button on, Logical button off), the Filters section is subdivided into five columns, starting with Category and ending with Instrument. By making Filter selections, you can quickly narrow the Results column to the sounds you're looking for. The more columns in which you enable Filters, the narrower your Results will be.

You can explore this concept further by clicking Piano in the Category column. Instantly the scope of the other columns becomes narrower. Now the Sub Category column displays filters for A. Piano (Acoustic), E. Piano (Electric), and Other. Click on the A. Piano Sub Category. Now you can further refine your search by choosing a filter in the Style and Character columns. For now, leave those filters off. Instead, click on HALion Sonic SE in the Instrument column. That way, the Results column will only display sounds that come from the HSSE VST Instrument.

With those filters enabled, the Results column will display a list of sounds that meet the criteria you chose in the Filters section. At the top of the Results section, you will see the sound named "[GM 001] Acoustic Grand Piano." Single-click on that sound, and a green highlight will appear on it, indicating its selection. After a short pause, the sound and its samples will be loaded, and you'll be able to audition it by playing your MIDI controller. Your Browser will appear as it does in Figure 7.3.

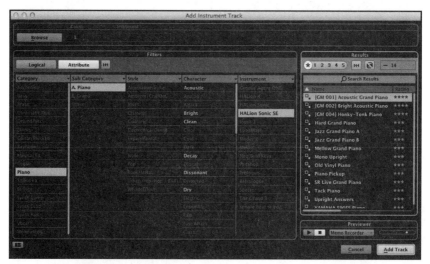

Figure 7.3. The Browser with filters enabled.

After auditioning the first sound, you may find it's not quite what you're looking for. You can single-click on other sounds in the Results column to explore other possibilities. On the right side of the Results column, you might miss the razor-thin vertical scroll bar. Dragging the scroll bar up and/or down will reveal more sounds. (If no scroll bar appears, then the Results column is displaying all the sounds that meet the criteria specified in your Filter selections.) You can also hover your mouse pointer in the Results column and use your mouse wheel to scroll the list.

Once you've found the sound you want to use, you could click the Add Track button. However, first try choosing something other than Piano. Click the Filter reset button. Then click on the Drum&Perc Category, then the Drumset Sub Category, then HALion Sonic SE in the Instrument column, and then scroll to the sound titled SR Alta Kit. Play some notes on the lower end of your MIDI keyboard to audition the sounds, and then click the Add Track button in the lower right-hand corner. The Add Instrument Track dialog box will disappear, and you will notice a new Instrument track added to your Track column. This track will have the same name as the sound you chose.

Verifying Track Settings Prior to Recording

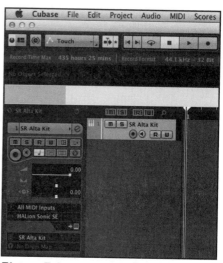

Before you press the Record button, take a look at your new Instrument track in Figure 7.4 and verify that all the settings are correct.

You will need to make sure that the track is record enabled and the MIDI Input and Output settings appear as they do in Figure 7.4. If you have a different section selected in the Inspector, make sure to click on the top section. Since the Add Instrument Track procedure set the Output to HALion Sonic SE, the only thing you'll need to do is verify that the Input is set to either All MIDI Inputs or the name of your MIDI controller that appears in the MIDI Port Setup of the Device Setup window. (See "Configuring Your MIDI Interface" in chapter 3.)

Figure 7.4. The new Instrument track.

FILTERING MIDI AFTERTOUCH DATA

Although it's not critical, I would recommend filtering MIDI aftertouch. If it gets recorded onto the Instrument track, it won't be a big deal. However, it will make it more difficult for you to see and interpret the MIDI data. The MIDI Filters are located in the Preferences, which can be accessed from the File menu (Windows) or the Cubase menu (Mac). When the Preferences window appears, locate the MIDI Filter in the left column, then check the Aftertouch box in the right column.

Click the Apply button, then the OK button, both of which are at the lower left-hand corner of the Preferences window. The Preferences are systemic, meaning that any changes you make affect Cubase globally. Therefore, aftertouch will be filtered during MIDI or Instrument track recording in every project from here on out. If you need to record aftertouch, repeat the procedure and disable (uncheck) the filter.

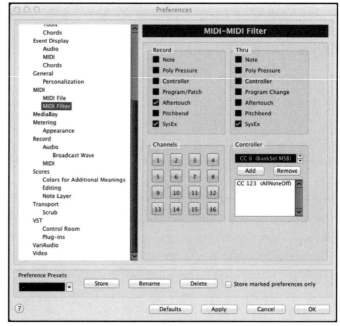

Figure 7.5. The Aftertouch MIDI Filter enabled.

The Logic Behind Starting with Drums

You may be asking why we're starting with drums. The reason is that when recording pop music, the drummer is usually the first musician to be recorded. This allows the drummer to provide the temporal grid upon which the other tracks will be recorded. After the drums are recorded, the other musicians will record their parts upon the foundation based on the drum tracks. This makes for a very tight recording.

In the same way, even though I'm recording MIDI and Instrument tracks instead of Audio tracks with a real drummer, I will create the foundation of the project with a virtual drum set. You can start with any instrument you'd like, but recording the drums first will allow the other tracks you'll be recording to groove and flow.

Drum Tracks Can Be Challenging

For nondrummers, creating a drum track can be tough. One of the best ways to learn what a drummer might play is to take some drum lessons from a drum teacher. That allows you to see and play the drums from a drummer's point of view. Armed with that knowledge and experience, you can record better virtual drum tracks in Cubase. Of all the money I ever spent on my recording studio, those drum lessons were probably the best investment I ever made.

To make it easier for you to get a drum track recorded, let's create arguably the simplest drumbeat found in pop music. Take a look at the drum notation in Figure 7.6.

If you haven't recorded drums or can't read drum notation, let me talk you through it. Notice the lowest note on the

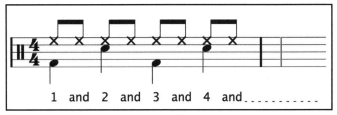

Figure 7.6. The drum beat you will record.

staff. That's the bass drum, and you can find it on your MIDI controller by playing the second C below middle C. The next note up is the snare drum, which is the second D below middle C on your MIDI controller. The highest note (represented with the X note head) is the hi-hat, which is found on the second F♯ below middle C. (Those are MIDI notes C1, D1, and F♯1, and MIDI note Nos. 36, 38, and 42, respectively.)

Now look at the counts beneath the notes. Notice that the bass drum notes land on 1 and 3, the snare drum notes land on 2 and 4, and the hi-hat notes land on 1–and–2–and–3–and–4–and. When you hear this beat played in its entirely, you'll probably say to yourself, "I've heard that drum beat before."

Let's Record...or Not

Now we're ready to record. However, if you'd rather not deal with drums right now, I've already recorded them for you. All you need to do is locate the folder named "The Right Track" on the disc that came with this book and load the project named "The Right Track Matt R01 drums only.cpr." When the project loads, it will be activated. Your project will still be loaded but will become deactivated. Now single-click on the yellow event in the Event Display, and type Ctrl/Command + C to copy the event. Then type Ctrl/Command + W to close the "drums only" project, at which time your project will be reactivated. Type the "." key on your keypad to return the cursor to the beginning of the project. (You could also move the Left Locator to bar 1 and type the "1" key on your keypad to move the Cursor to the beginning of the project.) Verify that the Instrument track you added is still selected (see Figure 7.6), and then type Ctrl/Command + V to paste the yellow event onto your Instrument track. You can then proceed to "Recording Your Second Instrument Track."

However, if you're the adventurous type, go ahead and record the drum part. Verify that your Instrument track is record enabled (see Figure 7.4), and then click on the Transport menu and verify that Metronome On/Off and Precount On/Off are both checked. If they're not, click on them to activate them. If they're both unchecked, you'll need to go to the Transport menu twice to activate each one. As a precaution, go to the Transport menu and click on Metronome Setup. Take note of the numeric value in the Precount Bars field.

Engage recording either by clicking the Record button on the Transport Panel or by typing the "*" (asterisk) on the keypad. You will hear the beeping of the Metronome during the Precount Bars, then the recording will engage. During the recording, you'll see an event being drawn in real-time on the Instrument track. You only need to record one bar of drums at this point. When you're finished recording, press the Stop button on the Transport Panel or type "0" on your keypad. To review your recording, press Play on the Transport Panel or type Enter on the keypad. If you're not happy with the recording, type Ctrl/Command + Z to undo the recording. Then repeat the recording process until you get a good take. (Note: I'm going to be talking about the mouseless recording workflow in a moment; afterward, you will not be clicking on the Transport Panel buttons.) If you get the notes right but the timing is a little (or a lot) off, don't worry about that right now. We'll deal with timing in a moment. For now, let's take a closer look at what we've recorded in Figure 7.7.

Figure 7.7. The MIDI event on the Instrument track (drums).

If you look closely at the MIDI event, you'll see some little specks through bar 1, after which they stop. Those specks are the MIDI notes you played. But you'll notice that the event continues on past bar 2. That's because it took you a moment to move your hands from the MIDI keyboard and press the Stop button, during which time the recording proceeded.

BASIC EVENT EDITING

Now that we've recorded an event, you can start learning the basics of editing, including resizing, repeating, and quantizing.

Resizing the Event

Before going any further, you'll need to resize the event length so that it's precisely one bar long. Precision editing will require that Snap is enabled. (See "Cubasic No. 5: Snap" in chapter 5.) Hover your mouse pointer over the event. Notice that when you do, you'll see small boxes in the lower corners of the event. These are known as Event Handles.

CUBASIC NO. 9: THE EVENT HANDLES
The Event Handles allow you to make different types of edits to an event, including repeating, which you'll learn about in a moment.

Figure 7.8. Event Handles revealed by hovering mouse pointer over an event.

The most common function of the handles is to allow you to increase or decrease the length or duration of an event. Move your mouse pointer over the right handle. You'll notice your pointer turns into a "Left/Right Arrow" Resize tool. Click and drag the handle very close to bar 2. (Snapping will resize the event precisely to bar 2.) When resizing the event, it will turn a much darker color. Don't worry, it just means the event is selected. When you release your mouse button, the event will appear as it does in Figure 7.9.

Figure 7.9. The event after it was resized.

Cubasic No. 10: Creating Repeats

Repeating an event is similar to a copy-and-paste command. But using the handles is a much more sophisticated method. Hover your mouse pointer over the right handle, at which time the pointer becomes a Resize tool. Now type and hold Alt/Option to turn the Resize tool into a Repeat tool, as seen in Figure 7.10.

Figure 7.10. The Repeat tool.

The Repeat tool resembles a pencil. While holding Alt/Option, click and drag the right handle to the right. You will see the Repeat count appear to the right of the Repeat tool, as it does in Figure 7.11.

Figure 7.11. The Repeat tool and the Repeat count.

The Repeat count will indicate how many times the event will repeat. The further to the right you drag the handle, the more repeats you will create. Go ahead and drag the event to create seven repeats so that it appears like Figure 7.12.

Figure 7.12. The result of repeating the event seven times.

Now start playback from the beginning of the project. You'll hear that the original event repeats all the way through bar 8. This method is a great way to repeat events that occur over several bars. However, the Repeat tool can get overused. No musician can play the exact same performance over and over again. Every repetition would have differences in style, volume, timing, and other nuances that are not created by the Repeat tool. But since you're just getting started, you have a right to overuse these tools.

Quantizing MIDI Data

Speaking of tools that get overused, let me introduce you to the concept of quantizing. Quantizing is a fancy term for quickly correcting your timing errors. In other words, when you play back a MIDI track and you hear some timing problems, quantizing the MIDI data can make the recording sound as though it were played much tighter. When MIDI recording programs first hit the market, they sort of autoquantized the data. This was due to their low timing resolution. I remember using a pre-MIDI program that had 16 PPQ (pulses per quarter note) resolution. That meant that when I recorded a track, it would connect each note to the nearest sixteenth-note within the bar. The playback didn't sound like the freestyle performance that was recorded. Instead, it had the human groove stripped out of it and sounded more like a computer with perfect timing.

That's exactly what quantizing does: it makes the timing perfect. But perfect timing usually sounds boring. It certainly allows nondrummers to create much tighter-sounding MIDI drum tracks. But in stripping out the human timing element, "it-can-sound-ve-ry-mech-an-i-cal." For example, when you quantize a MIDI event to sixteenth-notes, the notes will be pushed or pulled to the nearest sixteenth-note. That's identical to that old program with 16 PPQ. When you consider that the timing resolution of Cubase is 480 PPQ, reducing it to 16 PPQ seems like a step backward.

FOR NOW, LET'S QUANTIZE

Now that I've told you that quantizing will strip the soul from your MIDI recordings, let's go ahead and do it anyway. Fortunately, Cubase gives us a number of quantizing methods, only one of which will result in a soulless mechanized feel. There's Quantize, Iterative Quantize, and Part to Groove. Each method will offer a different level of timing correction. Before you can quantize an event, it has to be selected.

SELECTING ONE EVENT

If you single-click on an event in the Event Display, it will become selected. Selected events are darker than unselected events on the same track. For example, single-click on the first event in your drum track, and it will look like Figure 7.13.

Figure 7.13. One event selected.

If you were to perform a Quantize command now, it would only affect the selected event. However, since our drum track is made up of eight events, we'll need to select all eight of them.

SELECTING MULTIPLE EVENTS

There are a number of different ways to do this. Holding the Shift key and double-clicking the first event will select all of the events to the right. Typing and holding the Ctrl/Command key will allow you to select a series of contiguous or noncontiguous individual events. You can also type and hold the Shift key, and click and drag a selection box around the events, as in Figure 7.14.

Figure 7.14. A selection box.

When you release the mouse button, all of the events between the start and end of the selection box will be selected. But if you want to select all of the events on a track, let me show you the fastest method. Right-click on the track (not the event), and choose Select All Events from the submenu in Figure 7.15.

You will notice that all of the events on the track will become selected. Now the Quantize command will affect all of the selected events.

Figure 7.15. The Select All Events command.

SETTING A QUANTIZE VALUE

The basic Quantize settings are located on the left side of the Cubase tool bar.

Figure 7.16. The Quantize settings.

The Quantize settings are divided into three sections. Clicking on the Quantize value in the center will open a list of Quantize values. For our drum event, a setting of 1/8 (eighth-notes) will be appropriate. So if it isn't set to the default of 1/8, click on it and choose that Quantize value. Then verify that the "Q" button (indicated by the letter "Q" in Figure 7.6) doesn't say iQ. If it does, click on the button to return it to the default Q. Q means the quantization will be perfect, whereas iQ will turn Iterative Quantize on. I'll talk more about the iQ setting in a moment.

PERFORMING THE QUANTIZE

Now go to the Edit menu and select Quantize or type "Q" on your computer keyboard. Then play the project to audition the Quantize results. Unless your timing was way, way off, the events will sound exactly like they look in Figure 7.6. The timing will be perfect, therefore sounding somewhat boring. Wouldn't it be nice if you could correct the timing with an adjustable level of perfection? Well, you can, and it's called Iterative Quantize.

PERFORMING AN ITERATIVE QUANTIZE

Type Ctrl/Command + Z to undo the first Quantize, then click on the Quantize/Iterative Quantize button (see Figure 7.16) so that it turns white and displays iQ instead of Q. That will indicate that Iterative Quantize is enabled. Verify that all of the events are still selected, then repeat the Quantize procedure by selecting Quantize from the edit menu or typing "Q." When you play the results, you'll notice that some of the looseness of the original recording is retained, therefore making it sound more human than the first Quantize command. If it's still not as tight as you'd like it, repeat the Quantize command, and the Iterative Quantize will further tighten the timing. The default strength of the Iterative Quantize is 60 percent, which means that the notes are pushed or pulled within 60 percent of perfection. If you repeatedly use Iterative Quantize on an event, it will eventually become completely quantized.

UNDOING ANY QUANTIZE AT ANY TIME

If the Quantize command was the last command you performed, you can type Ctrl/Command + Z to undo it. However, one of the magical things about Cubase is that you can undo the quantization anytime you'd like to, either now or at any time in the future. In other words, Cubase always retains the original recording and allows you to reset the quantization of any event or events. The events you'd like to have returned to their original timing will first need to be selected. Then go to the Edit menu and select Reset Quantize.

THE MOUSELESS RECORDING WORKFLOW

When you recorded your first Instrument track, I provided you with the option of using either the Transport Panel or keypad for transport control. However, I would strongly recommend that, from now on, you use the keypad. You'll be using the Transport controls repeatedly throughout the recording process. By using the keypad and other key commands such as Ctrl/Command + Z for undo, you can dramatically increase the speed of your recording workflow. I call this the "mouseless recording workflow."

On the disc that accompanies this book, you will find a PDF folder that contains a file named "Keypad and Transport.pdf." It is a printable version of Figure 5.23 and shows the keypad and its associated Transport controls. Please print that PDF and place it where you can easily see it. It will help you learn this fantastically fast workflow. To that end, I will no longer be including the Transport Panel instructions during any recording process. You can still use the Transport Panel, but it will be much slower than using the keypad.

THE CONCEPT OF MULTITRACK RECORDING

Before you record your next Instrument track, it's a good time to talk about the concept of multitrack recording. Cubase, like all DAW software, allows you to record one track while you're listening to the previously recorded tracks. This is known as multitrack recording and remains one of the biggest revolutions in music production. But we have not always had the luxury of multitracking.

A Brief History of Audio Recording

When audio recording became possible in the late nineteenth century, recording a musical performance meant that all the musicians had to play at the same time. Most ensemble groups didn't have a problem with this, because they always performed together in the same way. But it was also because the recording equipment of the era could only provide one track at a time. In the 1930s, magnetic (analog) tape recorders were invented. Recording suddenly became more accessible and affordable. The tape recorder also brought another revolution to market: stereo recording. In other words, some tape recorders had two tracks: one for the left and one for the right. Both tracks were recorded simultaneously and provided a much more realistic reproduction of sound.

Then in the early 1950s, a brilliant man named Les Paul (for whom the iconic Gibson Les Paul electric guitar is named) invented the process of ping-pong recording. Basically, he'd record his guitar onto a mono track on the tape recorder's left channel. Then he'd record the output of the left track into the input of the right track while he was playing a new guitar track. After the recording, the right track would contain the sound of the original track along with the new guitar track. He'd repeat the process back to the left track, which would then contain three guitar tracks. That left-to-right, right-to-left procedure is how it got the name ping-pong recording. Using the ping-pong method, individuals could make ensemble-style recordings even if they were the only musician.

The Invention of the Multitrack Recorder

In the '60s and '70s, the tape recorders became more than stereo recorders. By widening the tape and putting more magnets into the record/playback heads, track counts increased dramatically. The Beatles recorded on some of the earliest 4-track recorders. Before long there were 8-, 16-, and 24-track recorders, some of which could be linked together for even higher track counts.

Then in the early 1990s, Keith Barr of the company Alesis created the first affordable digital multitrack recorder, named the ADAT (Alesis Digital Audio Tape). Each ADAT machine had eight tracks that could be recorded onto an S-VHS tape. You could link up to sixteen ADATs together for a total of 128 digital tracks. Each ADAT cost about $4,000, so you did have to save your money to afford one, plus a mixer, outboard processors (such as compressors and reverbs), and a DAT (Digital Audio Tape) machine to mix down to. But if you really wanted to be on the bleeding edge, you could get a 1X CD burner for about $1,300. The blank audio CDs were around $60 each. (Making a toaster [a bad disc] back then was enough to ruin your whole day.)

Cubase Has Spoiled Us Rotten

You are about to record your second track, thereby your first multitrack recording. Consider this: fifty years ago, what you're about to do could not be done at any price! The technology simply hadn't been invented yet. But now that you have Cubase, you can record unlimited MIDI, Instrument, and Audio tracks. The only limitations are the speeds of your computer and hard disks, and how much room you have left on your hard drive. All of the outboard processing can be done from within Cubase, and those processors are included in Cubase. Lest we forget that Cubase comes with over twenty-eight hundred built-in sounds you can add to your compositions, you can see that Cubase has provided us with an entire recording studio for less than $499. Sure, we still have to buy the computer along with an audio interface, microphones, and other essentials. But the bottom line is that you have more power at your fingertips than the Beatles ever had when they were recording their iconic albums. Cubase really has spoiled us rotten. To that end, let's get back to recording.

RECORDING YOUR SECOND INSTRUMENT TRACK

After the drummer packs up his drums, it's time for the bass player to lay down his or her tracks. In this case, you're going to repeat the Instrument track recording process, but this time you're going to record the bass guitar part. Therefore, you'll be repeating the recording process outlined in "Recording Your First Instrument Track" earlier in this chapter, except you'll need a different sound. When you get to the Browser as shown in Figure 7.17, click the Filter Reset button. Then choose the Bass category, the E. Bass subcategory, the HALion Sonic SE instrument, and then the Dry Finger Bass sound. To create the Instrument track, click the Add Track button in the lower left-hand corner.

Figure 7.17. Choosing the bass sound for the Instrument track.

You might have an idea of what you'd like to record for the bass track. Just in case you're feeling uninspired, Figure 7.18 will offer a suggestion.

Figure 7.18. A possibility for the bass track.

Bass guitar parts are generally monophonic, meaning that only one note is played at a time. (Being a bass player myself, I know that's not always the case. But let's keep it simple.) Go ahead and record this example or your own inspiration on the new Instrument track, and remember to use the mouseless workflow.

Using the Legato Function

When you have your bass line recorded, give it a listen. If it's anything like the bass line in Figure 7.18, it probably sounds choppy. Bass lines like my example are usually played legato, meaning that notes flow one to the other without any pauses in between. When a bass player plays legato notes on a real bass, the string continues to ring until the next note is played. But that's hard to recreate on a keyboard. So make the notes sound more like a real bass player is playing them by making the MIDI notes legato.

First, resize the event so that it is exactly eight bars long. Then make sure the event is selected, click the MIDI menu, go to Functions, and choose Legato. Now play the track, and you'll notice that the bass line is much smoother. The Legato function extends the end of every MIDI note to the beginning of the next note. It may not work every time, but when it does, it makes a huge improvement.

USING MIDI TRACKS WITH THE VST INSTRUMENTS RACK

You have seen how quickly your music can be recorded using MIDI data with Instrument tracks. However, using MIDI tracks along with VST Instruments loaded into the VST Instruments rack can provide you with options you don't get with Instrument tracks. The biggest advantages are accessing multitimbral VST Instruments and using more than one stereo audio output.

Loading Instruments into the VST Instruments Rack

For this example, you're going to continue using HALion Sonic SE (which I will hereby refer to as HSSE). HSSE has both monotimbral and multitimbral operational modes. When you use an HSSE sound with an Instrument track, it's monotimbral. But when you install it into the VST Instruments rack and address it with MIDI tracks, HSSE becomes multitimbral.

You can access the VST Instruments rack by clicking the Devices menu or by typing F11 on your computer keyboard.

The VST Instruments rack is comprised of up to sixty-four numbered slots. In Figure 7.19, you can see

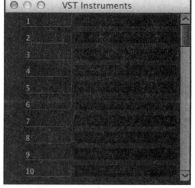

Figure 7.19. An empty VST Instruments rack.

ten empty slots. Click on the first slot where it says "no instrument" to reveal the VST Instrument list. (Note: The number and variety of VST Instruments that appear in the list may be more varied if you have installed third-party VST Instruments. Therefore, Figure 7.20 may contain instruments you do not have.)

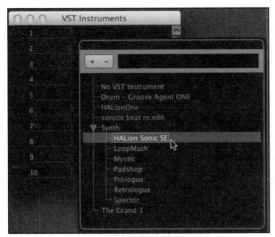

Figure 7.20. Choosing the HALion Sonic SE instrument.

When the list appears, choose the Synth category, and then click on HALion Sonic SE. You will be prompted to add a MIDI track, so go ahead and click the Create button. A new MIDI track will be added to your project, and it will automatically be assigned to channel 1 of HSSE. You will also see the HSSE control panel.

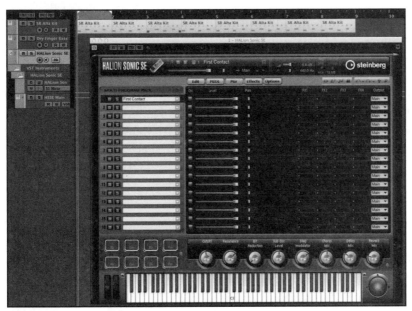

Figure 7.21. The MIDI track and HALion Sonic SE control panel.

The HALion Sonic SE Control Panel

Think of the control panel as the front panel of a hardware synthesizer, which usually contains all the knobs and switches. On the left-hand side of the control panel, you will see sixteen numbered slots. These Program slots are similar to the slots on the VST Instruments rack. However, instead of being used for VST Instruments, the Program slots are where you load HSSE sounds, also known as programs. You can take a

Figure 7.22. The Inspector and Program slots of HALion Sonic SE.

closer look at those slots and some of the Inspector settings in Figure 7.22.

You'll notice that the MIDI track has been created for you, its MIDI Output is assigned to HSSE, and the MIDI Channel is set to 1. There are sixteen MIDI Channels just like there are sixteen slots on the HSSE control panel. Next to the channel number is the Edit Instrument button. Clicking this button will hide or reveal the control panel of the VST Instrument to which the MIDI (or Instrument) track is assigned.

LOADING SOUNDS (PROGRAMS) INTO HALION SONIC SE

This is another case of Cubase referring to "sounds" as programs, but the terms are synonymous. However, there is a significant difference between using VST Instruments and creating Instrument tracks: no specific sound selection takes place. There's a default sound called "First Contact" loaded into the first Program slot, but HSSE chose that for you. Therefore, you'll need to add the programs you want to use.

In the far right of each Program slot is a small triangle. That's the Load Program button. Clicking on it will open a Browser very similar to the one in Figure 7.17. The main item that's missing is the Instrument column, which makes sense, because you're looking at the HSSE control panel and therefore loading HSSE sounds/programs. Go ahead and load three different sounds into the first three slots of HSSE, as I have done in Figure 7.22.

The MIDI track that was created for you should still be record enabled. That will allow you to audition the programs you're loading into the first slot. However, you won't be able to hear the sounds in any other slot. That's because the MIDI track is assigned to channel 1, therefore slot 1 of HSSE. To audition and record those programs, you'll need to create two more MIDI tracks.

ADDING MORE MIDI TRACKS

Click on the Project menu, click Add Track and then MIDI, or right-click on the Track column and select Add MIDI Track. The Add MIDI Track dialog box will appear, but if you see the Browser, click the Browse button in the upper left corner. Change the Count to 2, then click Add Track. You'll see two more MIDI tracks added to the Track column, and they'll have default names such as "MIDI 02" and "MIDI 03." You can, and I recommend that you do, change their names.

The next step is to change their MIDI Output and MIDI Channel settings in the Inspector. Click on the first new MIDI track, then change its MIDI Output to 1-HALion Sonic SE - MIDI (at the top of the selection box) and its MIDI Channel to 2. Repeat the process for the second new MIDI track, but assign its MIDI Channel to 3. Now when you record enable the associated MIDI track and play notes on your MIDI controller, you'll hear the sounds you've assigned to the HSSE Program slots 2 and 3.

In the "The Right Track" folder of the disc that accompanies this book, you can load the project "The Right Track Matt R01.cpr" to listen to the ideas I came up with in this chapter.

USING MIDI TRACKS WITH HARDWARE SYNTHS AND DEVICES

Up until this point, I've been totally ignoring any hardware synthesizers, sound modules, samplers, drum machines, or other MIDI-compatible devices you might have. But it's quite easy to add these devices into your Cubase Project as long as you follow two very important rules.

Rule No. 1: Assign the MIDI Tracks to the Proper MIDI Output and Channel

The MIDI Output will need to be assigned to the MIDI port to which the device is connected. For example, in Figure 7.23, I've created a new MIDI track and assigned it to Taurus-3 Bass Pedal. That's Moog Taurus-3 bass pedal synthesizer, which has its own built-in USB MIDI interface (along with enough "bull power" to knock down walls). The setting you use will need to correspond to the MIDI interface to which your hardware device is connected. Bear in mind the device could have a built-in USB interface like my Taurus pedals.

Figure 7.23. Inspector MIDI settings for an external device.

The MIDI Channel assignment will depend on the capabilities of your device. Some devices (like my Taurus pedals) are monotimbral and therefore only receive on one MIDI Channel. The device itself will have its own internal channel assignment, so the MIDI Channel setting for the MIDI track will need to equal that channel. However, if your device is multitimbral (like the Yamaha Motif), then you can create up to sixteen MIDI tracks and assign each to a different channel.

Rule No. 2: The Device Audio Outputs Must Be Connected to Be Heard/Recorded

You now know that MIDI is not sound. Therefore, making the proper settings in the Inspector is not enough to hear your external hardware device. The last step is to plug the audio outputs of each device into your sound system and/or audio interface. I use a multi-input audio interface (Steinberg MR816CSX) so that I can leave all of my external synths plugged in at all times. That also allows me to record an Audio track after I've recorded and edited the MIDI tracks. (That step is critical to incorporate the sound of your hardware synth[s] into the MP3 or audio CD mixdown file.)

To demonstrate this, let me assume you have one hardware synth you want to use in your Cubase Project. The synth audio outputs (the physical connectors on the device) need to be connected to something in order to be heard. If you're using a mixer, you could plug the device into that. However, I would recommend plugging the device directly into your audio interface, like I've done in Figure 7.24.

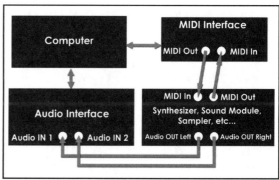

Figure 7.24. Recommended external synth wiring configuration.

Now you need to create an Audio track and turn the Monitor button on. For my purposes, the Taurus pedals have a mono output, so I've created a mono Audio track. If your external synth is stereo, then use a stereo Audio track. Also make sure to set the audio input to the physical input of the audio interface to which you've connected the external synth.

Leaving the Audio track in Monitor mode (Monitor button on) will allow you to hear the synth while you're recording the audio being generated by the MIDI tracks. You'll also notice that I've changed the name of the MIDI track from "MIDI 04" to "Taurus-MIDI," and that track has been enabled for recording. This MIDI and Audio track setup allows you to record the MIDI while you're monitoring (listening to) the external synthesizer audio output. Then when you're done recording and editing the MIDI data, you can record enable the Audio track and record the output of the synth onto that track. After the recording, you can disconnect the audio cables and power off the synth, because the Audio track will contain all the sound that external synthesizer was generating.

TESTING 1, 2, 3, 4

While you can make a lot of music with MIDI and Instrument tracks, I'm guessing you'll be adding Audio tracks to your Cubase Projects. With that in mind, I'll be discussing Audio tracks in the next chapter.

Figure 7.25. The new Audio track in Monitor mode.

Recording Audio Tracks

Many of the processes of recording Audio tracks are identical to those of recording MIDI and Instrument tracks. Therefore, it's a really good idea to read through chapter 7, because I cover many of those fundamental recording operations. This chapter will deal strictly with the fundamentals of audio recording in which you will learn about:

- Choosing a monitoring strategy.
- Configuring Direct or Software monitoring.
- Setting proper input levels.
- The "line of sight" recording philosophy.
- Recording your first Audio track.

CHOOSING A MONITORING STRATEGY

Before the invention of multitrack recording, there wasn't a need for sophisticated monitoring. Since all the musicians in the studio played at the same time, they just heard a monitor mix in their headphones. But with multitrack recording, each individual musician will record his or her tracks while listening to the prerecorded tracks. Therefore, he or she will need to hear a balance between the previous track(s) and the track(s) currently being recorded. That balance is critical for the musician to properly play against the tracks that have been recorded earlier. Too much of one and not enough of the other will result in a poorly performed recording.

So how do we achieve a proper balance? There are two monitoring strategies with differing benefits. Basically, direct monitoring is when the performer hears the audio interface inputs and outputs simultaneously. Software monitoring is when the performer hears only the audio interface outputs. Here's a closer look at these strategies.

Direct Monitoring

This is by far the best choice for monitoring. The biggest advantage is that the performer will hear what he or she is playing precisely in time with the prerecorded tracks. This is known as zero-latency monitoring, wherein the performer monitors the inputs of the audio interface and the outputs of the prerecorded tracks simultaneously.

The disadvantage of direct monitoring is that it's harder to configure. The monitoring of Cubase is different with every audio interface. You'll learn about these differences in a moment. But there is another possible disadvantage: any processing added by Cubase (such as compression, EQ, and guitar-amp effects) will not get recorded on the Audio track. However, the disadvantage isn't as big as you might think, because any processing can be applied after the Audio track has been recorded.

Software Monitoring

Software monitoring allows the performer to hear his or her tracks along with any Cubase processing while listening to the prerecorded tracks. That processing will also become a permanent part of the recording. Software monitoring is also very easy to configure.

The biggest disadvantage is the latency performers will experience. Software monitoring requires Cubase to process the audio before it can be sent to the output of the audio interface. (This is a disadvantage shared by all DAW programs.) Performers will notice a slight delay between when they play a note and when they hear it in their headphones. The severity of that delay (or latency) will depend on the speed of the computer, sample frequency of the project, buffer size setting, and the number and type of processors being applied by Cubase.

My Monitoring Advice

I would recommend configuring Cubase for direct monitoring and using the Tapemachine Style Auto Monitoring preference. (See "Auto Monitoring" below.) However, if you do want to record through plug-in effects (such as VST Amp Rack or the Vintage Compressor), you'll need to use software monitoring. I'll go over both strategies in a moment, but you'll also need to learn how to set up Auto Monitoring in Cubase.

Auto Monitoring

No matter which monitoring strategy you're using, you'll need to set the Cubase Auto Monitoring preference. Different settings will alter the functionality of the Monitor button on an Audio track. For Windows, click on the File menu and select Preferences. For Macs, type Command + , (the Command key plus the "," [comma] key), or click the Cubase menu and select Preferences. The Preferences window will appear as it does in Figure 8.1.

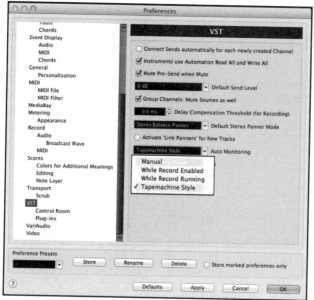

Figure 8.1. Auto Monitoring setting in the Preferences window.

On the left side of the window, click on VST. Then locate the Auto Monitoring preference on the right. Click on the triangle to display the four Monitoring preferences.

MANUAL
The default setting is manual. This means that the Monitor button on the Audio track will need to be enabled and disabled manually.

WHILE RECORD ENABLED
When you record enable an Audio track, the monitor will also be enabled. However, during playback, the monitor will need to be manually disabled so that the Audio track will be audible during playback.

WHILE RECORD RUNNING
This enables the monitor only when recording is occurring. However, when recording has ceased, neither you nor the performer will be able to hear the input.

TAPEMACHINE STYLE
This is the setting I would recommend. It handles monitoring identically to that of an analog multitrack. When you record enable an Audio track, the monitor is also enabled. During recording, the monitor remains active. During playback, the monitor disengages, so that both engineer and performer can listen to the newly recorded track. When transport is stopped, the monitor reactivates.

Figure 8.2. The Project & MixConsole preferences.

Disable Record on Selected Tracks Preferences

You may have noticed that when you select an Audio, MIDI, or Instrument track, the track automatically becomes record enabled. Up until this point, this has made the recording process easier. But now that you're going to use monitoring while recording Audio tracks, you need to disable the automatic record enabling. Otherwise, when you select an Audio track, the record enable and monitor will become active, and you won't hear the track play back. While you're still in the Preference window, locate Project & MixConsole in the Editing category, as shown in Figure 8.2.

Locate both the Enable Record on Selected Audio Track, and Enable Record on Selected MIDI Track (which includes Instrument tracks). They're both enabled by default. Uncheck each box, and then click the Apply button.

CONFIGURING CUBASE FOR DIRECT MONITORING

As I mentioned previously, direct monitoring is more work to configure. However, both performer and engineer will enjoy its advantages. The most difficult part of describing the configuration will involve your choice of audio interface. Every manufacturer and model will employ direct monitoring in a different way. Therefore, I have to generalize the configuration of your audio interface.

Enable Direct Monitoring in Cubase

Click on the Devices menu, and select Device Setup. From the Devices column on the left side, locate VST Audio System. Clicking on whatever appears below will display the driver options for your audio interface. In the case of Figure 8.3, it's my Steinberg UR28M audio interface. With the driver options highlighted, enable the Direct Monitoring on the right side of the window, as it is in Figure 8.3.

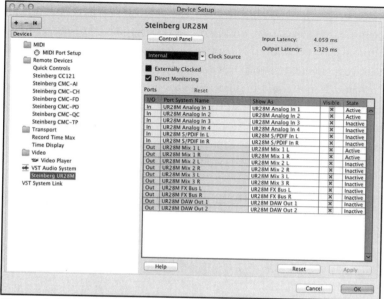

Figure 8.3. Direct Monitoring enabled on the driver options screen.

You may need to hit the Reset and Apply buttons at the bottom of the Devices window to engage Direct Monitoring. You can then close the Devices window; however, you need to further configure your interface.

The Two Common Facilities for Direct Monitoring

This is where the configuration of Direct Monitoring gets difficult. Basically, your audio interface will have one or both of these facilities for configuring the all-important "input to output" balance.

MIX OR BALANCE KNOB

Many of the sub-$500 interfaces have a mix or balance knob. The position of the knob will determine how much input versus how much output you're hearing. For example, the Steinberg UR22 interface has a mix knob, as shown in Figure 8.4.

You'll notice that the extremes of the knob are labeled INPUT and DAW. Turning the knob toward INPUT will introduce more input signal and less playback signal. The opposite is achieved by turning the knob toward DAW. In other words, if you can't hear the performer you're recording (or the performer can't hear himself or herself), you'll turn the knob toward INPUT. If you (or the performer) is hearing too much of the performance you're recording, turn the knob toward DAW.

Figure 8.4. The mix knob on a Steinberg UR22 audio interface.

SOFTWARE-BASED MONITOR APPLICATIONS (PROGRAMS)

Many of the more expensive audio interfaces (such as Apogee, PreSonus, and RME) come with a monitor mixer application. That application is commonly installed during the driver-installation process. Therefore, you probably already have it installed on your computer. You'll need to launch and configure that monitor application in order to take advantage of direct monitoring in Cubase. Consult either your audio interface owner's manual or the manufacturer website for more information.

However, to give you an idea of what I'm talking about, Figure 8.5 shows the console program that comes with the Universal Audio Apollo audio interface.

Figure 8.5. The Universal Audio Apollo console program.

The best way to think of the monitor application is that it provides mixer functionality to your audio interface. Some of the sliders will control how much signal is coming from the hardware audio inputs, while other sliders control the playback output of Cubase to both you and the performer(s). By configuring the monitor application properly, you'll be able to achieve the requisite input-to-output balance.

A Word About the Control Room

Cubase has a very sophisticated Control Room that allows you to customize all of your monitoring needs, including the creation of four separate headphone (studio) mixes. This allows you to feed different mixes to each performer of both prerecorded tracks and the tracks currently being recorded. For example, if the drummer needs more snare drum in his or her mix, you can increase the signal from that track without changing the balance in the three other headphone mixes. You can also assign the Click to any mix and adjust its volume. The Control Room is a very powerful tool for studio monitoring.

However, not everyone can take advantage of the multiple headphone mixes in the Control Room for monitoring. First, your audio interface must have multiple outputs or multiple independently programmed headphone outputs, which most mid- to high-end audio interfaces will have. But you must also have multiple headphone amplifiers and multiple headphones. The most important thing to realize is that you'll have to rely on software monitoring. That is, unless you have a Steinberg UR- or MR-series audio interface such as the UR824. Steinberg made it possible to use the UR- and MR-series with all the features of the Control Room and still use direct monitoring. Other hardware manufacturers can add that functionality to their interfaces, but most of them still use a proprietary application to create monitor mixes. Personally, I love to have the Control Room and my UR or MR interfaces handling the monitoring, because then I don't have to switch between Cubase and a monitoring application.

Configuring Cubase for Software Monitoring

Software monitoring is easier to configure than Direct Monitoring. However, there are some critical settings that will affect the monitoring operation and the latency it will induce.

DISABLE DIRECT MONITORING

Refer to Figure 8.3 and disable Direct Monitoring. You may also need to hit Reset and Apply for the changes to take effect. Also, if your audio interface has a mix knob, turn it all the way to DAW, or totally opposite the inputs. If your interface came with a monitor application, make sure to turn down all of the input sliders.

SETTING THE LOWEST POSSIBLE BUFFER SIZE

The round trip (input to output) the audio signal will make through your audio interface will introduce some latency—or the time it takes for the signal to enter the interface, be processed by Cubase, and then be played back through the audio interface outputs. The audio interface buffer setting controls the amount of latency. Refer to Figure 8.3, and look at the Input and Output Latency. For my UR28M, the round trip will take about 4 ms (milliseconds) at the input, and about 5.3 ms at the output. That's a round-trip latency of about 9.3 ms. In an ideal world, the round trip would be 0 ms, but that is impossible with software monitoring. So it's imperative to reduce the latency as much as possible by lowering the buffer size. At the top of Figure 8.3, you'll find the Control Panel button. Clicking on that button will reveal a screen that will allow you to set the buffer size. If you're using Windows, the

Figure 8.6. Control Panel with buffer size.

screen will vary depending on manufacturer. On a Mac, it will appear as it does in Figure 8.6.

The current setting of 64 samples will allow for the 9.3 ms round-trip latency. By increasing the buffer size to a value such as 128 or 192 samples, the latency times will be increased as well. For example, if your project is set at 44.1 kHz, a setting of 64 samples would give you a round-trip latency of 9.3 ms. However, even if your driver allows for these extremely low buffer sizes, you may not get reliable performance.

KEEPING YOUR LATENCY EXPECTATIONS REALISTIC

It takes a really fast, modern computer and a great audio interface with robust device drivers to achieve such low latencies. Even then, low buffer sizes can cause audible pops and clicks to appear in the audio signal. In some cases, the audio system may completely stop and require you to hit the Reset button on the Device Setup/driver options window. If you were recording at the time, the audio would contain anomalies and may not have recorded completely. Either way, the recording would be ruined. Therefore, low buffer-size performance should be thoroughly tested before recording any Audio tracks you want to keep. This limitation of software monitoring reveals the huge advantages of direct monitoring, wherein you can set very high buffer sizes and never hear the latency during the recording of Audio tracks.

However, the buffer size has a direct impact on the latency when recording Instrument tracks and VST Instruments with MIDI tracks. With all of this in mind, it's likely you'll be adjusting the buffer sizes several times while you're working on a project. It's a bit of a drag, but so is putting gas in your car and checking the tire pressure. Configuring latency is just something that has to be done when using any DAW software.

SETTING UP YOUR AUDIO TRACK

Now that you've made most of the preparations for audio recording, you can start making tracks. There will be a few more concepts I'll cover throughout the process. But at this point, make sure you have your "The Right Track X R01 Project" loaded. (See "Recording Your First Instrument Track" in chapter 7.) Then go to the File menu, select Save As, and save a version of the project as "The Right Track X R02." (Remember, X = your first name.) This is so that you'll have a version of the project without the Audio tracks. That way, you can always revert to the earlier R01 version or any of its contents or settings.

Adding an Audio Track

Adding an Audio track is similar to adding any track to Cubase: click on the Project menu, select Add Track, and then select Audio. You can also right-click in the Track column and select Add Audio Track. The Add Audio Track dialog box will appear as it does in Figure 8.7.

Figure 8.7. The Add Audio Track dialog box (Browser closed).

If the multicolumn Browser appears, click the Browse button. But before you add the track, you'll need to determine its configuration.

CONFIGURING THE AUDIO TRACK

At the top of the Add Audio Track dialog box, you can choose how many tracks you want to add, the channel configuration, and what speakers the sound will come out of. The latter will be set automatically depending upon the mono or stereo configuration. (M = Mono, and L R = Stereo.) If your project was in a surround-sound configuration, you could choose which speakers to assign the track to. The count is set to 1 by default, but you could add several tracks at once if you so desired.

The configuration is the setting that takes the most consideration. In "When to Record in Mono, Stereo, or Multichannel" in chapter 4, I talked about counting your sources to determine whether a mono or stereo track was appropriate. In my case, I'm going to record my acoustic guitar using its built-in pickup. In other words, I'm going to take an instrument cable and connect the guitar's output to the audio interface input. That's one source, so I'll choose a mono configuration. However, if you're recording from more than one source

(such as a stereo keyboard output or multiple mono sources), you'll need to choose a stereo configuration or add multiple mono tracks. When your configuration is set properly, click the Add Track button.

In previous chapters, the new track would automatically be record and monitor enabled. Due to your changes in the Preferences window, they'll need to be enabled manually. But don't do it yet! If you do, you (and your ears) might be sorry.

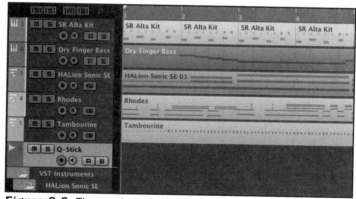

Figure 8.8. The new Audio track.

ONE ROOM + MICROPHONE + MONITORS = HEADPHONES

If you are lucky enough to have a studio room (where your performer resides during recording) and a control room (where you and your computer are), you'll need to provide the performer with headphones and a monitor mix. However, most of us don't have separate rooms, which means our microphone(s) and monitors are contained in one room. This presents a feedback problem. In other words, the sound from the microphone goes into the audio interface, then gets played out to the studio monitors, and then goes back into the microphone. This vicious cycle goes round and round, over and over again. The least it will do is color (in a very negative way) the sound of the recording and make it useless. The most it will do is cause uncontrollable squealing and howling to pour from and quite possibly damage your studio monitors. That will make the recording process impossible. Many try to control the feedback by turning down the studio monitors, but that will not solve the problem.

The only way to record with microphones in one room is to turn off (or completely turn down) the studio monitors and put on your headphones. If you are recording someone else, he or she will need to wear headphones too. In my case, even though I'm not using a mic, I prefer to wear headphones, because they'll provide a more intimate sound from my instrument. Plus, the disruption of air molecules (i.e., sound) emanating from the studio monitors can cause my guitar strings to vibrate and transfer that unwanted sound to the track. That's something you'll want to avoid too; you'll want the Audio track to be recorded as purely as possible.

THE "LINE OF SIGHT" METHOD OF RECORDING SIGNAL FLOW

Every audio engineer has his or her own philosophy regarding the signal flow getting to the audio interface. Some prefer to put signal processing (such as compressors, limiters, and equalizers) in between the source and input of the audio interface. That has the advantage of incorporating the processing directly onto the track. Others, like myself, prefer to leave the signal path as pure and simple as possible—in other words, connecting the source directly to the audio interface with one cable. I call this the "line of sight" method. This method presumes that any signal processing will be done after the track has been recorded. By using line of sight, you'll have plenty of options for treating the track with effects during the mixing process. You won't have those options if you incorporate the processing during the recording, meaning you'll have to get it right during the recording. Getting it right the first time can certainly be achieved but usually requires years of experience.

If you have an audio source that requires constant processing to achieve a characteristic, then line of sight won't work. But I would recommend that you keep the signal flow as simple as possible for another reason: noise. Every electronic device you add to the signal flow will add noise such as hum and hiss. That noise will get progressively more noticeable with every device you add to the signal path. The noise will become part of the recording, and if it's too noticeable or distracting, you'll need to rerecord the track(s) without the preprocessing.

SETTING AN APPROPRIATE INPUT LEVEL

I almost added this as a Cubasic, but setting an appropriate audio input level is universal to the science of audio recording regardless of the device you're recording onto. The concept is to record with as much signal as possible without clipping (also known as peaking or distorting) the input of the audio interface. If you exceed the maximum input level of the audio interface, you'll be adding unwanted (and unflattering-sounding) distortion to the recording. Once it's there, you cannot remove the sound of clipping.

So why do we want to set a level as close to clipping as possible? The reason is to maximize the signal-to-noise ratio. The louder the signal, the less noticeable any noise will become. There's a control on every audio interface for setting the input level. Usually it's a knob or slider labeled "gain" or "level." In the case of a Steinberg CI2 (see Figure 8.9), it's called gain, and each input has its own control. Along with that control is usually some sort of peak, clip, or OL (overload) indicator. The CI2 has red peak indicators on each input channel, as shown in Figure 8.9.

Figure 8.9. The gain knobs and peak indicators on a Steinberg CI2.

Setting the input level is actually a very simple process. The best way to do it is to sing or play the instrument as loudly as it will be played during the recording, and increase the gain knob (or equivalent) until the peak indicator (or equivalent) shows clipping. Then decrease the gain until the peak indicator no longer lights up. The rule is: you should never, ever, ever see the peak indicator during the actual recording. That's about it. (Note: I added a little "flash" indicator around the peak indicator on channel 1 to make it more visible.)

But with vocalists, they'll start to emote during the recording. When they do, they might sing more loudly than they did when you set the input level. Or in the case of instrumentalists, they might play more loudly or turn their own volume up without telling you. Either situation will result in an increase of input level that might cause clipping, thereby ruining the recording. Therefore, I always recommend setting the gain a little lower, just in case. Since your project is set to either 24- or 32-bit (see "Project Setup" in chapter 5), you'll have a very wide dynamic range with which to process and edit the audio after the recording.

Some musical instruments will also have volume controls. For example, a synthesizer or keyboard will have a volume control, as will a pickup-equipped acoustic guitar or electronic drum set. If that's the case, make sure it's turned all the way up when you set the input level. That will further maximize the signal-to-noise ratio and also prevent the performer from manually increasing his or her volume beyond the point of clipping. (That's just one of a million tricks you'll pick up from working with volume-obsessed musicians.) However, if your gain control is turned all the way down and the input is still clipping, you might need to enable the PAD switch on the audio interface. If your audio interface doesn't have a PAD switch, decrease the volume control of the device you're recording or invest in an in-line PAD circuit (like the Dayton Audio XATT10), available at your local music store or online.

RECORDING YOUR FIRST AUDIO TRACK

Now that you've added your Audio track, set its input channel and input level, and likely dawned your headphones and turned off your monitors, you can record and monitor enable the track. (See Figure 8.8.)

Record on Measure 2, Not Measure 1

In Figure 8.10 (which is part of the "The Right Track Matt R02" on the disc that comes with this book), you'll notice that I've moved all of the events in the Event Display one measure to the right. I did this by performing a select all command (Ctrl/Command + A), then clicking on any event and dragging to the right. Then my recording starts at measure 1, but I didn't actually start recording until measure 2…or did I? When you listen to the guitar track, you'll notice it plays before all the other tracks. That's because it has a few pick-up notes that occur inside of measure 1. If I had left the other events on measure 1 and started performing at that point, the recording would have missed those pick-up notes. But even if your performance doesn't include any pick-up notes, there's usually a few milliseconds of sound before the downbeat. If you miss them by recording too early, the track will sound chopped off at the beginning. For that reason, I recommend that you never place your Left Locator upon the measure where the performance begins. Always give yourself a measure to ensure that you capture the entire performance, including any pick-up notes or fleeting "human elements" that occur prior to the downbeat of the recording.

Your Last Chance to Change Tempo

Up until this point, you've been using MIDI and Instrument tracks. That has allowed you the freedom to adjust the tempo (see "Project Tempo and Time Signature" in chapter 5) at will. However, by recording an Audio track into this project, you have effectively set the tempo in stone. It's easy to change tempo with MIDI and Instrument tracks, but a bit more difficult with Audio tracks. You'll usually end up with audible artifacts if you change the tempo of audio data, so it never sounds better than if you set the right tempo prior to recording. To that end, I've adjusted the tempo of "The Right Track Matt R02" from 120 BPM (beats per minute) to 112 BPM.

Using Methods from Chapter 7

During the recording process, you'll be using many of the conventions you learned in chapter 7, including the mouseless recording workflow, the Locators, and multitrack recording. Go ahead and do some recording, but remember that you're just practicing. If you take the recording too seriously at this point, the mistakes you'll be making might disillusion you. I really don't want that to be the case. I'd much rather you treat the recording process like that of learning a new musical instrument; you'll try, make mistakes, and learn to avoid them next time, and the process will get faster and better each time. For example, take a look at Figure 8.10.

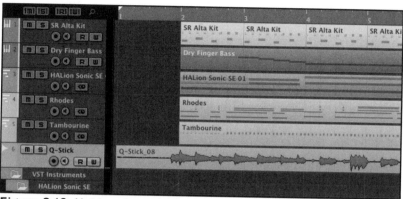

Figure 8.10. Matt is no "one-take wonder."

You'll notice I wasn't happy with my performance until take 08. While I'm embarrassed to admit it, that's an extraordinarily low number of takes for me. It's not uncommon for me to get into double, even triple, digits! I guess I practiced more when I was paying for studio time.

DON'T LET ME STOP YOU

From here, the world is truly your oyster. (Or if you're a vegetarian like me, the world is your tomato.) Using the MIDI, Instrument, and Audio track recording methods you've just learned about, you should keep recording. Remember that learning Cubase is exactly like learning a musical instrument. Therefore, you'll learn more when you practice every day. You'll also be making plenty of mistakes along the way. But it is learning from those mistakes that will move your education forward. I've provided you with some ideas to get started, but I'm guessing you have a lot of your own music to record. Get those ideas out of your head and into your Cubase Project with dispatch.

Editing in the Project Window

If I were writing this book twenty-five years ago, this chapter on editing would be very short. That's because there was very little editing that could be done. Audio recording was taking place on open-reel analog tape decks. And other than the cutting and splicing of the analog magnetic tape with a (properly demagnetized) razor blade, the format simply didn't offer much in the way of editing. But when technology gave way to digital recorders, and ultimately DAW (Digital Audio Workstation) programs such as Cubase, the editing process exploded with an ever-expanding palette of creative and practical tools. Or in a more Cubase-specific sense, editing is the moving and rearranging of events in the Event Display of the Project window.

It's also important to know that with very few exceptions, any edits you make while you're in the Project window are nondestructive. Removing MIDI events can result in permanent erasure. That's one reason I rely on the Mute tool, which you'll learn about later in this chapter. However, with Audio events, you can cut, copy, and paste to your heart's content and never lose the original recording. In this chapter, I'll be exploring the basic editing concepts shared by MIDI, Instrument, and Audio tracks, including:

- Methods for the Cut, Copy, and Paste commands.
- The Toolbar and how it pertains to editing.
- The editing tools in the Toolbox.
- The Status, Info, and Overview lines.
- Zooming the Event Display.

MORE THAN CUT, COPY, AND PASTE

One of the most amazing and useful functions of early computers was the ability to cut, copy, and paste (CCP) data within one document or into another. Undo and Redo were and are a fantastic remedy for those "oops" moments. Any of you who ever used a typewriter know what I'm talking about. I'll never forget the aggravation of making an irreparable mistake at the end of a page and having to start all over again, or the elation I felt when my mom bought an IBM Correcting Selectric II typewriter with the "last character erase" feature. Lest we forget, typewriters didn't autocorrect ourr speling errers, ether.

When MIDI sequencing programs allowed composers to record music in the 1980s, CCP opened a new world of creative and time-saving possibilities. Then in the 1990s, that same functionality could be performed on audio data as well. Today, the CCP commands are ubiquitous in practically all software programs, including Cubase. They're usually located in the Edit menu, which is where you'll find them in Cubase. However, the tools found in the Toolbar of Cubase go far beyond the basic CCP commands. That's not to say that CCP commands aren't useful, but I'm sure you'll see that the tools offer many more possibilities.

Basics for Cut, Copy, and Paste

If you're accustomed to relying on CCP commands, let me take a moment to discuss how they work in Cubase. For cut and copy commands, you must use the Object Selection tool, Range Selection tool, or other select command to define the events you'll be cutting or copying. (See "Object Selection Tool (Normal Sizing Mode)" and/or "Range Selection Tool" later in this chapter.) To paste the data you've cut or copied, you must both select the track and move the cursor to the temporal location to define the coordinates of the paste to occur.

EXPLORING THE TOOLBAR

The Toolbar is located at the top of the Cubase Project window and is not visible unless you have started a new project or loaded an existing one. Hopefully, you've been doing a lot of recording and have plenty of material upon which to edit. If not, you can load the project titled "The Right Track Matt R02.cpr," located on the disc that accompanies this book. (See Appendix A: "Using the Included Disc.")

Locating the Toolbar

You can find the Toolbar at the topmost margin of the Cubase Project window, as seen in Figure 9.1.

Figure 9.1. The Cubase Toolbar (upper right-hand corner).

You should already be familiar with some of the items on the Toolbar, including the Transport controls and Snap functions. But now that you're going to edit your material, I'll need to go over the Toolbox and the editing tools it contains.

The Toolbox is divided into several icons that depict their operation. Some tools have different operating modes, indicated by a small, white triangle that will appear when the tool is selected. For example, the Object Selection tool in Figure 9.2 is in a selected state, and the Mode indicator is shown at the bottom.

Figure 9.2. The Toolbox and Mode indicator under Object Select tool, far left.

Selecting the Tools

You can select a tool at any time simply by clicking on its corresponding icon in the Toolbox. However, there are more and even faster ways to select tools. For example, you can right/Ctrl-click in the Event Display to reveal an additional and identical Toolbox, as seen in Figure 9.3.

Using the right-click method with a mouse will reveal the small Toolbox on the left of Figure 9.3, while Mac trackpad users (Ctrl-click) will see the vertical list on the right. Either way, holding the mouse button down, you simply drag your mouse to hover over the tool you wish to use, and release the mouse button.

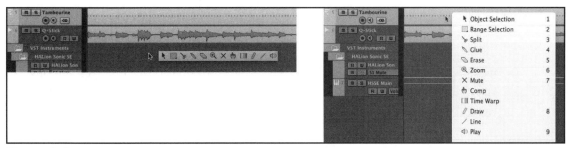

Figure 9.3. Right/Ctrl-clicking in the Event Display.

My favorite method is to use the top row of number buttons on the computer keyboard. In Figure 9.4, you'll see how the number keys correspond to the tools.

Typing the number key will select the corresponding tool. For example, typing the "3" key will select the Split tool. Typing the "1" key will select the Object Selection tool. Additionally,

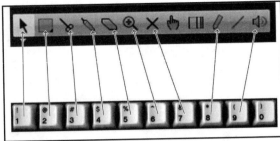

Figure 9.4. Corresponding number keys and tools.

repeatedly typing the "1" key will cycle through the three modes of the Object Selection tool.

You'll also notice that there are twelve tools, but only nine can be accessed by the number keys, and they're not selected concurrently. That's because some of the tools have more specialized functions. So you might wonder why Steinberg didn't group the specialized tools together in the Toolbox. The reason was to maintain the number-key-to-tool behavior that Cubase users have used for years. (Old timers, like me, rejoice!)

Tool Behavior and the Snap Settings

The behavior of the tools is highly influenced by the Snap settings. When Snap is off, the events and edits can be made freely at any temporal position. When Snap is on, the edits and movements made with the tools are constrained based upon the Snap settings in Figure 9.5.

Figure 9.5. The Snap settings.

Snap can be turned on and off by clicking the Snap button or by typing the "J" key on your computer keyboard. For this chapter, the Snap type should be set to the default of Grid. The Grid Type can be set to varying degrees of constraint, depending upon how fine a control is desired. For example, the default of Bar will constrain the edits to the bar lines of the Event Display. A setting of Beat will constrain the edits to the quarter-note resolution of the Event Display.

If an even finer degree of control is desired, setting the Grid Type to Use Quantize will allow you to define the constraint based upon the Quantize Preset. For example, selecting the Quantize Preset of 1/16 (sixteenth-notes) will constrain the edits to the sixteenth-note resolution of the Event Display.

Temporarily Disabling Snap

If you find yourself making a series of edits and want to quickly disable Snap, you can hold down the Ctrl/Command key while making the edits. When you release the Ctrl/Command key, the Snap behavior will be reengaged.

USING THE TOOLS

Each of the twelve tools in the Toolbox has a specific function. That functionality is only applicable to the events in the Event Display. For example, if you select the Split tool, the Mouse icon will resemble the Scissors icon, but only when the mouse is moved to the Event Display. When you move the mouse to any other region of the Cubase Project window, the mouse returns to its default "pointer" appearance. That allows you to see which tool you have selected during editing but leave the default appearance for other mouse operations outside of the Event Display.

The tools also make appearances in other editors, such as the Key and Drum Editors. Their functionality is virtually identical no matter which editor you're using them in. As

you'll see in some of the subsequent chapters, the other editors offer a finer degree of detail. For now, I'll go over each of the tools as they appear in the Toolbox from left to right, as shown in Figure 9.6.

Figure 9.6. The tools in the Toolbox.

Object Selection Tool (Normal Sizing Mode)

The Object Selection tool in Normal Sizing mode is the default and most commonly used tool in the Toolbox. With it, you can click on events to select them. Selected events will turn black, making it easy to identify selected versus unselected events. For example, in Figure 9.7, the first track has one event of many selected, whereas the third track has a larger event selected. Those selected events are blackened.

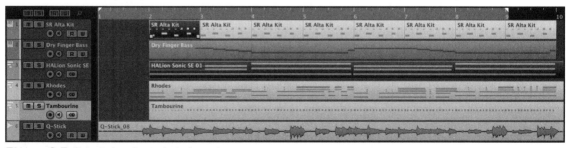

Figure 9.7. Selected and unselected events.

OBJECT SELECTION WITH THE SHIFT KEY
Shift-clicking and/or Ctrl/Command-clicking allows you to select multiple events.

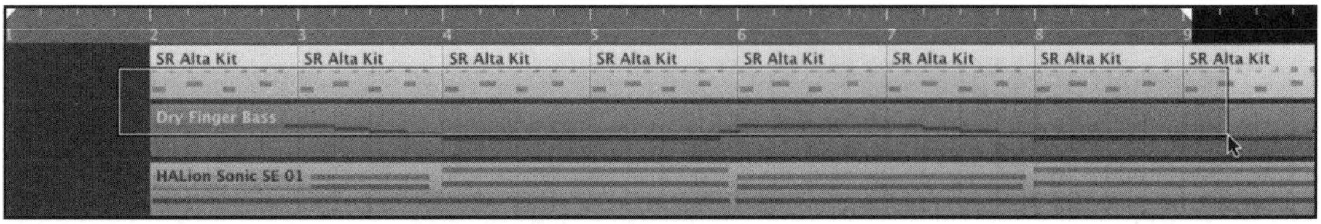

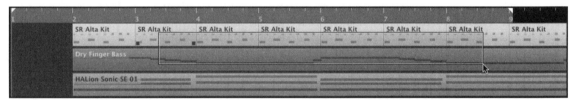

Figure 9.8. Clicking and dragging from an empty area.

You can also select a series of events by clicking and dragging from an empty area across several events, even across multiple tracks, as shown in Figure 9.8.

If you want to select several events that don't have any empty area from which to drag, hold the Shift key prior to clicking and dragging, as shown in Figure 9.9.

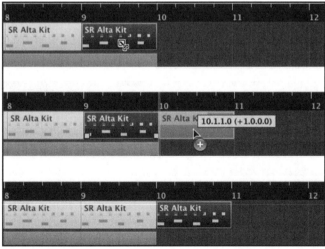

Figure 9.9. Shift-clicking and dragging.

Figure 9.10. Drag copy before, during, and after.

MAKING DRAG COPIES
When you hover over an event and press the Alt/Option key, the Object Selection Tool icon will turn into a small scissors pointing at a box. Clicking on an event (or series of selected events) while holding the Alt/Option key will create copies of the events that you can drag to different temporal locations, as shown in Figure 9.10.

During the drag, a small "+" sign will appear underneath the Mouse icon to indicate that you are making a copy. (That "+" sign has a square, clear background on Windows and a round, green background on a Mac.) If you want to make a drag copy and you forgot to hold the Alt/Option key prior to the drag, you can hold Alt/Option before releasing the mouse button to complete the Drag Copy operation.

You can also hold the Shift key along with Alt/Option to make a Shared copy. Any editing you make on that event will be reflected in all the events with which it is shared. (See "Making Shared Event Repeats" later in this chapter.)

RESIZING EVENTS

When you hover your mouse over an event, two very small squares will appear at the lower corners. Those are called the Event Handles, as shown in Figure 9.11.

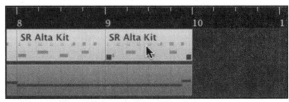

Notice the mouse is hovering over the event at measure 9 and the Event Handles are visible, whereas the event at measure 8 has no Event

Figure 9.11. The Event Handles.

Handles. It's the hovering that makes the Event Handles visible. Clicking on the handles and dragging left or right allows you to resize the event. Audio events can be resized to the extent of their contents. In other words, if an Audio event were originally thirty seconds long, you could shorten it to any size. However, you could not extend the length to longer than thirty seconds.

MAKING EVENT REPEATS

Another highly useful technique is to hold the Alt/Option button while dragging the right handle. When you hover the mouse over the handle while holding Alt/Option, the Mouse icon turns into a pencil similar to the Draw Tool icon. Clicking and dragging then creates Event Repeats, as shown in Figure 9.12.

Be aware that each Event Repeat is independent of the original. This allows you to make further edits to each event or the data contained within without altering the original from which it was made. However, Shared Repeats work differently.

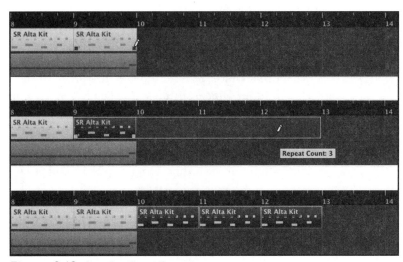

Figure 9.12. Creating Event Repeats.

MAKING SHARED EVENT REPEATS

Shared Repeats allow you to make edits to one Shared Event, and all Shared Repeats will reflect the same edit. For example, if you edited the MIDI notes on a Shared Event to play the cowbell instead of the snare drum, all the Shared Repeats would also play cowbell. (Insert your own "more cowbell" joke here.) The process of making Shared Repeats is identical to that of making Event Repeats, except that after you've started making repeats, hold the Shift key at any time during the drag, as shown in Figure 9.13.

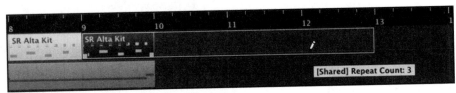

Figure 9.13. Creating Shared Event Repeats.

Shared Events, including the original from which the repeats were made, will all display small "=" icons in their upper right-hand corners.

SLIDE EDITING

Hovering your mouse over a MIDI or Audio event and pressing Ctrl-Alt/Option will turn the pointer into a small square with left and right arrows. Holding those modifier keys and clicking on the event will allow you to slide the data within the event to the left or right, depending upon which direction you drag the mouse. This allows you to leave the event in place, but move the data contained within the event.

There is no limit to how far you can slide MIDI data. However, audio data can only be slid to the boundaries of the audio data contained within the event. In other words, if the current size of the Audio event represents the complete audio recording contained within, you will not be able to slide the data in either direction.

OTHER OBJECT SELECTION TOOL MODES

By default, the Object Selection tool is in Normal Sizing mode. When you alter the size of an event by dragging its handles, the data contained within the event is not altered. The data may get truncated when making an event smaller, but the remaining data is unaffected.

When you click on the Object Selection tool in the Toolbox, a submenu will appear and display the other two modes, as shown in Figure 9.14.

You can choose a different mode either by selecting it from the submenu or by repeatedly typing "1" on your computer keyboard (see Figure 9.4) to cycle through all

Figure 9.14. Object Selection Tool modes.

three modes. Pay attention to the Tool icon, as it depicts how the Object Selection tool will appear in the Event Display.

Using the Object Selection tool in these other modes is identical to resizing events; however, the results are quite different. Sizing Moves Contents will move the data contained within the event. Sizing Applies Time Stretch will keep all the data within the event, but apply time compression/expansion to alter the tempo of the event. Depending on the amount of the resizing, the sonic quality of the time stretch will vary slightly on Audio events. MIDI data, on the other hand, will retain its original sonic quality, because MIDI is not sound. The notes are simply placed at different temporal locations.

Range Selection Tool

The Range Selection tool is very useful for editing, copying, or deleting events across multiple tracks, and especially when the events have differing sizes. For example, Figure 9.15 shows events with both MIDI and audio data and of varying sizes. If you wanted to remove all of the data between measures 5 and 7 across all the tracks, you would use the Range Selection tool to click and drag around that range.

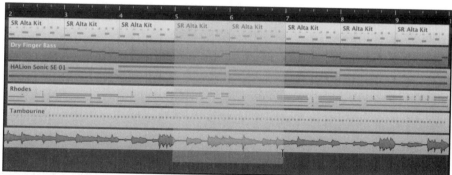

Figure 9.15. The Range Selection process.

The range will appear as an opaque blue box to reveal the selected data. To erase the data within the range, type the Delete key on your keyboard, and the result will appear as it does in Figure 9.16.

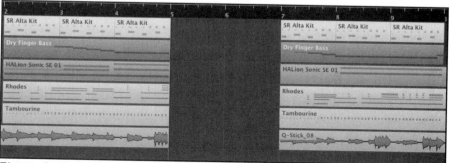

Figure 9.16. The range after the delete process.

Notice that the deletion of the range resulted in the creation of more events. The lower tracks used to have one long event. But after the deletion of the range, there are now two events: one preceding and one following the range.

OTHER RANGE
SELECTION PROCEDURES
For these functions to work, you must first use the Range Selection tool to define the range. (See Figure 9.15.) When you hover your mouse over a selected range, the Mouse icon will appear as a hand. Clicking and dragging the range will move the data to a new location and leave a gap similar to the one in Figure 9.16. Holding Alt/Option while dragging will create a copy of the range while leaving the original range intact. (Note: Shared copies cannot be created with the Range Selection tool.)

Split Tool

The Split tool appears as a scissors and is the modern equivalent of using a razor blade on analog tape. That is, it splits one event into two events, or multiple events into many more events. For example, the Audio event in Figure 9.17 (Q-Stick_08) is one large event. If you want to split it into two separate events, use the Split tool to click on the event at the desired location.

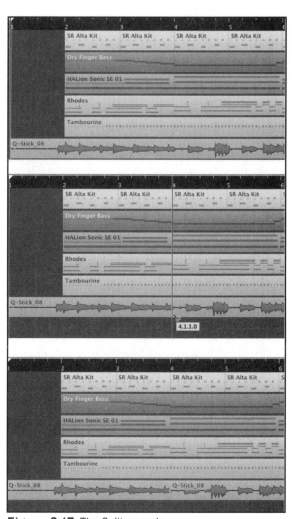

Figure 9.17. The Split procedure.

OTHER SPLIT PROCEDURES
You can use the Split tool on a series of events, as long as they are selected first. For example, Figure 9.18 shows two selected events that are not vertically contiguous. But using the Object Selection tool and Shift-clicking each event will select them both. Then clicking with the Split tool will split both events.

Figure 9.18. Using the Split tool across multiple events.

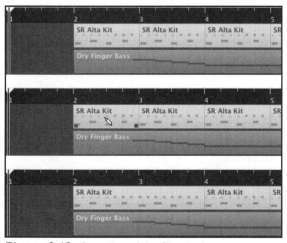

Figure 9.19. Operation of the Glue tool.

Similarly, if you want to use the Split tool across all of the events, use the Select All command (Ctrl/ Command A) to select all the events. Then click with the Split tool on any event and at the desired location.

Glue Tool

The Glue tool is the antithesis of the Split tool. Rather than making many from one, it makes one from many. It resembles a small tube of glue and is the digital equivalent of adhesive tape. When using the Glue tool on single events, it has a "left to right" behavior. In other words, clicking on an event will glue the next event to the right. That's true even if there is a void area between the events. Because of this left-to-right behavior, clicking on a right-most event (or a solitary event on a track) with the Glue tool will not produce any result. Figure 9.19 depicts the operation of the Glue tool.

OTHER GLUE PROCEDURES

Another important behavior is that the Glue tool only works one track at a time and across like data. The latter is easy to understand, because you cannot glue MIDI events together with Audio events. However, the former means you cannot glue the events from one track to another. You could use the Object Selection tool, Range

Selection tool, or Select All command to select multiple events. Then clicking with the Glue tool will join right events to the left events but keep the events relative to their original tracks.

Erase Tool

This is perhaps the most basic of the tools. It resembles the eraser used on chalkboards. Clicking on an event with the Erase tool will erase it from the Event Display.

OTHER ERASE PROCEDURES

You can erase multiple events across multiple tracks by first selecting the events with the Object Selection tool. You can also use the Range Selection tool to define a range of events, and then click on the range (opaque blue area, see Figure 9.15) to erase the contents. Additionally, you can hold Alt/Option while clicking on an event. Doing so erases all the events to the right but leaves the clicked event intact.

Zoom Tool

The normal behavior of the Zoom tool is as a horizontal zoom-in tool. Clicking and dragging over events with the Zoom tool will zoom in to reveal finer details. Clicking and dragging while holding Ctrl/Command will also zoom all tracks heights as well as zooming the events. I don't use the Zoom tool very often, but when I do, I like to keep the Overview line (see "The Status, Info, and Overview Lines" later in this chapter) visible so that I can use it to zoom out. Additional provisions for zooming the Event Display will be discussed later.

Mute Tool

This is an extraordinarily powerful, yet misunderstood, tool. But after I describe how it works, you'll find yourself using it more and more. You see, when you remove MIDI events from the Event Display, they're gone forever (that is, unless you use the Undo command to restore them). But after you close the project, the MIDI events are unrecoverable. Audio events are quite different, because Cubase always remembers every audio recording you make, in a special place called the Pool. Space constraints won't allow us to discuss the Pool in this book, so for now, it's time to learn how to use the Mute tool.

When you click on an event with the Mute tool, it gets grayed out and will not be audible during playback. So why not just delete the event with the Erase tool or by typing the Delete key on your keyboard? Because a muted event can be unmuted, thereby leaving it in place. Simply click on the muted event with the Mute tool, and it will become audible again during playback. This is perfect for when you think, "I don't want to use that event," but you change your mind later on.

The Mute tool resembles an "X." When you click on an event with the Mute tool, it will become grayed out and inaudible during playback, as shown in Figure 9.20.

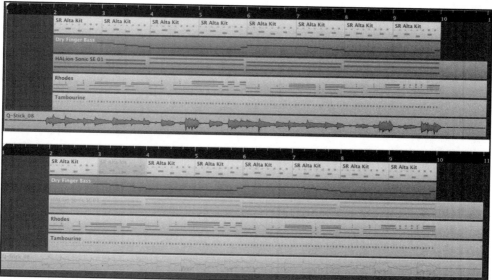

Figure 9.20. Operation with the Mute tool.

OTHER MUTE PROCEDURES

You can mute multiple events by using the Object Selection tool or Select All command prior to Shift-clicking one of them with the Mute tool. You can also click and drag across multiple events to mute a range of events.

Time Warp Tool

Due to space constraints, the Time Warp tool will won't be covered in this book. Suffice it to say you cannot use the Time Warp tool to create clichéd plots for television and cinema.

Comp Tool

The Comp tool is a powerful and multifaceted tool that will be covered in Chapter 10.

Draw Tool

The Draw tool resembles a pencil and can be used to create blank events. This is especially useful on MIDI and Instrument tracks when you want to create new data in the Key, List, or Score Editors. While you can create empty Audio events, there isn't much facility to use, edit, or create data inside of them. The Draw tool can only be used on a track-by-track basis. In other words, you cannot create multiple events across multiple tracks.

Line Tool

The Line tool will be covered in Appendix B: "A Primer on Automation."

Play Tool

The Play tool resembles a speaker and can be used to listen to individual events in the Event Display. The Play tool works on both MIDI and Audio events. Using the Play tool and clicking and holding on any MIDI or Audio event will start playback from the click location. Only the clicked event will be audible, and playback will adhere to the project tempo. If playback proceeds past the boundary of the clicked event, no sound will be produced by subsequent events. If you'd like to hear those events, click and hold on them with the Play tool in Play mode.

Scrub Tool

Clicking and holding the Play tool button will allow you to select the Scrub tool. *Scrubbing* is a term that comes from the days of reel-to-reel analog tape. With the playback head engaged, you could manually wind the reels back and forth to listen closely for edit points. That's exactly how the Scrub tool works, but be aware that it only works on Audio events. Click and hold the Scrub tool over an Audio event, and drag the mouse slowly from left to right. Then drag right to left. The speed of the scrubbing will depend on how quickly or slowly you're dragging the mouse. It even sounds like old analog tape going forward and backward. This allows you to listen to the audio contained in the event in a nontemporal fashion and make other edits (such as splitting) based on what you're hearing and seeing.

You can also use the Scrub tool to adjust the handles of Audio events and hear the results of adjustment. This makes it much easier to move the handles to the audible start and finish of the audio data. Be aware that the temporal adjustment is quite a bit slower with the Scrub tool than it is with the Object Selection tool. I recommend that you make the gross edits with either the Object Selection or Range Selection tools, then use Scrub tool to trim up the shortened events.

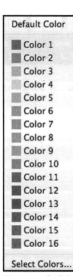

Figure 9.22.
Color list.

CHANGING EVENT COLORS

While the Select Colors menu is not one of the Cubase tools, it is located to the right of the Toolbar, as shown in Figure 9.21.

Figure 9.21. Location of the Select Colors menu.

Changing the color of an event can make it easier to see during editing. For example, if you want to see all of the drum fills on a drum track, you could use the Object Selection tool to select each drum fill event, then use the Select Colors menu to choose a new color for the selected events.

When you click on the Select Colors menu, a list of sixteen selectable colors will appear, as shown in Figure 9.22. If you're really into specific colors or you are color-blind and wish to define your own colors, you can choose Select Colors from the bottom of the menu to open a palette of colors from which to choose or design.

After you've selected a color, all of the selected events will reflect the new color.

Other Color Selection Procedures

You can use the Range Selection tool, Select All command, or Ctrl/Command-click method of selecting multiple events to change event colors of many events simultaneously. You can also right/Ctrl-click on a track and choose Select All Events from the mini-menu to select all of the events on that track. Once you've made your selections, click the Select Colors menu to choose the desired color.

THE STATUS, INFO, AND OVERVIEW LINES

The Status, Info, and Overview Lines can be very useful during the editing process. However, they're not always visible. Clicking on the Window Layout button located at the upper left-hand corner of the Project window shown in Figure 9.23 will allow you to make each of the lines visible.

Figure 9.23. The Window Layout settings.

When the Window Layout settings are visible, a blue, opaque mask will cover the rest of the Project window. That mask indicates there's another window open. This is a common behavior in Cubase. Now put checks next to the Status Line, Info Line, and Overview boxes. To close the Window Layout settings, simply click anywhere else on the Project Window.

The Location of the Lines

Each of the lines is located directly underneath the Toolbar, as seen in Figure 9.24.

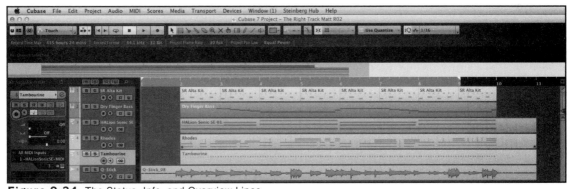

Figure 9.24. The Status, Info, and Overview Lines.

The Status Line

The Status Line displays the current settings in the Project Setup window, which can be revealed by clicking the Project menu and selecting Project Setup, or by typing Shift + S. You can also click on the Status Line to reveal the Project Setup settings. The Status

Line itself displays four fields: Record Time Max, Record Format, Project Frame Rate, and Project Pan Law. However, there are many more settings in the Project Setup window, the most significant of which I'll go over in a moment.

All but Record Time Max are configured in the Project Setup window. Instead, Record Time Max keeps a running tally of how much recording can be performed on the drive where the Project (and Project Folder) is stored. This is especially useful to monitor when you're recording audio projects with lots of tracks, or when you've done so much recording that your hard disk is filling up. (Lucky you!) If you want to hide the Status Line but still monitor the record time, there's a larger Record Time Max window located under the Devices menu.

THE PROJECT SETUP WINDOW

It's very important to configure these settings before you do any recording. That's because making changes afterward can be very problematic. For example, if you've recorded audio files at 48.000 kHz and then change the Project Settings to a sample rate of 44.100 kHz,

the speed and pitch of the 48 kHz files will be altered during playback. That's why it's critical to set them right the first time. I would recommend that unless you have the specific need to do otherwise, you configure your Project Setup window as it is in Figure 9.25.

The most common sample frequency for musicians using DAW programs is 44.100 kHz. That's because audio CDs and consumer-friendly MP3 files are 44.100 kHz. However, if you're working on audio for film or video, you'll want to set the sample rate to 48.000 kHz. If you are working on projects you know will be converted to other DAW programs that are incapable of deciphering 32-bit files (such as Pro Tools 9 or earlier), you should set the bit resolution to 24-bit. Most modern DAW programs can read 24-bit files, so only in the rarest of circumstances would you need to choose 16-bit.

If you want to avail yourself of the high-resolution sample-rate capability of your audio interface, you can choose from all of its supported rates. If you have such an audio interface, the sample frequencies of that device

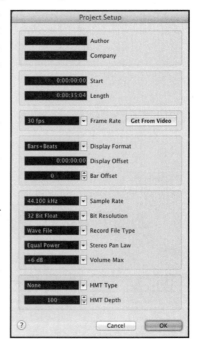

Figure 9.25. Recommended Project Setup settings.

will appear in the Sample Rate dropdown box. You might be able to choose 88.200 kHz, 96.000 kHz, 192.000 kHz, or even 384.000 kHz, regardless of the destination medium of the final product. But bear in mind that the sample rates of most consumer audio products max out at 48.000 kHz. Therefore, your end-listener will not be able to fully enjoy the sonic advantages of high-resolution sample rates. Recording in high resolution is mainly for your benefit, but can be important for "future proofing" your music if compatible consumer products are introduced at a future date.

The Info Line

The Info Line displays very detailed information on one or more selected events. The data that appears in the Info Line will differ somewhat depending on what type of event is selected. For example, Figure 9.26 shows the Info Line values for a single MIDI event.

Figure 9.26. Info Line values for a MIDI event.

For now, I'll concentrate on the Info Line as it pertains to MIDI and Audio events.

INFO LINE DATA COMMON TO MIDI AND AUDIO EVENTS
- Start: Start location of the event.
- End: End location of the event.
- Length: Overall length of the event.
- Offset: Timing offset of the data within the event.
- Mute: Mute condition of the event. (See Mute tool.)
- Lock: Indicates if an event is locked out of editing.
- Transpose: The value to which the event is being transposed.
- Global Transpose: Whether the event follows the Transpose track or not.
- Root Key: Establishes the root key of the event.

INFO LINE DATA FOR MIDI EVENTS
- Name: The name of the event.
- Velocity: The positive or negative velocity offset.

INFO LINE DATA FOR AUDIO EVENTS
- File: The name of the Audio file depicted by the event.
- Description: The name of the event.
- Volume: The volume of the event in dB (decibels).
- Fine-Tune: Tuning values finer than a semitone.

EDITING THE INFO LINE VALUES

Editing values on the Info Line is accomplished by a variety of methods. If the data is alphanumeric (such as Name or Description), you can double-click the current value and use your computer keyboard to enter the desired value. For timing data (such as Start and Length), you can employ the double-click method, or you can click and drag to increase or decrease the value. For finer control, you can hover the mouse over the value. Hovering slightly above the horizontal midline of the value will add a small "+" icon to the mouse, and clicking will increment the value. Similarly, hovering below the horizontal midline of the value will reveal a small "-" icon to the mouse, and clicking will decrement the value. Strictly numeric values (such as Volume and Fine-Tune) can be double-clicked, or Alt/ Option-clicking will reveal a vertical value slider you can adjust up or down. Data that have predetermined values (such as Global Transpose or Mute) can be edited by clicking the data, which will reveal a list or switch between two different values.

EDITING MULTIPLE SELECTED EVENTS

By using the Object Selection tool to select multiple events, you can edit the values of all the selected events. When a single event is selected, the alphanumeric values in the Info Line are a light blue. When multiple events are selected, the values turn orange. When you edit timing values, the selected events will retain their positions relative to one another. However, you can hold Ctrl/Command while editing the timing values to adjust all the events identically. This is useful for selecting several events at varying locations and placing them all at a specific location.

The Overview Line

The Overview Line is simply a very small depiction of the events in the Event Display. It is useful for monitoring your current position, especially on lengthy projects. It also offers some very useful zooming capabilities that I'll discuss in a moment. (See "Zooming with the Overview Line.") The Overview Line depicts both events and the visible region of the Event Display, as seen in Figure 9.27.

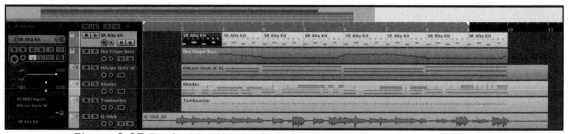

Figure 9.27. The Overview Line and Event Display

As you can see, the Overview Line looks like a vertically compressed version of the tracks in your project. All the event colors are represented identically both in the project and the Overview Line. It displays all events, whether they're currently visible in the Event Display or not. But it also depicts the entire length of the project at all times. If you notice that there's a bit of void area on the right side of the Overview Line, you'll want to adjust the Length setting in the Project Setup window (see Figure 9.25) to accurately depict the overall length of the project. However, if you start recording past the project Length setting, it will be lengthened automatically.

ADVANCED ZOOMING TECHNIQUES AND THE EVENT DISPLAY

Zooming refers to how much data you can currently see. Think of a camera with a zoom lens. A wide zoom reveals a broader spectrum but less detail. A tight zoom reveals a smaller spectrum but more detail. In the same way, you can alter both the Vertical and Horizontal Zoom settings of many windows, including the Event Display. Therefore, many of the techniques I will discuss in this section are applicable to the Key Editor, Sample Editor, and many other windows. Changing the zoom allows you to customize the display to make the process of editing easier.

Horizontal Zoom

While there are more conventional methods, I'm going to show you my favorite zoom technique first. Once you start using it, you'll wish every temporally based software program (DAW programs, nonlinear video editors, scientific programs, etc.) would use this zoom technique. I call it the "drag" zoom. Click and hold your mouse on the Time Ruler at the top of the Event Display, then drag up to zoom out or down to zoom in. Figure 9.28 further demonstrates this powerful zoom method.

Figure 9.28. Drag zooming.

Holding the Shift key while drag zooming will lock the Cursor position. This is useful for maintaining the focus of your zoom without accidentally moving the cursor to the left or right.

There are also key commands for zooming: "G" to zoom out and "H" to zoom in. And if you're really into convention, there are Zoom sliders in the lower right-hand corner of the Event Display, as shown in Figure 9.29.

The horizontal slider on the bottom can be adjusted left or right, left to zoom out and right to zoom in.

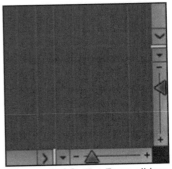

Figure 9.29. The Zoom sliders.

ZOOMING WITH THE OVERVIEW LINE

When you move your mouse into the Overview Line, it will resemble a pencil. That allows you to click and drag a range inside of the Overview Line to define a zoom. The zoom will appear as a slightly dark box around the range you drew. Then if you hover over that range, the mouse becomes a hand, allowing you to drag the entire zoom range from left to right. Or if you hover near the left or right boundary of the zoom range, the mouse becomes left and right arrows, allowing you to stretch or shrink the zoom range.

Vertical Zoom

When you zoom vertically in the Event Display, you're essentially making the track heights taller or shorter. Locate the vertical slider on the right-hand side of Figure 9.29, and adjust it up and down. Both the events and the heights of the tracks they reside on will become taller or shorter, as shown in Figure 9.30.

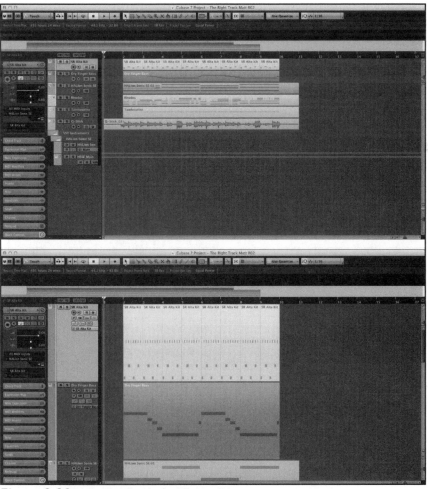

Figure 9.30. Adjusting the Vertical Zoom slider.

ZOOMING TRACK HEIGHTS

When adjusting the Vertical Zoom slider, it will adjust the track height of all tracks equally. Another method is to use the Zoom tool while holding Ctrl/Command. You can also adjust the Vertical Zoom on a track-by-track basis by adjusting the track heights. Simply hover over the top or bottom boundary of a track in the Track column, as shown in Figure 9.31.

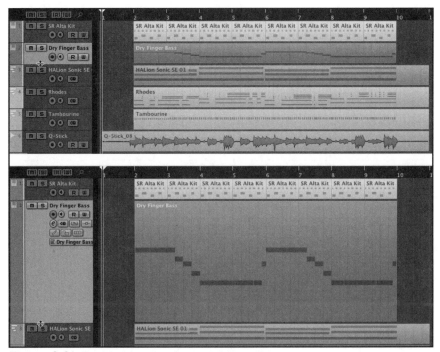

Figure 9.31. Track height adjustment, track by track.

The mouse will appear as two small, parallel lines with arrows at the top and bottom. Clicking and dragging up and down will adjust the height of the track. Holding Ctrl/ Command, then clicking to drag, will adjust all track heights simultaneously. You can also select multiple tracks (the tracks, not their associated events) and adjust all their heights by adjusting only one selected track.

Zoom Commands and Their Key Commands

The Zoom commands are a great way to adjust the gross zoom of the Event Display. Click on the Edit menu, select the Zoom category, and select a command from the list that appears in Figure 9.32.

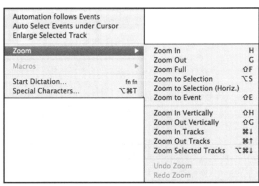

Figure 9.32. The Edit menu Zoom commands.

The commands are self-explanatory. You'll also notice that many of the commands have key commands assigned to them. A few of my favorites are Alt/Option + E to zoom one selected event, Alt/Option + S to zoom more than one selected event, and Shift + F to display all of the events horizontally.

ADDITIONAL ZOOM COMMANDS

There are additional Zoom Command menus located near the vertical and horizontal sliders shown in Figure 9.33.

Clicking on the Zoom menus will reveal the associated Zoom commands shown in Figure 9.34.

The horizontal commands are time based, allowing you to zoom to specific time ranges. The vertical commands are based on the number of tracks you'd like displayed. My favorite command is Zoom N Tracks. After you select it, a dialog box will appear, allowing you to type in a numeric value. This is very useful when you have multiple associated tracks. For example, if you have ten drum tracks you'd like visible for editing, enter a value of 10, and all the track heights will be zoomed to view ten tracks at a time.

ZOOM MEM AND ZOOM ZAP

These zoom commands are very useful; however, they do take a little work to set up. You see, Zoom MEM and Zoom ZAP are not commands that are accessible from a menu; rather, they are only implemented via a key command. Strangely, neither command has a default key command, which will require that you assign them before you can use them.

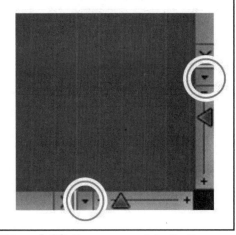

Figure 9.33. Zoom commands by the Zoom sliders.

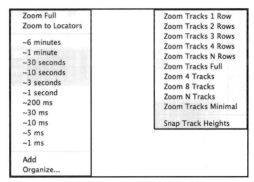

Figure 9.34. Horizontal and Vertical Zoom Menu commands.

Before you assign the key commands, let me tell you more about Zoom MEM and Zoom ZAP. Sometimes you'll find yourself doing a lot of manual zooming in and out, and that can take a toll on the speed of your editing workflow. Zoom MEM allows you to memorize your current zoom level, and Zoom ZAP allows you to toggle back and forth between the levels zoomed in and zoomed out. For example, if you're editing the Event Handles of a track with many Audio events, you could zoom in and use the Zoom MEM command to remember that zoom level, then manually zoom out. The next time you want to zoom in to that memorized level, you could use the Zoom ZAP command to zoom in, complete the edit, and then Zoom ZAP again to zoom back out.

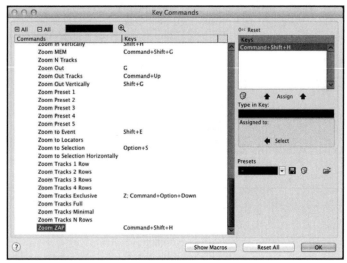

Figure 9.35. The Key Commands window.

Now assign some key commands to Zoom MEM and Zoom ZAP. Go to the File menu and select Key Commands. That will open the Key Commands window, as seen in Figure 9.36.

Zoom MEM and Zoom ZAP are located in the Zoom category in the left-hand column. Figure 9.36 also shows the keys to which I've assigned the commands: Ctrl/Command + Shift + G for Zoom MEM (top of left column), and Ctrl/Command + Shift + H for Zoom ZAP (bottom of left column). You don't have to use the same commands, but here's how to assign them. On the right-hand side, you'll see a blank window labeled Type in Key. Single-click on the Zoom MEM command on the left, then single-click in the Type in Key box. The box will turn blue, indicating that it's waiting for you to type the preferred keys on modifiers on your computer keyboard to which you want to assign the command. When complete, the keys you pressed will appear in the box; then single-click the Assign button (with two black arrows) to complete the operation. Repeat the procedure for Zoom ZAP, but make sure to choose a different key and modifier combination. Close the Key Commands window when finished.

Here's a few things to know about Zoom MEM and Zoom ZAP. You have to be manually zoomed in prior to memorizing the level with Zoom MEM, and you must zoom back out manually after executing the command. The Zoom ZAP command is a toggle between zoomed in and zoomed out. The position of the cursor specifies where the zooming will occur. Therefore, it's important to move the cursor along the timeline prior to "zapping" to the new zoom level. If you don't, the zoom might not occur at the currently desired location. Make sure you move the cursor before using the Zoom ZAP command.

Event Zoom

The Event Zoom slider is located at the upper left-hand corner of the Event Display. Its location and function are shown in Figure 9.36.

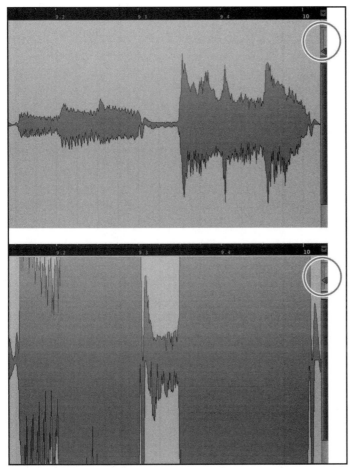

Figure 9.36. Event Zoom slider.

The Event Zoom only affects Audio events. But as you can see, the audio waveform contained within an Audio event will become magnified. This will allow you to see quiet passages more easily, and therefore, editing will become easier.

A common misconception of the Event Slider is that it affects the volume of the audio data. This is not the case. Even though the data looks like it's getting louder, only visual representation of the audio data is being affected.

OVERLAPPING EVENTS

Before you can start editing your events, you'll need to understand how Cubase handles events when they overlap. That overlapping concept is also critical for understanding a powerful feature called Comping. So significant is Comping that I'll need a separate chapter to discuss it in. I'll do that next.

Overlapping Events, Comping, and the Comp Tool

At this point, I hope you've been doing a lot of recording and that you've been using MIDI, Instrument, and Audio tracks. You should also be familiar with how MIDI events and Audio events differ from one another. But it's easy to get the behaviors of MIDI and Audio events confused. Since both MIDI and Instrument tracks use MIDI, their events are interchangeable. However, MIDI events cannot be placed on Audio tracks, and vice versa. In fact, most of the fourteen track types that Cubase uses contain specific noninterchangeable events. But now you need to learn about overlapping events and a wonderful creative Cubase function known as Comping and the Comp tool. In this chapter, you will learn:

- That MIDI events can overlap.
- That Audio events should not overlap.
- The basics of Comping.
- How to create composites with the Comp tool.
- How to reveal and edit the Comping Lanes.

UNDERSTANDING EVENT OVERLAPS

When you start editing the events in the Event Display, it's very easy to move, delete, copy, and rearrange the events. However, it's critical to understand how only certain events can be moved to specific track types. To illustrate this, you'll be using a project from the disc that comes with this book. It's located in the Cubase Projects Folder, and the folder name is "Overlaps." (See Appendix A: "Using the Included Disc.") Inside that folder, load the project "Overlaps R01.cpr."

Exploring the "Overlaps R01" Project

The "Overlaps R01" project contains three Instrument tracks and two Audio tracks, and should appear similar to Figure 10.1.

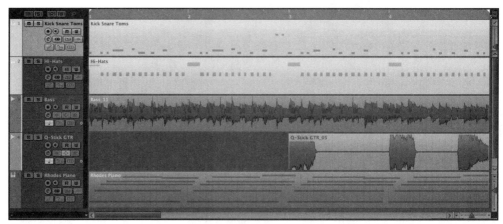

Figure 10.1. The Track Column and Event Display of the "Overlaps R01" project.

The project was created in Cubase, so it's possible that if you're using Cubase Artist or a lower level, the Instrument tracks may not contain the same sounds. If that's the case, go ahead and assign different yet similar sounds to the Instrument tracks. In other words, tracks 1 and 2 are drum sets, and track 5 is an electric piano. Then start playback, and have a listen to all the tracks. The cycle mode is on, so the same four measures will repeat over and over until you stop playback. While it's playing, solo each track so that you get an idea of the sounds contained within the events. Also notice that when you hover your mouse over any of the events, it will darken slightly and its Event Handles will become visible.

Identifying Event Overlaps

When your mouse hovers over overlapping events, their appearance is quite different. Instead of only a slightly darker background, you'll see vertical pinstripes running across the events. For example, with your Object Selection tool, drag the Hi-Hats event over the Kick Snare Toms event. You can do this whether Cubase is playing or not. But if you are in Playback mode while you do this, you'll notice that the characteristics of the Hi-Hats sounds will be slightly different. That's because the Hi-Hats track has a different instrument assigned to it than does the Kick Snare Toms track. However, the MIDI notes for the Hi-Hats are identical to both tracks, which is why you'll still hear the Hi-Hats sounds. But the most significant thing to realize is that you can still hear both events. When MIDI events overlap, they'll both be audible. Now when you hover your mouse over the events on track 1, they appear with the vertical pinstripes that indicate an overlap, as shown in Figure 10.2.

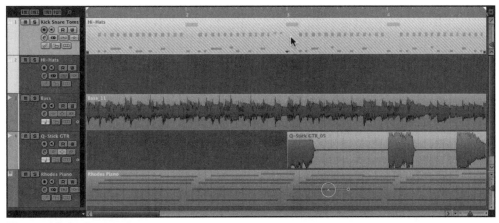

Figure 10.2. Overlapping events.

Since both events had identical start and end times, the pinstripes will appear across the entire range of the overlap. However, if you adjust the handle of the Hi-Hats event, you will see how the overlap range follows the topmost event, as shown in Figure 10.3.

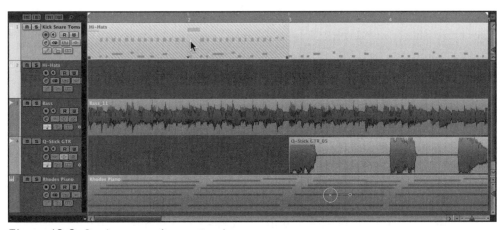

Figure 10.3. Overlap range after event resize.

Now type Ctrl/Command + Z (Undo) to return the Hi-Hats event to its original size. (See Figure 10.2.)

Overlapping MIDI Events

You've already discovered how overlapping MIDI events can coexist on the same track. This offers both creative freedoms and creative conundrums. The ability to layer multiple MIDI events can create very dense results. But then the editing gets a little foreboding. For example, the Object Selection tool will always select the topmost event. When using the Split, Erase, Mute, or Play tool, only the topmost event will be edited. However, when using the Range Selection tool, all of the events (even several layers deep) get selected. Try some of these edits on the Hi-Hats event, and see how and if the Kick Snare Toms event is affected. After you've tried a few edits, undo to the point where you first opened the project. (See Figure 10.1.)

WHEN OVERLAPPING MIDI WON'T WORK

When you were listening to the overlapping Hi-Hats and Kick Snare Toms events, the audible difference was in what type of hi-hat sound was being produced. As I mentioned before, this is because the MIDI notes were identical between the instruments loaded on tracks 1 and 2. But what if you overlapped MIDI events that had very different track sounds? To find out, with the Object Selection tool, click and drag the Rhodes Piano event on top of the Hi-Hats event. Release the mouse button, and start playback (if you haven't already done so). Notice how the sound of the piano goes away but has been replaced with some cymbal and percussion sounds. This is the result of incompatible MIDI performances. Basically, the lesson to be learned is that the sound comes from the instrument assigned to the track, not from the MIDI event itself.

For a more dramatic example of this concept, drag the Kick Snare Toms event to the now-empty Rhodes Piano track. Solo the Rhodes track and listen to the results. If you're like me, you'll hear music that might accompany silly cartoon characters as they march down the street. But whatever you see in your mind's eye, you certainly won't be hearing drums. Now that you know you can overlap multiple MIDI events, remember that the track rather than the event determines the sound used for playback.

Overlapping Audio Events

The behavior of overlapping Audio events is much different than that of MIDI events. For example, the Overlaps Project has two Audio tracks: Bass and Q-Stick GTR. The "Bass_11" event plays throughout the entire four measures; however, the "Q-Stick GTR_05" event plays for only the last two measures. With the Object Selection tool, click and drag the "Q-Stick GTR_05" event over the top of the "Bass_11," and release the mouse button. When you listen to the playback, you'll notice that the "Q-Stick GTR_05" event cancels out the "Bass_11" event underneath. That's because as opposed to MIDI, only one overlapping Audio event can be played on a track. That event will be the topmost event, and events underneath that will not be heard.

HANDLING AUDIO EVENT OVERLAPS

You might conclude that since Audio events cannot be layered like MIDI events, you'll need to be thriftier with the number of Audio events you add to or record into a project. This is not true. Cubase (the full level) has unlimited Audio tracks; you can simply place those events onto their own tracks. Lower levels of Cubase will have finite track counts. (Cubase

Artist has sixty-four Audio tracks; Cubase Elements, forty-eight; and so on. . . .) When you consider that many Beatles recordings were made on 4-track recorders, even entry-level varieties of Cubase can provide you with more tracks than you may need to complete your project.

There is one situation in which Audio events can overlap, albeit for brief moments. That can occur when joining two Audio events adjacently on the same track(s). In this case, it's very common to use a crossfade to smooth the transition between the end of one event and the start of another. I'll explore crossfades in chapter 12, "Editing Audio Data."

Using the "Move to" Commands

In a moment I'll be showing you the Comping capabilities of Cubase. Comping is a profoundly more powerful way of managing and editing overlaps. However, for some users, Comping may be overkill. So before I go on, I'll discuss the Move to commands.

After comprehending the limitations of overlapping Audio events, most people try to avoid them. However, there are situations, especially with MIDI events, where overlapping can offer some creative possibilities. For this reason, Cubase has ways of arranging the overlapping events. These are the Move to commands, and they're located under the Edit menu, as shown in Figure 10.4.

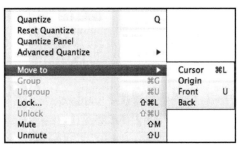

Figure 10.4. The Move to Front and Move to Back commands.

Using the Move to commands to rearrange the layers of events on a track: Move to Front will bring the selected layer to the surface of the track and can be invoked by typing the "U" key on your computer keyboard. Move to Back will submerge the selected event to the bottom of the track. For the Move to commands to work properly, you will first need to select one or more events. Move to Cursor will relocate the selected event(s) to the current cursor location, and Move to Origin will move an Audio event (not a MIDI event) to the position at which it was originally recorded. This can be very useful for resynching an Audio event if you've accidentally bumped it out of sync.

Merging Overlaps with the Glue Tool

In chapter 9, you learned how the Glue tool can merge adjacent events together into a larger single event. In a similar way, the Glue tool can merge overlapped events into a single event. If you glue Audio events together, their playback priority (topmost always audible) is maintained, and they will therefore be heard with their preglued priority. (Audio events glued in this way can be unglued later using the Dissolve Part command on the Audio menu.) Basically, gluing the overlapping events can make it much easier to move or otherwise edit a series of events. But with MIDI events, the Glue tool will combine all of the MIDI data from the overlapping events into a single event. For example, with the Object Selection tool, click and drag the Hi-Hats event over the Kick Snare Toms event. (See Figure 10.2.) Then select the Glue tool and click the Hi-Hats event to merge the contents of both events into one single event. The event will retain the name of the topmost event—in this case, the event is named "Hi-Hats."

There might also come a time when you want to glue all the events of a single track together. Right/Ctrl-click on the track (in the Track column), and choose Select All Events from the mini-menu. Then select the Glue tool and Shift-click on any selected event. All of the overlapping events, regardless of how many layers deep, will be glued together as one contiguous event.

COMPING FOR AUDIO EVENTS

Cubase has an amazing feature called Comping, which uses the unlimited Audio track playback capability of Cubase to composite best sections of several takes into one great take. But before you can fully understand the power of Comping, you need to understand how the need for it developed.

A Brief History of Multitrack Audio Compositing

In the days of analog recording, track counts usually ranged from two to twenty-four. While it was possible to synchronize multiple analog tape machines together to increase track counts, the cost of both equipment and tape stock was prohibitive to all but the big-name bands. So with only sixteen or twenty-four tracks, we still had to strive for the best "take"— that is, recording a performer over and over again until we captured the best performance. Every time we recorded a new take, the previous take was erased. Or in the rare case of leftover empty tracks, we could record multiple takes and later choose which ones to keep. Either way, the limits of technology forced us to "keep the best and punch the rest." That is to say, we kept the best take and used the technique of punch in/out recording to fix any remaining flubs on that take.

When digital recorders and DAW software entered the recording studio, track counts increased dramatically. Today with Cubase, the only limitation to track counts is the power of your computer. Modern computers can easily play back a lot of tracks, as shown in Figure 10.5.

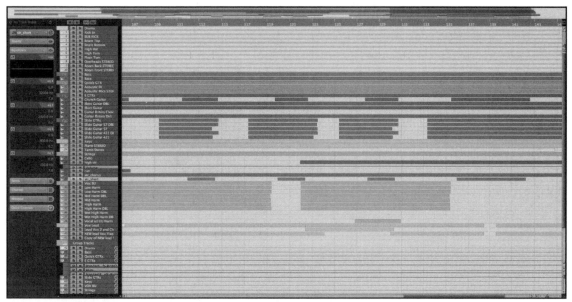

Figure 10.5. A midsized 41-Audio track project running on a MacBook Pro.

Higher track counts allowed us to record multiple takes onto multiple tracks and edit them to create the best take. This technique is known as compositing and is still used by many engineers on contemporary DAW programs.

Cubase Introduces Comping

When the developers at Steinberg took a close look at how Cubase users were using multiple compositing tracks, they realized there was a golden opportunity to make the process more elegant. This process is known as Comping. Instead of making users record onto multiple tracks, they added Comping "lanes" to every track, and every recording take was placed on the same track but in its own lane. Therefore, all of the takes exist on one track, rather than spanning across several tracks. Then, by editing the events on each lane, you can assemble the best event from multiple takes. So the results of Comping are identical to compositing. However, as you'll see, the Comping editing process is much easier.

RECORDING AUDIO TRACKS FOR COMPING

Before Comping, I would usually record a take, and if I thought I wouldn't use it, I would stop, hit Undo to remove the recorded event, and record a new take. But with Comping, unless the current recording is an obvious disaster, I'll keep every take. That means you're going to end up with a lot of overlapping Audio events. But as you already know, only the most recently recorded audio take will be audible, because it will be the topmost event.

Before you start recording your Audio tracks, you must make sure that Cubase will keep every take. Look at the far left of the Transport Panel, and take note of the current Audio Record mode, as seen in Figure 10.6.

If the mode is Keep History, you're all set. Keep History is the default setting, so unless you've changed modes, you shouldn't have to change it back. But if you do, click on the current setting to reveal the Audio Record Mode setting, and choose Keep History. Now every time you create new audio recordings on an Audio track, Cubase will keep every take.

Figure 10.6. Audio Record Mode setting.

Revealing the Comping Lanes

For the rest of this chapter, I would recommend loading the "Comping R01.cpr" project from the disc included with this book. (See Appendix A: "Using the Included Disc.") That way, you can follow along with the examples, and you won't put one of your own projects at risk.

When you've recorded several takes on an Audio track, it will appear as if you've only recorded once. That's because all the takes are overlapping on the track, as seen in Figure 10.7.

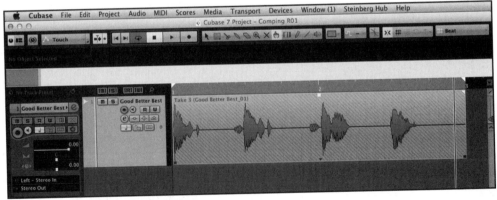

Figure 10.7. Several overlapping Audio events.

To reveal the Comping lanes, you'll need to click the Show Lanes button on the track. However, depending on the current track height and width, you might not be able to see the button. Increase the track height (see chapter 9, Figure 9.31) to reveal the Show Lanes button, as shown in Figure 10.7. (You may need to increase the track width by clicking and dragging the right edge of the track further to the right.) When you click on the Show Lanes button, the Comping Lanes will drop down below the track, as shown in Figure 10.8.

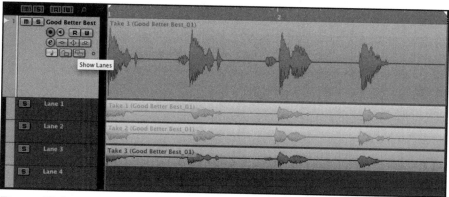

Figure 10.8. The Comping Lanes and Show Lanes button.

At first glance, you might presume that you're looking at a bunch of Audio tracks. However, instead of showing the track number and name, the lanes are identified by a number (Lane 1, Lane 2, etc.). The number of visible lanes will depend on how many takes have been recorded on the source track and will match the track color. If this is the first time you've opened the lanes, the last take on the highest numbered lane will probably be audible and appear normally, while the previous takes are inaudible and slightly dimmer in appearance.

Using the Comp Tool

The Comp tool can be found in the Toolbox and has an icon like a pointing finger. (It is the index finger pointing, rather than the one you see when you're driving in traffic.) The Comp tool can only be used in the Comping Lanes. Trying to use it on the track events will reconfigure the tool into a Move tool, as indicated by a Hand icon.

The Comp tool is a multifunction tool that can perform actions normally reserved for the Object Selection, Range Selection, Split, and Mute tools. However, because the Comp tool is used only in the Comping Lanes, it can perform all of those functions by itself without requiring you to select between four separate tools.

Every take you record will probably have some useful material in it. Confirm that the project has Cycle enabled on the Transport Panel, then start playback and listen to take 3. It should say, "Best, Best, Better, Good." (You'll see how you're going to use the words contained within these takes in a moment.) During the cycling playback, use the Comp tool to click on any event in a Comping Lane to make it audible. Doing so will mute out the previously selected take. For example, click on take 2, and you'll hear, "Good, Good,

Better, Best." Click on take 1, and you'll hear, "Good, Good, Best, Better." If one of those takes had the best overall performance, you could leave it selected and close the lanes by clicking the Show Lanes button shown in Figure 10.8.

However, it's more likely that you'll need to edit the events in the lanes with the Comp tool to get the best possible composite of all the takes. For instance, notice that among all of the takes you've auditioned so far, none of them says, "Best, Best, Best, Best." In other words, every take contains at least one "Good" and "Better" along with the "Bests." Since the goal of compositing and Comping is to build the best possible performance from all of the takes, you'll need to edit the events in the lanes to get the "Best, Best, Best, Best" result. (Now you understand why these events say what they say.)

Editing the Takes Within the Comping Lanes

The goal of this exercise is to get all the takes on the Comping lanes to say, "Best, Best, Best, Best." With that in mind, listen to take 3. It contains the most "Bests," so leave it selected. I did this on purpose, because it's very common to get the best recording on the latest take. But toward the end of take 3, the performance degrades, represented by the "Better" and "Good." Let's see if there are some "Bests" on the other takes.

EDITING WITH THE COMP TOOL

For this type of editing to work, verify that Snap is enabled and set to Beat. (See the upper right-hand corner of Figure 10.7.) Then use the Comp tool to click and drag across take 3 from measure 1 to the beginning of measure 2, as shown in Figure 10.9.

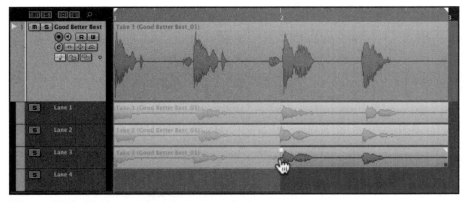

Figure 10.9. Clicking and dragging across take 3.

You'll see a light blue box appear around all of the takes in measure 1. One of the concepts of the Comp tool is that clicking and dragging across the desirable part of the take will leave it selected for playback. You could drag across any take, because, as you'll see, the split will affect all of the takes. But dragging across the desired take will keep you from having to remember or reselect the take you want to keep.

When you release the mouse button, you'll notice that all of the takes have been split at the beginning of measure 2, as shown in Figure 10.10.

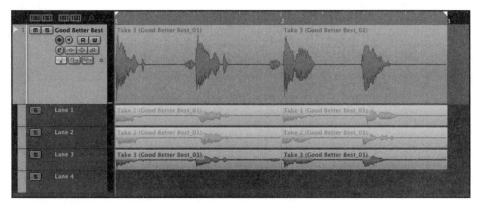

Figure 10.10. The completed splits and selections.

There are two things to notice. First, the split appears not only in the lanes, but also in the source event of the track. Second, even though you've split all of the takes, it's still take 3 that is selected for playback. Since you know that you won't be keeping the latter half of take 3, you'll need to audition the other takes for the best sections. Using the Comp tool, click on the second half of take 3. Now during playback, you'll hear "Best, Best" from take 3 and "Better, Best" from take 2, as shown in Figure 10.11.

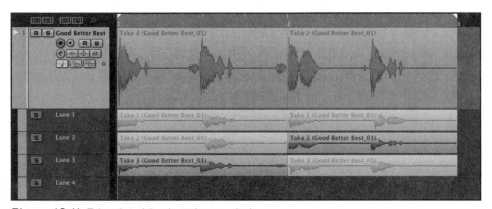

Figure 10.11. Takes 3 and 2 selected respectively.

Now if you're like me, you'll always strive for the best possible result. So perhaps take 1 has a "Best" with which you can replace the "Better" on take 2. To find out, use the

Comp tool to click and drag across take 1 from measure 2 to the third count (or middle) of measure 2. The resulting split is shown in Figure 10.12.

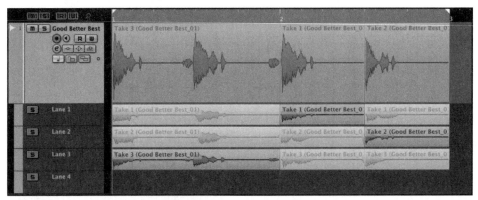

Figure 10.12. Takes 3 and 2 selected respectively.

Now when you listen to the results, you'll hear "Best, Best, Best, Best." So by using the Comp tool, you've built the best possible composite from all the available takes. But you're not done yet.

REFINING THE SPLITS

Listen to the takes in measure 2 and notice that the last "Best" sounds a little more like "est." That's because the "B" in "Best" got cut off when you made your last edit. In other words, the "B" was uttered a little early during the recording of that take and actually exists prior to the third count of measure 2. A sure fix would be to use the Comp tool to adjust the left event border (not the Event Handle) of take 2 and drag it to the left. However, because the Snap settings are currently active, an edit of that precision cannot be made. For example, using the Comp tool, hover your pointer at the beginning of the third take at measure 2, count 3. Your pointer will turn into an icon resembling two vertical parallel lines with arrows pointing to the left and right, as shown in Figure 10.13.

If you clicked and tried to adjust the border to the left, you'd notice it wouldn't move until you got near count 2, which is much further to the left than necessary. To make an edit of this precision, you'll need to consider the Snap settings. You could disable the Snap by typing "J," but you can also disable Snap temporarily by clicking your mouse to initiate the edit, then typing

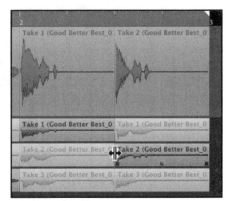

Figure 10.13. Adjusting an Event border.

and holding Ctr/Command while you drag left or right. Either way, drag the border slightly to the left to complete the edit, as shown in Figure 10.14.

Notice also that I adjusted the border of take 1 to the left so that it too was cleaner. Now listen to the entire recording, and you'll agree that the border adjustments have further improved the Comping results.

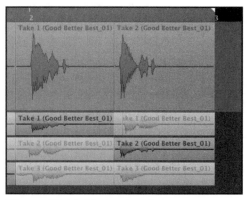

CROSSFADING THE TAKES

Sometimes the easiest way to solve clumsy-sounding Comping edits is to crossfade the takes. This can be done on an event-by-event basis by selecting only the desired events, or to all the events in the Comping Lanes. For this

Figure 10.14. The border adjustments.

example, apply crossfades to all the events by right/Control-clicking the track and choosing Select All Events from the dropdown menu. Then type "X" on your computer keyboard, and you'll see little crossfades applied to all the events, as shown in Figure 10.15.

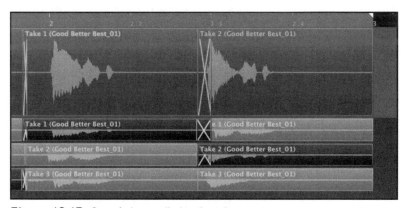

Figure 10.15. Crossfades applied to the takes.

See the little "X"s at the event borders? Those are the crossfades. A crossfade is a very brief fade-in and fade-out between two different takes or events. Crossfades can make edits sound more natural, and can also eliminate pops and clicks caused by colliding audio data.

Since you've completed your Comping edit, you can reclaim the vertical space in the Event Display by clicking the Show Lanes button (see Figure 10.8), which will close all the Comping Lanes.

(Note: If for some reason you got lost along the way, you can load the "Comping R02. cpr" project from the disc that came with this book [see appendix A] to hear and see the completed Comping edit.)

I can't overstate how powerful the Comping feature of Cubase can be. Without it, the compositing process would require us to mute and unmute multiple tracks and use a combination of resizing borders along with the Split and Mute tools on every single event to remove overlapping events. That would mean a lot more hassle and work for you and anyone who uses a DAW other than Cubase.

OTHER COMPING TECHNIQUES

My favorite technique for auditioning the takes with the Comp tool is to type and hold Crtl/Command and click on the events in the lanes. That will allow you to audition the audio data whether it's currently selected for playback or not. For example, when you were looking for the last "Best" to complete the edit, you could have used the Ctrl/Command-click technique on any take to audibly search for possibilities.

COMPING FOR MIDI EVENTS

All of the editing you've done with the Comp tool can also be used to edit MIDI events, with the exception of crossfading, which is an audio-only edit. However, because of the overlapping-friendly nature of MIDI events, editing with the Comp tool can be a little confusing. You see, since Audio events cannot overlap, only the most recently recorded event is enabled for playback prior to editing. However, all overlapping MIDI events will stay playback enabled, regardless of the order in which they were recorded. For that reason, it's a good idea to open the lanes of the MIDI or Instrument track you're recording and have the Comp tool selected. That way you can click a take in the lane to mute it prior to recording your next take.

Or if you like cycle recording, you can click on the MIDI Record Mode and MIDI Cycle Record Mode settings (see New/Mix in Figure 10.16) on the left-hand side of the Transport Panel and choose the settings listed in Figure 10.16.

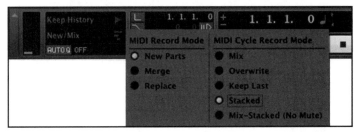

Figure 10.16. The MIDI Record Mode and MIDI Cycle Record Mode settings.

In the MIDI Record Mode column, the New Parts setting will ensure that every event created during the cycle recording is retained. Setting the MIDI Cycle Record Mode to Stacked will also keep every event, but it will always mute the recording prior to the current cycle recording pass. With those settings, you will not need to use the Comp tool during the recording process.

COMP-LETED

It's important to know that all of the edits you make during a Comping session are nondestructive. Therefore, you can edit to your heart's content without risk of losing any of your takes. You'll have the chance to explore more of this nondestructive editing concept later, especially when you start editing audio data in chapter 12. But next, in chapter 11, it's time to learn about editing MIDI data.

Editing MIDI and Instrument Data

When the MIDI Specification was released in the early 1980s, it brought unprecedented control and editing possibilities to musicians and producers alike. Not only could MIDI data be recorded and played back like audio recordings, but it could also be edited with microscopic precision. Individual notes within a chord could be manipulated or edited without disturbing the other notes around them. And since MIDI consisted of more than just note data, elements such as pitch bend, sustain pedal, and volume controllers could be edited with remarkable accuracy.

(Note: Before reading this chapter, you should be aware that a large part of the editing process is making proper selections. Therefore, it will be very important to have read chapter 9 before proceeding further.)

For almost thirty years, very little has changed about MIDI. However, the methods for editing MIDI data have become very refined. And when MIDI-controlled, computer-based virtual instruments hit the scene in the late 1990s, many musicians, producers, and music enthusiasts indoctrinated themselves into the MIDI world. In this chapter, I'll be looking at the many ways to edit MIDI in Cubase, including:

- The relationship MIDI shares with MIDI and Instrument tracks.
- The components of MIDI data.
- Editing MIDI events in the Event Display.
- Editing MIDI data in the Key Editor and In-Place Editor.
- Exploring the MIDI Functions and Logical Presets.

MIDI DATA IN CUBASE

There are two Cubase track types upon which you can record MIDI data: MIDI tracks and Instrument tracks. The ways in which the MIDI data is recorded, manipulated, and edited on the tracks are identical. The only difference is the ultimate destination for that MIDI data. MIDI tracks can send data to VST (virtual) Instruments in Cubase or to external MIDI devices via a MIDI interface. However, Instrument tracks can only send data to the VST Instruments to which they're assigned. But due to Cubase's flexibility, the events on MIDI and Instrument tracks can be freely exchanged or shared.

A Brief MIDI Primer

Over the years, the applications and advantages of MIDI recording have been wildly misunderstood. I still hear people say things like "MIDI is inferior to audio" and "MIDI sounds bad." Statements like those are usually perpetuated by folks who don't understand what MIDI is and how to use it. By now you should realize that MIDI data is not sound and that both audio and MIDI recordings have their own distinct advantages and disadvantages. So instead of going over all types of MIDI data at length, I'll only be briefly exploring the most common MIDI data you'll be using in Cubase. (Note: For a thorough description of MIDI, I recommend The MIDI Companion Book from Hal Leonard.)

MIDI NOTE DATA

Throughout the rest of this book, I'll be discussing MIDI real-time data—that is to say, the data used when recording musical passages from a MIDI controller (such as a keyboard or drum pad controller). MIDI is not sound. Rather, it is a series of actions. Those actions are representations of how the performer manipulates the musical instrument when he or she is playing it. For example, the most commonly recorded MIDI data is note on/off data. When a performer plays middle C on a MIDI controller (note on) that is then recorded on a MIDI track, Cubase captures the MIDI note number (pitch), how hard it was played (velocity), and when the note is released (note off).

MIDI CONTINUOUS CONTROLLERS

If MIDI could only represent note data, it couldn't depict the entire musical performance. For example, what happens when a pianist steps down on the sustain or other pedals? Plus, not all instruments generate notes the same way. When you press down on the keys of a piano keyboard, the piano will generate an audible sound. But when you press the strings against the fingerboard of a violin, no sound is produced. Audible sound is only generated when a bow is pushed across the violin strings. How are those actions represented differently in MIDI?

The developers of MIDI realized that they needed a specification that could depict all of the actions a musician could perform upon a real musical instrument. To that end, MIDI control numbers (known as continuous controllers, controllers, or CCs) were added to the spec. For example, when the sustain pedal attached to a MIDI keyboard is pressed, MIDI controller 4 is sent with a value of 127 (on). When the pedal is released, MIDI controller 4 is sent again, but this time with a value of 0 (off). Similarly, MIDI controller 11 is used to represent expression and can be used to represent the volume of notes being generated on a violin. MIDI controller 11 has a continuous range, as many controllers do, from 0 to 127. (Some hardware and software manufacturers represent MIDI controller values in a range of 1 to 128, which can result in numeric inconsistencies.)

OTHER COMMONLY USED MIDI DATA TYPES

While not an actual MIDI continuous controller, pitch bend is very common. Pitch bend is usually generated by the pitch bend wheel found on many MIDI keyboards, and can simulate the pitch effects created by musical instruments such as violins, woodwinds, and guitars. Similar to MIDI pitch bend, some keyboards can also transmit aftertouch, which is how much pressure is applied to a MIDI note while it's being played.

MIDI program changes are used to automate the selection of sounds within a synthesizer. Originally, MIDI had 128 program change numbers. That was more than enough, because early MIDI devices only had 32 or 40 onboard sounds. However, as technology progressed, it became possible for MIDI-compatible synthesizer manufacturers to install thousands of sounds inside of one device. How do you get to those sounds with only 128 program changes? Well, the MIDI Specification was modified to include a new data type known as bank select messages. They are MIDI continuous controllers 00 (MSB, Most Significant Byte) and 32 (LSB, or Least Significant Byte) and are used to determine which sound bank a MIDI program change will reference. For example, if you want to call up a synthesizer's eleventh sound located in the fourth internal sound bank, a 00 bank select message of value 4 followed by a program change of 11 might be the right combination. But since every manufacturer implements bank select messages differently, you'll need to consult the owner's manual or MIDI implementation chart to determine how to use them.

MIDI EDITING IN THE EVENT DISPLAY

Many of the most common MIDI edits, such as quantizing and transposing, can be performed in the Event Display. The advantage is that the edits are applied to all the data in the event, or multiple events across multiple tracks. So bear in mind that when you edit a MIDI or Instrument event in the Event Display, you're editing the MIDI data contained within that event.

It's also important to know that the types of editing you're going to learn about can be accomplished in a number of ways. I'll try to cover the most basic methods, but be aware that, as with most things in Cubase, there's more than one way to perform an edit. For the first part of this chapter, I would recommend loading "The Right Track R03.cpr" project from the disc that comes with this book. (See Appendix A: "Using the Included Disc.")

Quantizing MIDI Events

I already discussed the basics of quantization (a fancy word for the auto-correction of timing) in chapter 7. Now I'll go over more advanced features of this often used (and overused) MIDI edit. I'd like you to quantize some events in the Event Display. Mute the Q-Stick track and start playback to audition the MIDI and Instrument tracks. You can hear that the timing of the recordings are a little loose and could be improved by quantization. You're going to start with the Bass track, so go ahead and solo the Dry Finger Bass track, and listen to the playback. Since this track contains only single events rather than chords, it will be easier to hear the results of the quantize edit. Using the Object Selection tool, click on the Dry Finger Bass event, and then select the Quantize Preset of 1/16, as shown in Figure 11.1.

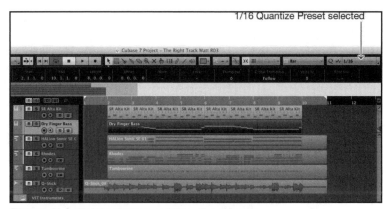

Figure II.I. Event selection and Quantize Presets.

Notice also in Figure 11.1 that the iQ setting is disabled. This is represented by the capital "Q" button to the left of the Quantize Preset of 1/16. I'll go over iQ in a moment, but for now, make sure it's set to Q rather than iQ. The Quantize Preset of 1/16 means that the MIDI notes on the selected events will be pushed or pulled to the nearest sixteenth-note. Since the shortest note played on the Dry Finger Bass event is an eighth-note, a sixteenth-note preset should work well. Choosing the appropriate Quantize Preset is critical but can also really mess up the timing, depending on how loosely the original recording was performed. Rest assured that Cubase can remove the quantization applied to MIDI events or data at any time to restore the original performance.

To execute the quantize, click on the Edit menu and select Quantize, or just type "Q" on your computer keyboard. You can leave the playback engaged to instantly audition the results of the quantize as long as the event (or events) remain selected. When you listen to the quantized event, you'll notice that the timing is perfect. (But perfect timing usually creates a musically boring result. More on that in a moment.) What you've just performed is known as a hard quantize. That is, the notes have been pushed or pulled to perfect sixteenth-note precision.

QUANTIZING MULTIPLE MIDI EVENTS ON MULTIPLE TRACKS

You might find yourself needing to quantize a whole bunch of MIDI events. In that case, all you need to do is make the proper selection of events. For example, in Figure 11.2, holding Shift and clicking on several events with the Object Selection tool has resulted in the selection of three events.

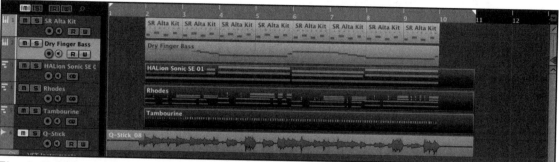

Figure 11.2. Three events selected for editing.

Since you've already selected an appropriate Quantize Preset (1/16), you can execute the quantize as you did before. (My preferred method is typing the "Q" key on the computer keyboard.) Now all three events have their MIDI notes placed perfectly on the nearest sixteenth-note.

QUANTIZING MULTIPLE MIDI EVENTS ON A SINGLE TRACK

The drum track in this project has eight events placed back to back. If you want to quantize specific events, all you have to do is select them first. However, if you'd like to quantize all of the events, right/Ctrl-click on the track, and choose Select All Events from the submenu, as shown in Figure 11.3.

Figure 11.3. The Select All Events command.

The results of the Select All Events command are shown in Figure 11.4, leaving you able to execute the Quantize command.

Figure 11.4. Results of the Select All Events command.

PERFECTION IS BORING

In the same way that the Borg on Star Trek diminish the human experience by creating perfection, so does the hard quantize. Humans are incapable of playing perfectly in time. That's something only a computer can do. Therefore, the results of a hard quantize sterilize the human nuance right out of a musical performance and make it sound "computerized." Fortunately, resistance is not futile, and quantization is not mandatory. But Cubase does provide you with alternatives, starting with iQ.

RAISING YOUR IQ

iQ is short for Iterative Quantize. iQ allows you to tighten up the timing of a MIDI recording without making the timing perfect—i.e., boring. But before you can use iQ on a track, you'll need to remove the hard quantize you've already performed. You can either type Ctrl/Command + Z several times, or select all the MIDI events and select Reset Quantize from the Edit menu. Either way, the original timing will be returned to the events. Then if you refer to Figure 11.1, you can click on the "Q" to enable iQ. Try executing a quantize with iQ enabled, and listen to the results. You should find them less computerized and more natural and human. If the timing is still too loose, you can execute another Iterative Quantize. You can even iQ as many times as you like, with each successive execution tightening the performance even more, although the end result will eventually be the same as a hard quantize. But how close to perfection will the notes be moved by the iQ? That setting is found in the Quantize Panel.

THE QUANTIZE PANEL

The Quantize Panel allows you to further customize the Quantize and iQ settings and even store them as your own Quantize Presets. If you refer to Figure 11.1, you can reveal the Quantize Panel by clicking to the right of the Quantize Preset or from the Edit menu. The Quantize Panel is shown in Figure 11.5 and is a separate window that can be placed anywhere on the screen and, if desired, be left open at all times.

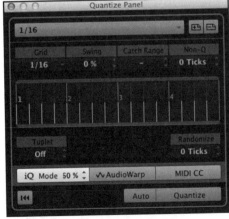

Figure 11.5. The Quantize Panel.

At the top of the Quantize Panel, you can select the Quantize Preset or use the Save/Remove buttons to save or remove your own custom presets. The Grid chooses the note value to which the Quantize command will place the notes. If your performance swings (as with the swung eighth-notes commonly found in jazz music), you can define the Swing percentage. Finally, the iQ Mode and Iterative Strength is located at the lower left-hand corner of the Quantize Panel. The Iterative Strength will indicate the degree to which the notes are being moved. For example, the default of 60 percent will move the notes within 60 percent of perfection. A setting of 90 percent will move the notes even closer to perfection. I usually leave this set to 50 or 60 percent and execute multiple iQ commands until the timing feels right. But if you do want to change the Iterative Strength, you can double-click the value and type in the desired percentage, or you can Alt/Option-click the current percentage to reveal a vertical slider with which to adjust the setting. (You can also click and drag your mouse up and down on the Iterative Strength, or hover your mouse over the setting and roll your mouse wheel up and down.) After you've made the adjustments, you can click the Quantize button in the lower right-hand corner of the Quantize Panel, but those settings will also be persistent. That will allow you to quantize with the new settings simply by selecting the desired events and typing the "Q" key.

Transposing MIDI Events

Prior to MIDI, the only way to transpose a recording was to rerecord the tracks in the desired key. If you had other band members, they'd usually do so grudgingly. On the other hand, if you'd hired session musicians, they'd be elated because you'd have to once again get out your checkbook. Either way, you'd have to take the time to record the tracks all over again. But with MIDI, you can simply transpose the events.

There are many ways to transpose events, but as with quantizing (or any edit), you must first make the proper selection. (Please review the steps for quantizing multiple events earlier in this chapter for more information.) The result of transposing an event will move the MIDI note numbers higher or lower in pitch. That pitch is represented in semitones or half steps. In other words, if you were to increase by 2 the transpose of an event containing a C major triad, the result would be a D major triad. Transposing by -2 would result in a Bb major triad.

TRANSPOSE IN THE INFO LINE

One of the easiest ways to transpose is to adjust the Transpose value in the Info Line (see "The Status, Info, and Overview Lines" in chapter 9), as shown in Figure 11.6.

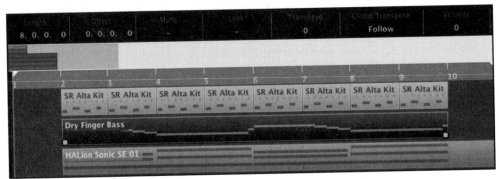

Figure 11.6. Transpose in the Info Line.

Double-click on the value, and type in the number of semitones you'd like to move the notes within the event (use a negative number for downward transpositions). Or you can Alt/Option-click on the value to reveal a vertical value slider.

You must always have at least one event selected for the Transpose value to be visible in the Info Line. If you have selected multiple events that currently have differing Transpose values, the text in the Info Line will appear in orange rather than the default light blue.

USING THE TRANSPOSE SETUP WINDOW

For more demanding Transpose results, there's the Transpose Setup window. Click on the MIDI menu and select Transpose Setup, as shown in Figure 11.7.

Unlike the Quantize Panel, the Transpose Setup window cannot be left open at all times. Therefore, it's important to make your event selections prior to opening the Transpose Setup window. The Semitones value is identical to that of the Info Line. However, one of the most powerful transposing features of Cubase is being able to change from one scale to another. For example, close the window and select the Dry Finger Bass, HALion Sonic SE 01, and Rhodes events; then reopen the Transpose Setup window. Enter the values shown in Figure 11.8.

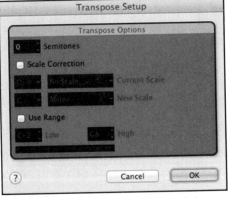

Figure 11.7. The Transpose Setup window.

Click on OK, and listen to the playback. You'll notice that not only have the notes been transposed, but the scale has been changed from major to harmonic minor.

DON'T TRANSPOSE
DRUM KIT EVENTS

Something really funny happens when you transpose drum events or tracks that have drum kit sounds assigned to them. To illustrate what I mean, right/Ctrl-click on the SR Alta Kit and choose Select All Events from the mini-menu. Then, using the Transpose value in either the Info Line or the Transpose Setup window,

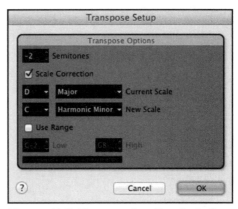

Figure 11.8. Transpose from D major to C harmonic minor.

transpose the events by 7 semitones. When you start playback, the drums sound very different. That's because when you transpose MIDI events that use drum kit sounds, the pitch of each drum sound won't change; rather, the MIDI note numbers will be transposed and change which sound is played by each note. As you can hear, the results are bizarre. The exception is if you're using a melodic percussion instrument, such as a xylophone or marimba. In those cases, transposing will function normally.

USING THE KEY EDITOR TO EDIT MIDI DATA

When more detailed MIDI editing is needed, Cubase comes with five MIDI editors: Key Editor, In-Place Editor (a variation of the Key Editor), Drum Editor, List Editor, and Score Editor. Each editor has strengths and specific uses, but they all allow you to edit your MIDI data with microscopic precision. Before exploring the editors, make sure to read chapter 9, because you'll need to know how to select data and use Zoom controls.

The Key Editor

The Key Editor is the default MIDI editor. You can access it simply by using the Object Selection tool to double-click on a MIDI event in the Event Display. (You can change the default editor in the Preferences.) You can also select a MIDI event and select Key Editor from the MIDI menu. Using either method, select the Dry Finger Bass event and open the Key Editor, as shown in Figure 11.9.

Figure 11.9. The Key Editor.

You'll notice many Key Editor features with which you're already familiar from the Event Display. Features such as the Window Layout button, Toolbar, Toolbox, and many others all work in the Key Editor as they do in the Event Display. However, you'll also see some new elements, such as the Keyboard, Note Display, and Controller Lane. Here's a closer look at these new items.

THE NOTE DISPLAY

The Note Display is very similar to the Event Display. But instead of showing events that contain the MIDI data, the Note Display shows the MIDI data itself. The little blocks you see in the Key Editor of the Dry Finger Bass are the MIDI note numbers. The vertical positions of the blocks represent the pitches of the notes, whereas the horizontal positions represent their placement in time. (Depending upon your level of vertical zoom, the blocks may also contain the pitches of the notes, such as D2, C1, etc.) The lengths of the blocks depict the note length. Since all of the notes on this event are eighth-notes, the blocks are all the same size. If we were to look at a musical representation of this MIDI data, it would look like Figure 11.10.

Figure 11.10. Notation of the Dry Finger Bass event in Figure 11.9.

At this point, you might understandably be wondering why Cubase doesn't always represent MIDI data in notation. This is because Cubase is able to display more musical nuance than notation. In other words, when musicians play the notation on the page, they are not able to play it with computer precision. (If they could, it would sound boring.) Instead, through their musical and human interpretation, they interject slight variations in timing. Cubase captures the performer's interpretation with a MIDI timing resolution of 480 PPQN (Pulses Per Quarter Note). Therefore, MIDI data needs to be represented with that same level of precision. Notation simply doesn't offer that level of precision, but the Key Editor does.

ACOUSTIC FEEDBACK

Referring to Figure 11.9, you'll see a small button in the upper left-hand corner that resembles a speaker with a Mouse Pointer icon. That's the Acoustic Feedback button. This is not to be confused with the feedback that occurs whenever anyone in movies or TV touches a microphone. Rather, when Acoustic Feedback is enabled, it allows you to click on and hear the MIDI notes in the Note Display. The notes will be played in context with their corresponding note lengths and velocities. (More on velocity in a moment.) You can also click on the Keyboard to hear the notes.

THE KEYBOARD

The Keyboard is located on the left side of the Key Editor. It is a musical keyboard rotated counterclockwise by 90 degrees and offers a melodic representation of the MIDI data. In fact, if you look closely, the grid that appears behind the Note Display has lighter and darker areas that correspond to the white and black notes of the keyboard. This makes it much easier to edit MIDI notes when they are in the middle or right-hand side of the Note Display.

A CLOSER LOOK AT THE EVENT
DISPLAY AND CONTROLLER LANE

To get a better idea of how the Event Display and Controller Lanes represent MIDI data, load the "MIDI R01.cpr" project from the disc that comes with this book. (See Appendix A: "Using the Included Disc.") In that project, you will find one Instrument track with a short MIDI event on it. Double-click that event to open the Key Editor, as shown in Figure 11.11.

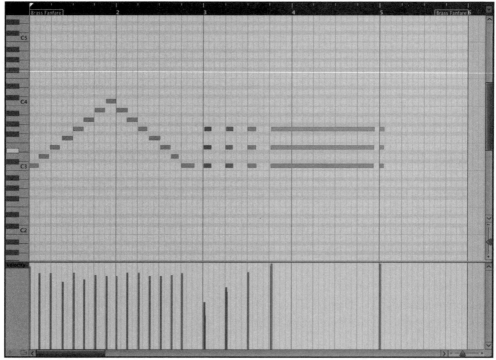

Figure 11.11. Event Display and Controller Lane of the event in the "MIDI R01.cpr" project.

The MIDI notes in the Note Display start with single-note events that are similar to Figure 11.9. To the right of the single notes, you will see some stacked notes that represent chords. The notes themselves vary in color, and I'll explain why in a moment. For now, listen to the notes by starting playback. What you will hear is a C major scale, followed by five C major first-position triads. The Instrument track is using a brass-section sound. The notation of the MIDI notes is shown in Figure 11.12.

Figure 11.12. Notation of the MIDI notes in Figure 11.11.

Now that you've seen and heard these MIDI notes, you'll need to know how you can use the Key Editor to edit the MIDI data. The process is very similar to moving events in the Event Display. Using the Object Selection tool, you can drag notes to the left or right to alter their timing. Your Snap settings will, of course, have a lot to do with where notes can be placed. Dragging notes toward the top or bottom will alter the MIDI note number and therefore the note pitch. And as you may have surmised, dragging multiple notes up or down is yet one more way to perform a Transpose Edit.

EDITING WITH THE INFO LINE

The Key Editor and Event Display each have their own Info Line. If the Info Line is not visible, click on the Window Layout button (first button at the upper left-hand corner of Figure 11.9), and put a check next to Info Line. The Info Line can display very detailed information about selected MIDI events, and you can also edit those values. For example, in Figure 11.13, the Info Line is displaying the data values for the highest C note in the scale.

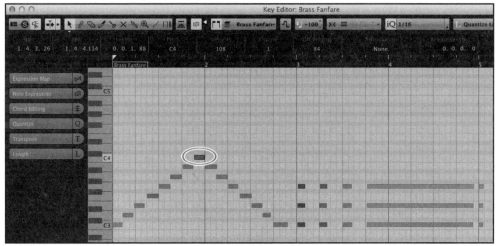

Figure 11.13. Info Line showing values for selected note.

You can see the Info Line displaying timing data such as note start, end, and length values. You can also see the pitch, velocity, and MIDI Channel values. You can alter any of those values to edit the selected data.

Editing MIDI Note Velocity

Velocity, or how fast the note is played, represents the note dynamics. In other words, velocity is how hard the note was played. Every MIDI note has a velocity value that is variable from 0 to 127. Values below 63 are quieter, while values above 63 are louder. It's easy to confuse velocity with volume, but be aware that they are two different things. In Cubase (and all DAW software with MIDI sequencers), velocity represents how hard the musician was playing his or her instrument, whereas volume represents the loudness of the track. Or another way to look at it is that velocity represents dynamics, such as mezzo forte or crescendos/decrescendos, while volume would be used to adjust the volume of the track for a fade-out.

Velocity is depicted in the Key Editor in a number of ways. I've already talked about editing the value in the Info Line, so what follows are other ways to edit velocity.

VELOCITY IN THE NOTE DISPLAY

As I mentioned earlier, every MIDI note in the Note Display is colorized. By default, the color represents the velocity. (See Figure 11.9, and confirm that the Event Color setting at the upper right-hand corner is set to Velocity.) Quieter notes are bluer, while louder notes are redder. For example, the chords in Figure 11.11 get progressively louder. The first two chords are quieter than the following four. You can edit a note's velocity by typing Shift + Ctrl/Command while clicking on an event, and moving the mouse up and down. A small black box showing the velocity value will appear to the left of the event, as shown in Figure 11.14.

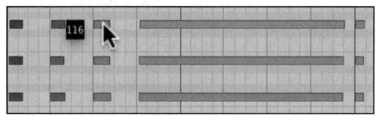

Figure 11.14. Adjusting velocity in the Note Display, velocity value box visible.

VELOCITY IN THE CONTROLLER LANE

In Figures 11.9 and 11.11, you will find the Controller Lane underneath the Note Display. While MIDI velocity is not a continuous controller, the velocity values are represented here by default. The taller the vertical bars, the louder the notes. The velocity bars are also color coded identically to the notes to which they correspond in the Note Display. To edit a velocity value, use the Object Inspector to click on the vertical bar to adjust it higher or lower. Try this on the single notes in bars 1 and 2. But when you try to adjust velocity on chords, all of the notes will have their velocity values adjusted at the same time. Therefore, it's important to use the Object Selection tool to first make selections of which notes you'd like to adjust. Then velocity edits will only occur to the selected event or events, as shown in Figure 11.15.

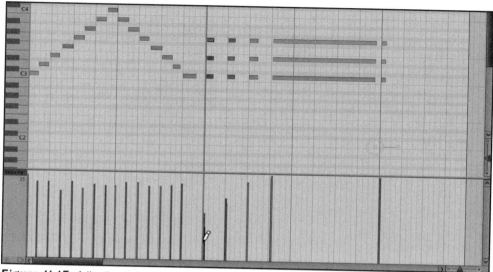

Figure 11.15. Adjusting the velocity of one note in a chord.

If you have selected multiple notes in the Note Display, you can adjust multiple velocity values by clicking and dragging across the Controller Lane.

DRAWING VELOCITY VALUES WITH THE LINE TOOL

With multiple notes selected in the Note Display, you can select the Line tool from the Toolbox and draw a line across the Controller Lane. This will create uniform velocity values, as shown in Figure 11.16.

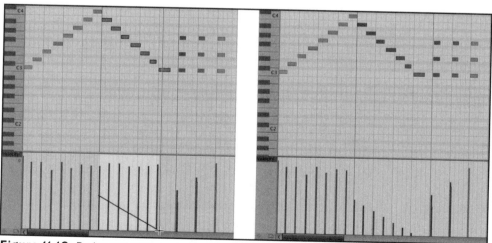

Figure 11.16. During and after a velocity edit with the Line tool.

If a nonlinear result is desired, you can click on the Line Tool icon in the Toolbox and choose from the shapes shown in Figure 11.17.

Of all the shapes, my favorite is the parabola. It is capable of creating exponential velocity curves that are very musical, whereas the default Line shape tends to create velocity curves that are a little mechanical sounding.

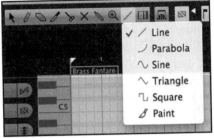

Line
Parabola
Sine
Triangle
Square
Paint
Brass Fanfare
C5
Figure 11.17. Line tool shapes.

Editing Controllers in the Controller Lane

The Controller Lane (see Figures 11.9 and 11.11) can be used to edit a variety of different continuous MIDI data, including velocity (default), aftertouch, pitch bend, and all 128 MIDI continuous control numbers. You've already used the Controller Lane to edit velocity. Now it's time to explore how to edit other MIDI data.

SELECTING THE MIDI CONTROLLERS TO EDIT

At the upper-left corner of the Controller Lane, you will find the Controller Selection and Functions menu. (See Figures 11.9 and 11.11.) Look for a small box containing the word Velocity. When you click on that box, you will see a list of the most commonly edited MIDI controllers, along with any other controllers that currently exist on the selected event, as shown in Figure 11.18.

Articulations/Dynamics
Velocity *
Pitchbend
Aftertouch
Poly Pressure
Program Change
System Exclusive
CC 1 (Modulation) *
CC 2 (Breath)
CC 4 (Foot)
CC 7 (Main Volume)
CC 8 (Balance)
CC 10 (Pan)
CC 11 (Expression)
CC 64 (Sustain)
Setup...
Create Controller Lane
Remove this Lane
Select All Controller Events
Figure 11.18. The Controller selection and Functions menu.

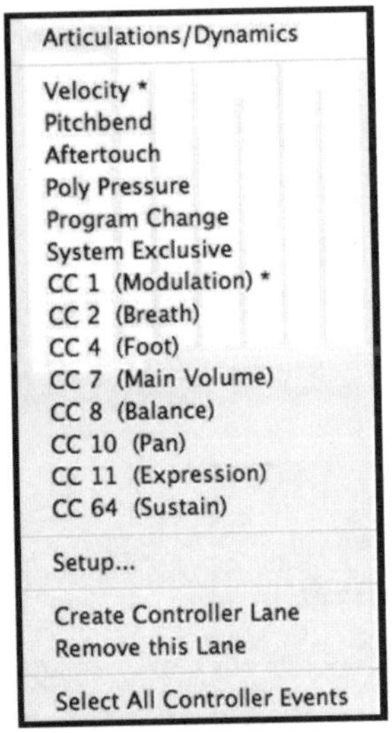

Notice that two of the controllers have asterisks next to them. The asterisk indicates that the controller exists on the selected event. The Brass Fanfare event in the "MIDI R01.cpr" project contains both velocity and CC1 (Modulation) controllers. By selecting CC1 (Modulation), the Controller Lane will show the values of the modulation data, as shown in Figure 11.19.

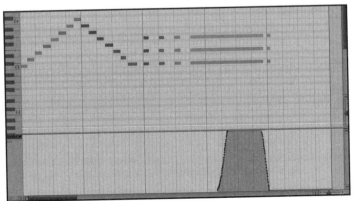

Figure 11.19. Controller Lane showing CC1 (Modulation) data.

CC1 is MIDI continuous controller 1, and usually represents the movement of the modulation wheel on a MIDI keyboard controller. CC1 is used for a variety of effects, including expression, filter cutoff, and effect control, such as the speed of a rotating speaker effect. However, the most common use of CC1 is to modulate the strength of a synthesizer's LFO (Low Frequency Oscillator) to create vibrato or tremolo effects. When you start playback on this project, you'll hear the vibrato added to the brass sound throughout measure 4. This CC1 data was created at the time of recording. But now you could use either the Draw or Line tools to edit the data or create new data from scratch. Be aware that most controllers (such as CC1) start at 0 and end at 127, while others have a midpoint (such as MIDI pan, not to be confused with Peter Pan) that starts with 0 in the middle of the Controller Lane.

THE IN-PLACE EDITOR TO EDIT MIDI DATA

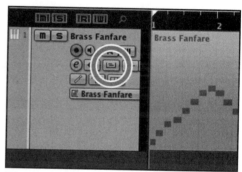

Now that you know how to use the Key Editor, using the In-Place Editor is a breeze. It is a smaller version of the Key Editor and is located in the Event Display. Each MIDI and Instrument track has an Edit In-Place button, as shown in Figure 11.20.

Be aware that the track height might need to be adjusted to reveal the Edit In-Place button. Alternatively, you can select the desired track and click the MIDI menu and select Open In-Place Editor.

Figure 11.20. The Edit In-Place button.

Using the In-Place Editor

The biggest advantage of the In-Place Editor is that you don't have to leave the Project window to edit MIDI data. And since it looks and functions exactly like the Key Editor, you needn't learn a new editor, nor close the Key Editor window. The track height will be automatically increased to accommodate the In-Place Editor, as shown in Figure 11.21.

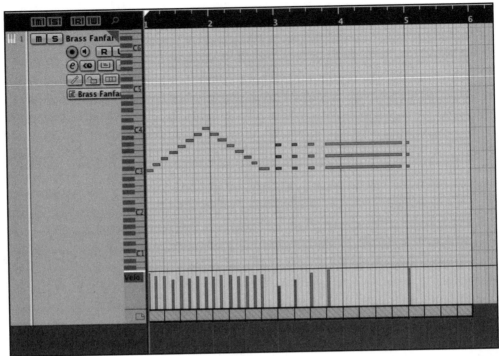

Figure 11.21. The In-Place Editor.

Since the In-Place Editor is part of the Project window, you can use those tools to make edits. However, the zooming and other visual adjustments of the In-Place Editor are not quite as fully featured as is the Key Editor, and the size might make precision editing more challenging.

OTHER MIDI EDITING COMMANDS

Edits such as quantizing and transposition are some of the most common MIDI editing commands. However, Cubase has many others, and I'd like to show you a few that I think you'll find useful. For this section, I would recommend loading "The Right Track R03.cpr" project from the disc that comes with this book. (See Appendix A: "Using the Included Disc.")

Dissolve Part

This is by far one of the most powerful MIDI edits you can perform in Cubase. Since MIDI events can contain multiple note pitches on different MIDI channels, the Dissolve Part command can separate them onto their own tracks and events. A perfect example would be taking the SR Alta Kit and separating the MIDI notes onto their own tracks, thereby creating a track for each drum sound. This allows the data to be freely and discretely edited without affecting the other data in the event. (A fringe benefit for Instrument tracks is the creation of discrete MixConsole Channels for each drum sound. I'll discuss this more in chapter 14, "The Art of Mixing.")

Right-click on the SR Alta Kit and choose Select All Events, then click on the MIDI menu and select Dissolve Part. The Dissolve Part window will appear, allowing you to make the settings as they appear in Figure 11.22.

Make sure that Separate Pitches and Optimized Display are both selected, then click OK. The results are shown in Figure 11.23.

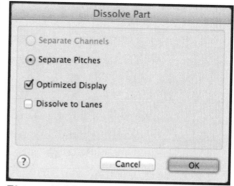

Figure 11.22. The Dissolve Part window.

Figure 11.23. Results of the Dissolve Part command (tracks reordered for clarity).

The dissolved tracks will be placed at the bottom of the track list. I've dragged those tracks underneath the original SR Alta Kit track to make the results clearer. As you can see, each note has been dissolved onto its own track. The original track and its events have been left intact. However, the events have been muted. This leaves them in place for future editing, but they won't be heard during playback.

Velocity

Up until this point, I've taken a "note by note" approach to editing note velocity. But there's also a way to make velocity edits on an eventwide or trackwide basis. Select an event (or use the Select All Events command), and then click the MIDI menu, select Functions, and select Velocity. The Velocity dialog box will appear, as shown in Figure 11.24.

There are three types of velocity editing you

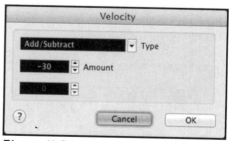

Figure 11.24. The Velocity dialog box.

can choose from. The default is Add/Subtract. To add value to the velocities, enter a positive value into the Amount field. Conversely, negative values will reduce the velocities. If some notes within the event exceed the minimum (0) or maximum (127) range, their values will not be altered past the limit. However, remaining velocities will be adjusted to the defined amount.

The Compress/Expand type will either smooth a wide range of velocities or expand the velocities to create a more dynamic range. The Amount field becomes a percentage from 0 to 300. Values of less than 100 percent will compress the velocities to create a less dynamic track and are useful when the recording contains too wide a range of dynamics. Values above 100 percent will expand the velocities of a track with a narrow dynamic range, so that the differences between soft and loud dynamics are more pronounced.

The Limit type will allow you to define an Upper and Lower limit into which all the velocities will be squeezed. In other words, the louder velocities will be adjusted to but not exceed the Upper limit, while the softer velocities will be adjusted to but not exceed the Lower limit.

Delete Aftertouch

Aftertouch is a powerful controller. It allows the player to modulate parameters within the synthesizer even with both hands on the keyboard and both feet on the pedals. If you have a MIDI controller or keyboard with aftertouch, you may have already discovered how different sounds can be accentuated. However, you may have also noticed that many synthesizer sounds (both in Cubase and in external hardware synthesizers) don't have aftertouch assigned to a parameter, which means that pressing harder on the keys garners no results.

But the aftertouch data recorded on a track can diminish the performance of the synthesizer that's receiving it. This is because it takes more processing power to calculate the dense stream of aftertouch data. Many DAW users record aftertouch without even knowing or using it. If you start to see events that contain a lot of controller data, and you're not using aftertouch or any other controllers (such as pitch bend or modulation wheel), as shown in Figure 11.25, you might want to erase all the aftertouch. (Note: You can also set the Controller Lane Controller Selection to aftertouch to verify that the event contains superfluous aftertouch data.)

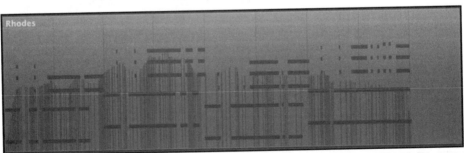

Figure 11.25. An event with a lot of possible aftertouch data.

If you're not using aftertouch, you may want to remove it from specific events or even all the events within your project. Select the event (or use the Select All command to select all of the events in your project); then click the MIDI menu; select Logical Presets, standard set 2; and then select del.aftertouch, as shown in Figure 11.26.

Unlike some of the other MIDI commands, Delete Aftertouch has no corresponding dialog box or settings. Selecting the command simply strips all the aftertouch from selected MIDI events.

FILTERING AFTERTOUCH

If you don't use aftertouch and don't wish to have it recorded into your Cubase Project, you can enable the aftertouch MIDI Filter in the Cubase Preferences. (Mac users: Click the Cubase menu and select Preferences. Windows users: Click the File menu and select Preferences.) Locate the MIDI Filters on the left side of the Preferences window, then enable the aftertouch filters in both the Record and Thru columns, as shown in Figure 11.27.

The Record filter prevents the aftertouch from being recorded, while the Thru filter prevents the aftertouch from being sent to the MIDI device, whether Cubase is in playback or stopped.

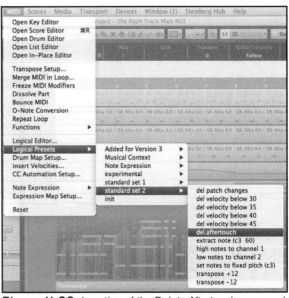

Figure 11.26. Location of the Delete Aftertouch command.

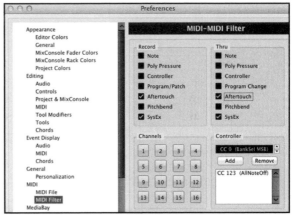

Figure 11.27. The MIDI Aftertouch Filter preferences.

EXPLORING MORE MIDI EDITS FOR YOURSELF

While perusing the MIDI menu, you undoubtedly noticed the myriad of MIDI commands, functions, and logical presets. I could write an entire book on these fascinating MIDI editing possibilities, and I urge you to explore them on your own. However, at this point, it's time to move on to editing audio data.

Editing Audio Data

When MIDI recording software first appeared in the mid 1980s, it ignited the fire of the digital-recording revolution. Today, the ability to not only record but also edit audio data provides a creative environment that many believed would never be possible, at least not without an investment of tens of thousands of dollars. In this chapter, I'll be exploring some of those formerly impossible edits. Newer editing features such as the VariAudio pitch correction were simply inconceivable only a few years ago. Yet today they have become an invaluable staple of modern music production.

(Note: Before reading this chapter, you should be aware that a large part of the editing process is making proper selections. Therefore, it will be very important to have read chapter 9 before proceeding further.)

I will be going over both the basics and some of the advanced editing features you'll come to rely on. For most of this chapter, you'll be using the "The Right Track Matt R04. cpr" project from the disc that came with this book. (See Appendix A: "Using the Included Disc.") In this chapter, you will learn about:

- The concept of a nondestructive editor.
- The difference between online and offline processing.
- Using the Event Audio Handles.
- Crossfading Audio events.
- Pitch and time correction with the VariAudio editor.

NONDESTRUCTIVE AND DESTRUCTIVE EDITING

Cubase is a nondestructive audio editor. In other words, most of the edits you'll perform will not affect the actual recordings in any way. This is a very different behavior from the analog and early digital recorders. Anyone who's ever used a tape recorder or VCR (video cassette recorder) understands how a destructive editor works. If you start recording on a piece of tape, any previously recorded material will be erased in favor of the new recording. And once that information is gone, there is no way of getting it back.

Examples of Destructive Editing

One famous, or rather infamous, example is the erased section of tape from (former US President) Richard Nixon's phone conversation that might have further implicated him in the Watergate scandal. Even using the most modern audio-analysis technology, that recording has never been recovered. And the cutting and splicing of analog tape is a destructive process because you are actually destroying the tape.

Early audio-editing software was the same way. Because computers didn't have the power to process the edits in real-time, the edits had to be performed on the actual audio files. In other words, if you wanted to apply a compressor to the bass drum track, you'd be destroying the original recording in favor of the compressed version. If you didn't like it, you'd need to undo it right away, because early editors did not offer unlimited undo. Rather, you'd get one undo to return the most recently processed file to its original state.

Cubase Is a Nondestructive Audio Editor

As I've previously discussed, when you record over or cut, copy, and paste in Cubase, the original material is always retained. The same is true for the commands found in the Audio menu and in the Audio Editor windows. Even though edits such as Reverse, Gain, and the VariAudio pitch correction behave like destructive editors, the original audio material is retained and replaced with processed portions that are automatically stored in the Edits folder of the Project Folder. This makes it very difficult to destroy the original recordings. It also gives you the freedom to try new things, with the confidence that you can always get back to where you started.

Offline and Online Processing

Whenever you perform an edit that appears to alter the original file, it is known as an offline process. In other words, Cubase magically replaces the original data with the edit but leaves the original intact. But most of the effects and other real-time processes you'll be learning about in chapters 14 and 15 can be created by the processing power of your computer and require no offline processing. As you've already guessed, adding effects such as compressors and reverbs in Cubase are known as online processes. They happen in real-time, and no additional edit files are generated.

USING THE AUDIO EVENT HANDLES

The Audio Event Handles function identically to those found on MIDI events. You can use them to trim, add repeats, and resize events. However, Audio Event Handles have additional functionality for adjusting the event volume, as well as fade-in and fade-out.

Revealing the Handles

Just like MIDI Event Handles, Audio Event Handles are revealed when your mouse is hovering over the event. But Audio events have additional handles, as shown in Figure 12.1.

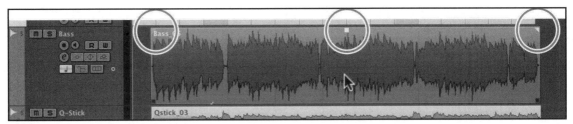

Figure 12.1. The Audio Event Handles.

These handles provide a fast and convenient way to alter the volume of an Audio event. I sometimes refer to these types of edits as "QD" or quick 'n' dirty automation, because the results are similar to mix automation (see Appendix B: "A Primer on Automation") but are performed on the event rather than a temporal location. But that means that copying the event will also copy the position of the handles. And while using the MixConsole is a more robust method for volume control (see chapter 14, "The Art of Mixing"), sometimes you'll find an event that's just a little too loud or soft, and adjusting a handle can make an appropriate edit quickly.

USING THE VOLUME HANDLE

Before you can use this method to adjust the Volume Handle, the entire scale of the event must be visible in the Event Display, or at least the midway point of the event must be visible, therefore making the Volume Handle visible. (There is an alternate method I'll discuss in a moment.) With the Object Selection tool, simply click and drag the Volume Handle up or down, as shown in Figure 12.2.

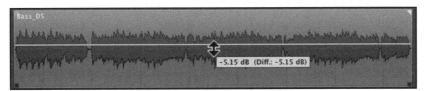

Figure 12.2. Adjusting the Volume Handle.

When the adjustment is being made, a small value box will appear next to the mouse. This will indicate both the current volume value of the clip and the difference between where the handle was and where it is currently being adjusted. In Figure 12.2, the original position of the handle was 0.0 dB, but it has been moved downward to -5.15 dB. (I guess I did that subliminally because I was just listening to the Who song "5:15.") That's a difference of -5.15 from the original position. However, if the original position was -2 dB and adjusted to -5.15 dB, the difference would appear as -3.15 dB. When making Volume Handle adjustments, the size of the waveform will increase or decrease to help you gauge the new setting.

Be aware that you can make increment or decrement adjustments to the Volume Handle even if the value exceeds 0 dB. This is because the dynamic range of the Cubase 32-bit floating point audio engine will allow you to exceed 0 dB without clipping the Audio track. However, it still might be possible to hear distortion during playback, because the increase in event volume might cause the Master Fader to be clipped (see chapter 14, "The Art of Mixing").

USING THE FADE HANDLES

Unlike the Volume Handles, the Fade-in and Fade-out Handles can be adjusted without requiring that the entire event be visible. Using the Object Selection tool, click on and drag either the Fade-in or Fade-out Handle sideways. Figure 12.3 shows an adjustment to the Fade-in Handle.

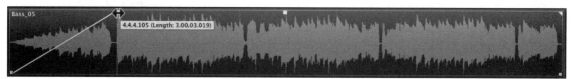

Figure 12.3. Adjusting the Fade-in Handle.

When you click on a Fade Handle, the entire event will become selected. That's why Figure 12.3 and 12.2 differ in appearance. During the adjustment, a value box will display the timing of the fade. Fade-outs are created the same way, except that you'll drag the Fade-out Handle to the left.

Adjusting the Handles in the Info Line

If you have your Info Line visible, you can edit the Fade and Volume settings of a selected event, as shown in Figure 12.4.

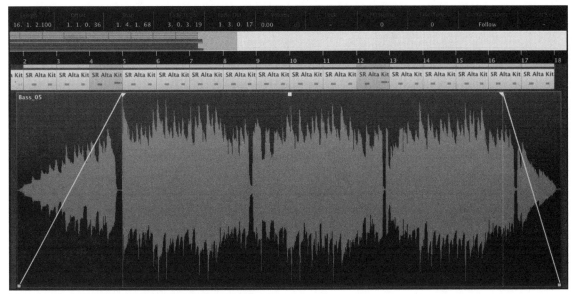

Figure 12.4. Fade and Volume settings in the Info Line.

The Fade-In, Fade-Out, and Volume settings are located at the top of Figure 12.4. Editing these values allows you to make handle edits even when the entire event is not completely visible within the Event Display. You can single-click, double-click, or mouse wheel to adjust any value, or Alt/Option-click to edit the Volume settings.

EDITING THE AUDIO EVENT ENVELOPE

Every Audio event has its own volume envelope. The envelope is similar to the Volume and Fade Handles, except that you can create very dramatic volume changes at any position within the event. Since the envelope is part of the event, every paste or repeat will also retain the envelope of the original event.

Drawing the Envelope

Normally you will not see the envelope until you have edited it. That's because it is a thin horizontal line at the very top edge of the Audio event. The envelope is programmed by using the Draw tool to create points along the horizontal envelope, and then dragging those points up and down to adjust the volume, as shown in Figure 12.5.

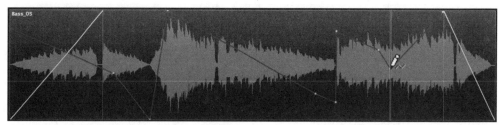

Figure 12.5. Drawing points onto the envelope.

Figure 12.5 might look a little chaotic, but as you can see when editing on your color computer monitor, the handles are white, while the envelope is blue. When creating new points with the Draw tool, you'll notice that a small, wavy line has been added to the Tool icon. That tells you that the Draw tool is in Envelope mode instead of the default mode. You can create new points by clicking on the envelope, or you can adjust a previously created point by clicking on it and dragging.

CROSSFADING AUDIO EVENTS

A crossfade is a quick fade from one Audio event to an adjoining Audio event, which can smooth out the audible transition. When joining Audio events together, you may get lucky and not have to apply a crossfade. However, if either or both events contain anything other than almost complete silence, there's a high probability that a crossfade will be required.

Setting Up the Crossfade Scenario

The need for crossfading will usually manifest itself as a popping, clicking, or other audible anomaly that occurs when playing through one event to another. Other times, the transition will not generate any anomalies but might just sound clumsy. Using the "The Right Track Matt R04.cpr" project from the disc that came with this book (see Appendix A, "Using the Included Disc"), you're going to create an edit that will require a crossfade. Load that project, then find the event named "Bass_05" on the Bass track.

Increasing the track height as I have in Figure 12.6 will make the editing easier. Then using the Split tool and with Snap set to Bar, click on the "Bass_05" event at measures 5, 9, 13, and 17, as shown in Figure 12.6.

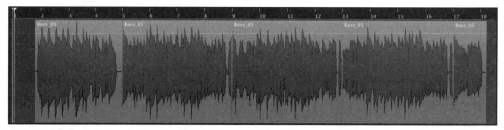

Figure 12.6. Results of using the Split tool.

You have now divided the "Bass_05" event into five separate events. Using the Erase tool, click on the second event. That will result in a gap between measures 5 and 7. Now, using the Object Selection tool, press and hold the Alt/Option key on your computer keyboard, and click and drag the fourth event. Drag that event to measure 5, and release the mouse. That will copy the fourth event into the gap where the second event used to exist. Refer to Figure 12.7 for more details.

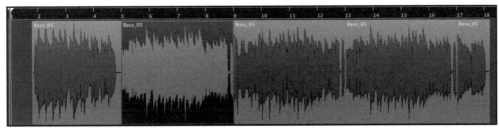

Figure 12.7. Results of copying event No. 4.

HOW POPS AND OTHER ANOMALIES OCCUR

Now solo the Bass track, and start playback from measure 2 or 3 to audition the transition at measure 5. You'll notice that there are two anomalies: a pop, plus the edit that just sounds clumsy. The pop occurs because the waveforms between event No. 1 and the copy of No. 4 create a jagged transition. If you zoom in very closely, you can see that quite a portion of event No. 1 runs directly into a louder portion of the copy of event No. 4, as shown in Figure 12.8.

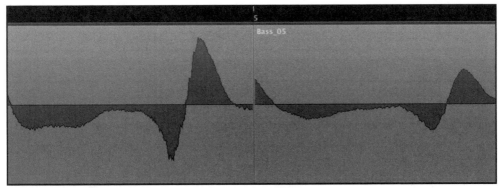

Figure 12.8. The jagged transition between event No. 1 (left) and copy of No. 4 (right).

In a perfect world, the events would always join together at what's called a zero-crossing. That is when both waveforms meet with complete silence on each end. This does occur from time to time, as it does when you listen to the transition at measure 9. Luckily, the waveforms of the copy of event No. 4 and event No. 3 join together at almost completely silent locations, as shown in Figure 12.9.

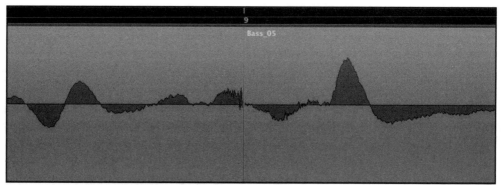

Figure 12.9. A lucky event transition at measure 9.

Because the transition is so smooth, there is no audible popping, and the edit doesn't sound clumsy like it does at measure 5.

HOW CLUMSY-SOUNDING EDITS OCCUR

Even without popping or other audible glitches, it's still possible that the transition from one event to another just sounds weird or clumsy. This normally occurs when the event you're copying sounds different from the one you're replacing it with. Sometimes it's caused by a difference in timing, while other times there's a slight difference in the performance. It's the latter that causes our clumsy-sounding edit in Figure 12.8. In other words, the performances in event No. 2 and the copy of event No. 4 are not identical. (If they were, you wouldn't be editing them in the first place, right?) To hear what I'm talking about, you can hit Undo a few times until event No. 2 is returned to its original position, and listen to the differences between No. 2 and No. 4. Then Redo until the copy of event No. 4 is back at measure 5.

Setting Up the Crossfade

Whether it's caused by a jagged or a clumsy transition, you're going to need to crossfade the end of event No. 1 into the start of the copy of event No. 4. Doing so will create a virtual zero-crossing and make the transition sound much more natural.

OVERLAPPING THE EVENTS

You've already learned that Audio events cannot overlap. If they do, only the topmost event will be audible. But crossfading the events will make them both audible for a very short period of time. So what you'll do now is use the Object Selection tool to click and drag the left Event Handle of the copy of event No. 4 (at measure 5) over the end of event

No. 1. Before you do, you'll need to disable Snap by typing "J" on your computer keyboard or holding the Ctrl/Command key after clicking and dragging the handle. Drag the handle so that it overlaps the waveform in event No. 1. The before and after of this procedure is shown in Figures 4.10 and 4.11.

The idea is to drag the event to overlap a very brief region. However, you can see in Figure 12.10 that event No. 1 has a little bit of audio data that precedes the copy of event No. 4. So dragging the handle over this audio data will create an edit that most closely resembles the transition between event No. 1 and the original event No. 2.

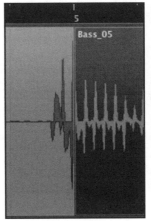

Figure 12.10. Before overlapping the events.

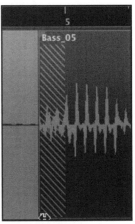

Figure 12.11. After overlapping the events.

EXECUTING THE CROSSFADE

Making the proper selection prior to executing the crossfade is critical. If you leave the only the copy of event No. 4 selected as it is in Figure 12.11, then crossfades will be applied to all the adjoining events, including No. 1 and No. 3. But you know that you don't need a crossfade between the copy of No. 4 and No. 3, as shown in Figure 12.9. What you want is a crossfade at measure 5 only. So use the Object Selection tool and click on event No. 1, then hold Shift on your computer keyboard and click on the copy of event No. 4. That will select both events, as shown in Figure 12.12.

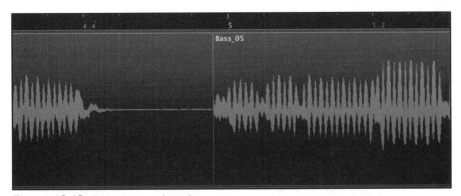

Figure 12.12. Both events selected.

Now that both events are selected, type "X" on your computer keyboard. Alternatively, you could choose Crossfade from the Audio menu, but hitting the "X" key is faster and resembles the shape of a crossfade, as shown in Figure 12.13.

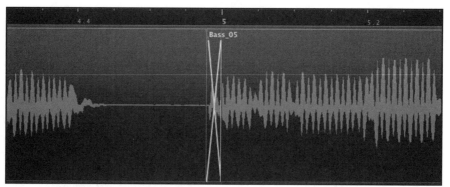

Figure 12.13. Results of the Crossfade command.

You can see that the crossfade creates a short fade-in and a short fade-out, thereby creating a virtual zero-crossing at the center of the crossfade. When you listen to the crossfade, you'll notice that the transition is void of popping and sounds less clumsy. (It was me playing bass, so it cannot be completely void of clumsiness.)

EDITING THE CROSSFADE

After the events have been crossfaded, you can make further edits to the placement of the event boundaries. However, the handles with which you would normally do this are no longer visible within the crossfaded zone. But now you can simply hover your mouse over either clip boundary inside the crossfade zone, and your pointer will turn into a Horizontal Arrows icon. Then click and drag the boundary sideways to adjust the event boundary, and you'll notice that the crossfade will adjust accordingly.

PITCH AND TIME CORRECTION WITH VARIAUDIO

There was a time when singing a bad note during an otherwise brilliant vocal recording required the section to be sung all over again. But ever since the late 1990s, there has been hardware and software that makes pitch correction possible. Today, the practice of pitch correction is as ubiquitous as double-tracking and the application of reverb. In fact, it has created a whole new class of audio editing known as Auto-Tune or autotuning, named after the first commercially successful pitch-correction product from Antares Audio Technologies. Autotuning used to be performed on only the noticeably out-of-tune vocal notes. But over the past decade, producers started autotuning an entire performance to create a very synthetic, yet striking, vocal quality. It all started with the hit song "Believe" by Cher, and whether you love autotuning or not, it has become a very popular effect.

Autotuning of pitches is similar to quantizing MIDI data, in that if you apply too much of it, the result will be a very sterile and boring version of the original. Both techniques can literally strip all the humanity from a recording. That's why many producers (such as yours truly) prefer to use it sparingly and only when absolutely necessary. A really good singer will rarely, if ever, need to be pitch corrected. However, as every studio owner can attest, if you feel like the performance can be enhanced or if the person paying for the studio time is asking for more and more pitch correction, you'd better acquiesce to his or her request. Either way, Cubase (the full level) comes with a fantastic pitch- and time-correction editor known as VariAudio. It can provide pitch and timing effects either gently or very strictly. In this section, I'll show you how to do both.

Pitch-Correction Requirements

Before you can start using VariAudio (or the vast majority of other pitch-correction programs), you'll need to be aware that the audio data must be monophonic. That's not to be confused with mono Audio tracks, because VariAudio can be used on stereo tracks as well. What I mean by monophonic in this case is that the event being edited must contain recordings of only single notes without chords or overlapping notes. Examples of monophonic musical instruments are a single human voice, a woodwind instrument (such as a clarinet or saxophone), or a brass instrument (such as a trumpet or French horn). However, as long as a polyphonic instrument (such as a guitar or violin) is only playing one note at a time, it too can be pitch corrected.

For the rest of this section, you'll be using the "The Right Track Matt R05.cpr" project located on the disc that came with this book. (See Appendix A: "Using the Included Disc.") In that project, you will find a vocal track that has some pitch issues. I sang them that way on purpose with this exercise in mind. (Really, I did!)

Opening VariAudio in the Sample Editor

The Sample Editor is very similar to the Key Editor. But instead of editing MIDI data, it's used to edit audio data. Start by locating the event called "Vox_19" on the Vox track (track 10) of the project. Then double-click to open the Sample Editor, as shown in Figure 12.14.

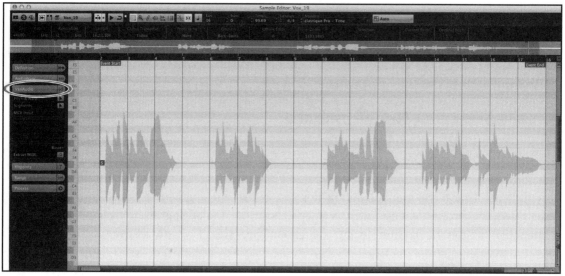

Figure 12.14. The Sample Editor and VariAudio tab

As you can see, many of the features from the Project window and Key Editor are present in the Sample Editor. It too has an Inspector, Window Layout button, and Toolbar, among others. Click the Window Layout button, and make sure that the Inspector, Info, and Overview Lines are visible. Then click on the VariAudio tab in the Inspector to reveal the controls for the pitch and time correction.

The Waveform Display will depict a lightly shaded version of the audio data. Go ahead and use the Vertical and Horizontal Zoom controllers to adjust the size of the waveform so that it appears as it does in Figure 12.14. Then notice that there is a vertical musical keyboard to the left of the Waveform Display. Now take a closer look at the VariAudio tab in the Inspector, as shown in Figure 12.15.

In the Toolbar shown at the upper left-hand corner of Figure 12.15, you will find the Solo Editor button. This will automatically solo the event during playback so that only the event you're editing will be heard. You'll also find the Acoustic

Figure 12.15. The VariAudio tab.

Feedback button that will allow the pitches to be heard during editing. Make sure that both of those buttons are enabled. Also notice the Segment Colors setting on the right side of the Toolbar in Figure 12.14, and change the default setting of Auto to Pitch.

Then there are two main tools you'll be using for VariAudio editing: the Pitch & Warp tool and the Segments tool. Each of these tools is located directly under the VariAudio tab with a mouse cursor–like icon to the right of Pitch & Warp and Segments, respectively. You'll need to switch back and forth between these tools on a regular basis, which you can do by clicking on the desired tool or typing the Tab key on your computer keyboard. For now, click on the Pitch & Warp tool. You will see a progress bar appear on the screen that depicts how long the pitch analysis will take. Longer events and longer audio files will require more time to complete. When finished, you'll see a series of segments added to the waveform display, as shown in Figure 12.16.

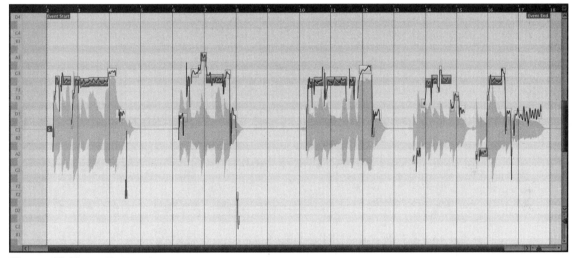

Figure 12.16. VariAudio segments.

These segments depict the pitch, length, and placement of every detected syllable within the "Vox_19" event. Start playback, and watch as the cursor moves across the segments. This will give you a better understanding of what the segments represent. Because the Solo Editor is enabled, you will only hear the vocal event during playback, even if the track Solo button is not engaged.

Most of the pitches in this vocal track are tolerable. However, when you get to the third line at measure 10 that says, "You cannot say you know how I feel," you'll notice that the "I" is very (okay, I'll say it: painfully) out of tune. This is the problem note you're going to correct, and it's a doozy. Not only is it out of tune, but the pitch drifts from flat to sharp. (Did I mention I sang it this way on purpose?) Using your favorite method for zooming, zoom in so that the entire vocal line from measures 10 through 12 are visible in the Waveform Display, as shown in Figure 12.17.

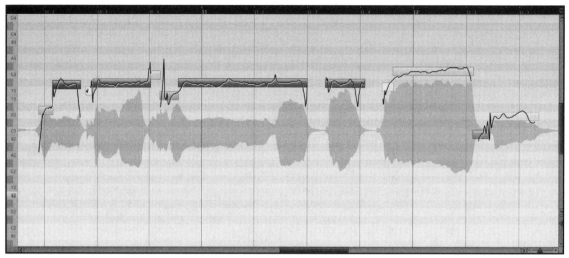

Figure 12.17. "You cannot say you know how I feel."

Using the Pitch & Warp Tool

In the background of the VariAudio editor, you can see the light and dark grid that depicts a pitch grid. To give you a better idea of how to view the grid, I've dragged the "I" segment closer to the vertical keyboard, as shown in Figure 12.18.

If you look closely at the "I" segment, you'll notice that the analysis detected that it is almost a G but that it is slightly sharp. When you click on the segment with the Pitch & Warp tool, you'll be able to hear the note. That's because the Acoustic Feedback is enabled. (See Figure 12.15.) Now type and hold the Shift key, and click and drag the segment down to G3. (You may get a small message in an orange border telling you that the algorithm has switched to Solo-Standard mode. This is normal because VariAudio uses that mode to shift pitches properly.) But before letting go of the mouse button, take a look at the Micro-pitch curves in Figure 12.19.

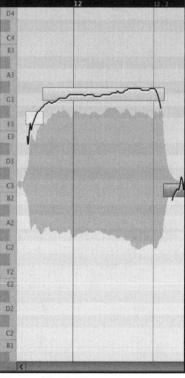

Figure 12.18. The pitch grid and vertical keyboard.

The Micro-pitch curves show how the pitch of a segment changes over time. When the event is first analyzed for pitch, you will only see the black or current pitch. But when you click and drag a note with the Pitch & Warp tool, the orange or original pitch will also be displayed. This gives you an idea of how far you're altering the pitch from its original position.

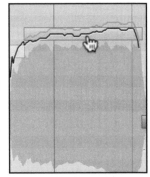

Figure 12.19. Orange (original) and black (current) Micro-pitch curves.

Now that the segment has been placed on G3, it sounds a lot better than when it was sharper. But the segment may sound better if moved in between G and F♯. To make those finer adjustments, remember to hold the Shift key during the edit to disable the chromatic snapping. However, the gross adjustments are usually made more easily by clicking and dragging notes without the Shift key so that they snap chromatically to each specific note. Then you can Shift-drag the note to make the finer adjustments.

You may also have noticed that the segment colors will change depending upon which note they're currently placed on. That's because you set the VariAudio Segment Colors setting to Pitches, and the color coding helps you see the pitch of each segment.

ALTERING THE MICRO-PITCH TILT

A simple adjustment like the one you just made might be all the editing you have to do to make the note sound properly intonated. However, this time you are not so lucky, because this segment drifts from in tune to sharp. To correct the intonation, you'll need to adjust the tilt. The Tilt control is located at the top of every segment and is much easier to see when the segment height is increased with the Vertical Zoom controller. Now take a look at the "I" segment in Figure 12.20.

Figure 12.20. The Tilt controls.

A fringe benefit of the increased segment height is that you'll be able to see both the note value and fine-tuning of the segment during editing. But now you can really see the Tilt controls represented by a thin horizontal line with small handles at the left and right. The tilt will allow you to correct the drift in pitch that the Micro-pitch curve represents in this segment. One way to adjust the tilt is to hover your mouse over one of the handles and drag up and down. Since the start of the segment is flat, click on the left handle and drag up. Then, since the note gets sharper, click on the right handle and drag down. The Micro-pitch curve should now appear as it does in Figure 12.21.

Once you've made those edits, the overall pitch of the segment might be pushed sharp or flat, requiring that you drag the segment back to G3. However, another way to adjust the tilt is to hold the Alt/Option key while moving the handle. I actually prefer this method, because the pitch of the segment is usually not altered as much as when editing either handle separately.

STRAIGHTENING THE PITCH

Now that the note is sounding good, there's room to make it sound better. You'll notice the Micro-pitch curve does wobble in and out of tune. In other words, the curve is not very horizontal. So using the Pitch & Warp tool, select the segment by clicking on it, then locate the Straighten Pitch slider under the VariAudio tab and drag it to the right, as shown in Figure 12.22.

For a segment like this, try moving the slider to about the halfway point. That will leave a bit of the human element in the segment but still improve the overall intonation of the note. When you compare Figure 12.21 to 12.22, you can see that the Micro-curve pitch has become more horizontal, and therefore more in tune. I would recommend repeating this edit on the last word of the event "true." I purposely added a little "bad lounge singer" vibrato to that note, which can be easily tamed by straightening the pitch. When you listen to the playback of the entire event, you won't have to plug your ears as you run out of your studio.

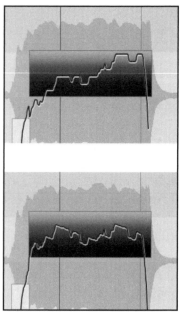

Figure 12.21. The Micro-pitch curve before and after editing the tilt.

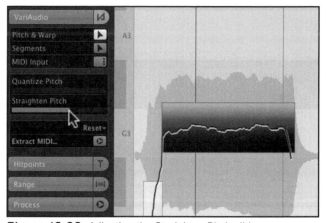

Figure 12.22. Adjusting the Straighten Pitch slider.

ADJUSTING SEGMENT START, STOP, AND LENGTH

Another function of the Pitch & Warp tool is to make segments longer or shorter, thereby changing the note start and end positions as well as the duration. This allows you to tighten up either the start or end of a note so that it lines up with a measure, bar, or beat. (It's similar to quantizing a MIDI note, but the audio segment length is not preserved, as it would be with MIDI.) Simply click and hold on the left or right boundary of the segment, and drag sideways. The degree to which the segment can be lengthened will depend on two factors: distance and sonic quality. When making notes longer, you might eventually run into the next adjacent segment, which will define the limits to which you can lengthen the segment. But even if the segment you're lengthening has no adjacent segments, dragging the note out too long might introduce some sonic artifacts that will degrade the quality of the result. You also run the risk of making it sound humanly impossible by making the segment longer than a human's lung capacity.

Using the Segments Tool

The VariAudio analysis does an amazing job of determining syllabic content. But sometimes a singer connects words and syllables together so seamlessly that the segments are not created accurately. When this occurs, you can use the Segments tool to define the locations of those segments. That will allow you to make pitch adjustments with the Pitch & Warp tool to individual words and syllables. This is why typing the Tab key on your computer keyboard to quickly switch from the Pitch & Warp tool to the Segments tool is such a convenient way to perform VariAudio editing.

SELECTING A SEGMENT

Within the event you've been editing is "say you know," which you can see in Figure 12.17. Because there aren't any hard consonants between those words, VariAudio analyzed them as one long word. That would make it very difficult to edit the pitch or warp. So type Tab to switch to the Segments tool, and take a closer look at the segment you'll be editing in Figure 12.23.

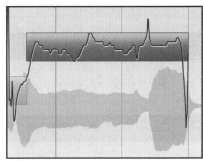

Figure 12.23. The "say you know" segment.

MAKING THE SPLITS

When you use the Segments tool and hover your mouse over the segment, you will see a thin horizontal line at the bottom. There isn't an official name for that line, so I'm calling it the Split line. Then move the mouse over the Split line (or toward the bottom of a segment if the Split line isn't visible due to short Vertical Zoom), and the mouse turns into a Split Tool icon. (It's identical to the scissors icon used by the Split tool in the Toolbox.) Now click on the Split line at the locations shown in Figure 12.24.

When you've made those splits, you'll notice that each event is moved to its newly analyzed pitch. In other words, "say" is now a little flat, "you" is properly intonated, and "know" is a little sharp. Now you can type Tab to switch back to the Pitch & Warp tool

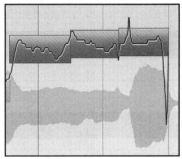

Figure 12.24. Splitting "say you know" into three segments.

to adjust the intonation of each segment. However, just for fun, drag "you" to E3 and "know" to D3, as shown in Figure 12.25.

Now when you listen to the playback, the melody line of the phrase has been completely retuned. You may notice some character differences between the original pitches and the retuned ones. But when you listen to the vocal track in context with the rest of the tracks (and especially after you add some effects to the track in chapter 15, "Effects: Inserts, Sends, and FX Channels"), those differences will be less discernible.

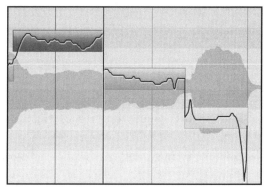

Figure 12.25. Retuning "say you know."

Making Multisegment VariAudio Edits

Sometimes you might need to tighten up the pitch of an entire event. If you did that note by note, segment by segment, it might take a very long time. Instead, you can select multiple segments within the Sample Editor and use the Quantize Pitch and Straighten Pitch sliders to adjust all of them simultaneously. Zoom your Waveform Display back to how it appears in Figure 12.16. Then you can Shift-click to select multiple individual segments, or type Ctrl/Command + A to select all of the segments. For this example, select all the segments, then move the Quantize Pitch slider about halfway to the right, as shown in Figure 12.26.

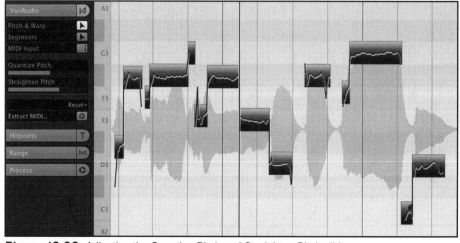

Figure 12.26. Adjusting the Quantize Pitch and Straighten Pitch sliders.

You'll notice that all the segments start to move closer to their analyzed pitches. Then if you want to straighten the Micro-pitch curves, move the Straighten Pitch slider about halfway, and listen to the results. The overall intonation of the entire performance has been improved. But be aware that the accuracy of the VariAudio analysis will depend greatly on how close to the correct pitch the original recording was sung. If you notice that segments are being adjusted erroneously either sharp or flat, you'll need to use the Pitch & Warp tool to make pitch corrections to those segments individually.

Creating the "Auto-Tune" Effect

Using the same procedure outlined above in "Making Multisegment VariAudio Edits," all you need to do is move the Quantize Pitch and Straighten Pitch sliders all the way to the right. When you listen to the result and depending on your point of view, you'll be either treated or subjected to the ubiquitous Auto-Tune effect.

BEYOND PITCH & WARP EDITING

You've seen how you can use the Pitch & Warp tool to correct the timing of individual segments. But what happens if you want to correct rhythmic timing across multiple tracks? For that kind of editing, Cubase provides Audio Quantizing and Group Editing. I'll discuss those operations and many more in the next chapter.

Advanced Audio Quantization, the Chord Track, and VarAudio 2.0

Along with pitch correction, being able to quantize multitrack drum recordings is another "holy grail" kind of editing. In a perfect world, drummers (and other musicians) would always practice with metronomes. That way, when they came into a recording studio and were told to play to the click track, the experience would seem more natural. Unfortunately, the world is not perfect, and many drummers find the process of recording to a click track very disconcerting. The results can be manifested as rushing, dragging, a lack of groove, and a generally sloppy-sounding drum track. Cubase has phase-accurate multitrack audio quantization, which when used in combination with Folder tracks and Group Editing can dramatically improve a multitrack drum or percussion recording. Plus the Chord track offers some exciting ways to augment both MIDI and Audio data, including the creation of up to four harmony voices. In this chapter, you will learn how to:

- Use multitrack audio quantization.
- Apply the techniques of Group Editing.
- Use Folder tracks.
- Analyze tracks for Hitpoints to detect drum notes.
- Slice, quantize, and crossfade drum tracks.
- Use the Tempo Detection feature.
- Create chord progressions with the Chord track.
- Create and edit harmonies with VariAudio 2.0.

MULTITRACK AUDIO DRUM QUANTIZATION

For many composers, whose forte is not drumming, the simple process of quantizing MIDI drum tracks is invaluable. But when it comes to quantizing the audio recording of a real drummer, the process is not so simple. In fact, up until a few years ago, it was an extremely tedious process. But Cubase has a really fast process with which you can quantize multiple Audio tracks. Since you haven't recorded a real drum set yet, I've provided a project called "Drum Audio Quantize.cpr" that can be found on the disc that comes with this book. (See Appendix A: "Using the Included Disc.") Go ahead and load that project before you continue.

Listening to the Drum Audio Quantize Project

This project is indicative of some of the timing anomalies I've mentioned. If you were to listen to it without the Click active, you might not immediately notice the timing problems. So go to the Transport menu and select Metronome Setup. (Remember, Click and Metronome are synonymous.) Make sure Metronome in Play is enabled, then click OK to close the window. If during playback you still don't hear the Click, type the "C" key on your computer keyboard.

Now you can really hear how far off this drummer gets from the original tempo of 92 BPM. His performance is pretty consistent right up until measure 14, where he starts to rush. Then he has to dramatically slow down to make up for all the rushing. Then at measure 22, he's dragging behind the beat and has to rush to catch up. This is a very common problem when a drummer is changing from one drumbeat to another. What you're going to achieve by quantizing these drum tracks is a solidly and consistently timed drum recording.

WHEN YOU CAN USE MULTITRACK AUDIO QUANTIZATION

Before you get started, you'll need to understand the prerequisites for this type of edit. It is critical that you perform the drum quantization prior to recording any other instrumentation. This is because the other musicians are going to be listening to the recorded drum tracks, the Click, or a combination of the two while they're recording their own tracks. So if they're playing a little out of time, like the drummer was during his recording, they're going to follow his prerecorded timing. Then if you quantize the drums afterward, the other tracks will suddenly sound out of time. And since you cannot quantize other instrumentation as easily as you can drums, you might find yourself in an editing and repair situation that will cost you time and money.

As you can see in Figure 13.1, the "Drum Audio Quantize" project you just loaded has five tracks: Kick, Snare, Hi-Hats (Hats), Overhead Left (OH_L), and Overhead Right (OH_R).

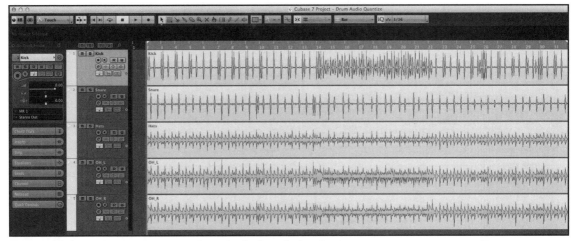

Figure 13.1. The Audio tracks in the "Drum Audio Quantize" project.

All of these tracks were recorded using the contemporary method of drum recording. That is, each drum and the hi-hat cymbals were miked with a separate microphone. Then a pair of overhead microphones was placed over the drum set to capture the other cymbals and a stereo image of the entire kit. The sound from each microphone was then recorded simultaneously onto its own individual Audio track. Since drums are very percussive, each drum note is clearly visible in the waveform display of each Audio event. With all of these things in mind, this project is a perfect candidate for drum quantization.

TRACKS YOU CANNOT MULTITRACK QUANTIZE

Audio quantization only works on percussive tracks like drums, so other instrument recordings are usually ineligible for this type of editing. You simply cannot quantize tracks such as vocals, guitars, pianos, or strings, because those recordings will lack the basic principles upon which audio quantization operates: percussiveness and track separation. Therefore, tracks that contain a mix of instrumentation (such as a stereo drum track containing the entire drum recording) or that don't have clearly visible note attack (such as a bowed violin or a human voice) cannot be quantized. The bottom line is that audio quantization only works on multitrack drum recordings, such as the "Drum Audio Quantize" project.

Creating a Folder Track

A Folder track does not contain performance data like Audio or MIDI tracks. However, a Folder track can contain many, many individual tracks. Moving Audio, MIDI, or any other tracks into a Folder track can provide a multitude of benefits, including reducing visible track counts and editing multiple tracks simultaneously. It is also a requirement for multitrack audio quantization. To create a Folder track, click the Project menu, select Add Track, and then select Folder. Change the name of the track to "Drum Kit," then drag the Folder track to the top of the Track Column, as shown in Figure 13.2.

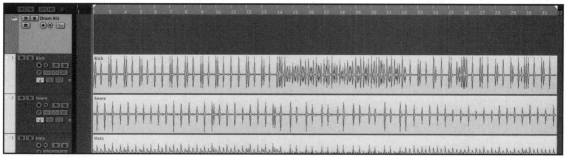

Figure 13.2. The Folder track at the top of the Track Column.

I usually change the color of drum tracks to yellow (it's a long story), so I prefer to make the Folder track the same color as the tracks it will contain. This makes it easier to identify the track simply by looking at it.

MOVING TRACKS INTO A FOLDER TRACK

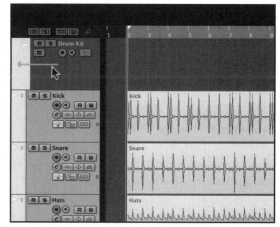

Figure 13.3. Moving the tracks into a Folder track.

To move the drum tracks into the Folder track, click the Kick track, and then Shift-click the OH_R track to select them all. Then click and drag on the Track name of any track to the midpoint of the Folder track. You will see a horizontal green arrow pointing left, as shown in Figure 13.3.

After you release the mouse button, the Audio tracks will be packed into the Drum Kit Folder track. The appearance of the Track Column won't be dramatically different from before. But there are two things to notice in Figure 13.4.

The Folder icon has two states: open and closed. The Folder track in Figure 13.4 is open; therefore, the tracks contained within can be seen in the Track Column and the Event Display. And to indicate that those tracks are in a Folder track, they are slightly indented to the right.

CLOSING AND OPENING THE FOLDER TRACK

Clicking on the Folder icon will close the folder and hide the tracks it contains. You can see how closing the Folder track can dramatically reduce the visible tracks in the Track Column. This makes it much easier

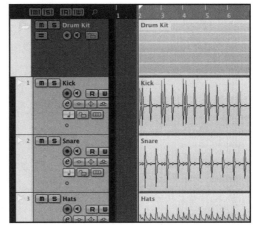

Figure 13.4. Folder Track icon and horizontal indent of tracks.

to manage a project when you've added more and more tracks. When you mute the Folder track, the tracks it contains will also be muted. The same is true for Solo and other track functions such as Record Enable and Monitor. Plus, when you use any of the tools (such as the Split or Erase tools) on the Folder track, all of the tracks inside will also be edited. You will see why this behavior is important when you start quantizing these tracks.

ANOTHER METHOD FOR CREATING FOLDER TRACKS

The reason I showed you the "long way" first was so that you could visualize the concept of a Folder track. But now that you understand the concept, let me show you a shortcut. With the desired tracks selected, click the Project menu, select Track Folding, and then choose Move Selected Tracks to New Folder. While you will still need to rename and (if desired) colorize the Folder track, you won't have to reposition the track or drag the tracks into the Folder track.

Analyzing Hitpoints

Hitpoints are what Cubase uses to indicate, among other things, where musically significant events (such as drum notes) are on an Audio track. In the case of multitrack audio quantization, you will need to analyze for Hitpoints on some, but not all, tracks. I would recommend using the Kick, the Snare, and one of the overhead tracks. Due to the differences in both the note quantity and volume, each track will have to be analyzed separately.

ANALYZING THE KICK TRACK FOR HITPOINTS

Double-click the Kick event to open the Sample Editor. Click on the Hitpoints tab in the Inspector, as shown in Figure 13.5.

Figure 13.5. The Sample Editor and Hitpoints tab.

Notice the oval circle on the left side of Figure 13.5. Directly underneath is the Edit Hitpoints button (to the right of Edit Hitpoints.) Click that button to execute a Hitpoint analysis. The results are shown in Figure 13.6. Pay attention to what happens to the Waveform Display.

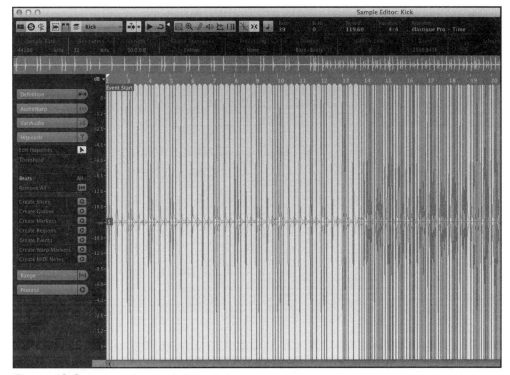

Figure 13.6. Results of the Hitpoint analysis.

The vertical gray lines that appear in the Waveform Display will indicate where the Hitpoint analysis has detected drum notes. You can see there are a lot of them, and in fact, there are too many Hitpoints. What you want to do is refine the detection so that Hitpoints are only created for the notes that come from the kick drum. In other words, because the sound of other drum instruments will bleed into the microphone during recording, not all of the detected Hitpoints are strictly kick drum notes.

ADJUSTING THE THRESHOLD

By default, the Threshold control (indicated by the oval circle on the left side of Figure 13.7) is set all the way to the left, which is its most sensitive position. That's why even the quietest notes have been detected as kick drum notes. By moving the Threshold slider to the right, you can refine the Hitpoint detection to only identify kick drum notes.

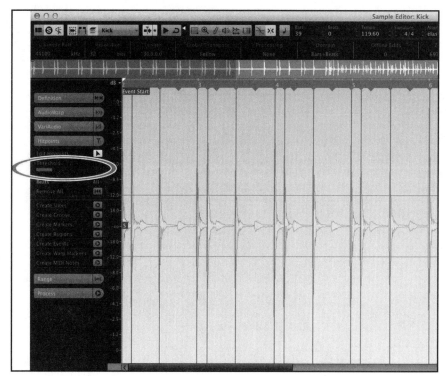

Figure 13.7. Adjusting the Threshold control (Sample Editor zoomed in).

As you adjust the Threshold, two horizontal lines will appear in the waveform display. These are the Threshold indicators, and they help you differentiate between loud notes and quiet notes. The loud notes are most probably kick drum, so you want to set the Threshold low enough that it detects the quietest kick drum. However, if you set it too low, it might detect quiet notes that are actually bleed-through from other drums. In the case of Figure 13.7, you'll notice that the kick notes (tallest waveform peaks) have Hitpoints, while the snare notes that bleed through (shortest waveform peaks) do not. This is an appropriate setting for the Kick event.

ANALYZING HITPOINTS ON THE SNARE AND OH_R EVENTS
Now you're going to close the Sample Editor and repeat the Hitpoint detection and Threshold adjustment on the Snare and OH_R tracks. Keep in mind that the Threshold setting for the Snare will be roughly the same as it was for the Kick. However, the OH_R event will contain notes from the Kick, Snare, and any other instrument on the drum set. Therefore, the OH_R Threshold will certainly need a lower, more sensitive setting.

Group Editing

The Folder track, when compared to other tracks, does not have as many controls. However, it does have one unique control called Group Editing. This is a small button that looks like an "=" sign, as shown in Figure 13.8. (Notice the circle in the upper left-hand corner.)

When Group Editing is enabled, it allows edits you make on one event to be applied to every event. Those events must be inside the same Folder track. Since multitrack audio quantization must be phase accurate, all the events must be edited equally. So go ahead and click the Group Editing button, but there's a catch.

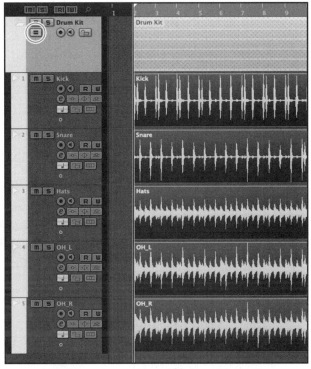

Figure 13.8. The Group Editing button and selected events.

ALL EVENTS MUST BE SELECTED

For the quantization to work properly, all of the events inside the Folder track must be selected. Notice in Figure 13.8 that this is the case. Making this selection can be a little tricky, but I've found the quickest solution. After the Group Editing button is enabled, you simply click on any event contained within the Folder track. The selection of any event in the folder will select all the events contained within.

OTHER GROUP EDITING SITUATIONS

Group Editing is the function that makes multitrack audio quantization possible. However, there are many other applications. For example, if you're simultaneously editing several tracks, such as background vocals or layered guitar tracks, Group Editing allows you to make identical edits across all tracks. Then if you find one event that needs a little individual editing, you can disable Group Editing, perform the edit, and then reenable Group Editing to pick up where you left off.

The Quantization Process

Now you're going to quantize all the drum events. This will require that you open the Quantize Panel either by selecting it from the Edit menu or by clicking the small button to the right of the Quantize Presets at the top of the Project window. If you've seen the

Quantize Panel while editing MIDI data, you'll notice that it has several more options in Group Editing mode, as shown in Figure 13.9.

The Slice Rules at the top of the Quantize Panel are only visible when you're in Group Editing mode. In the Hitpoint Tracks column, you'll see a list of the three tracks you've analyzed for Hitpoints. In the Priority column, you can change which tracks have the highest priority (more stars) or lowest priority (fewer stars). In this case, it set the priority by the order in which the events were analyzed. This order will usually garner the best results, so make sure that you follow the priority in Figure 13.9 regardless of the order in which they were analyzed.

MAKING SLICES

Take a look at Figure 13.10. On the left, you'll see the events at measure 14 (zoomed in for detail) prior to slicing. When you click the Slice button in the Slice Rules section, you'll see that every event will get split into multiple events, as shown in the right side of Figure 13.10.

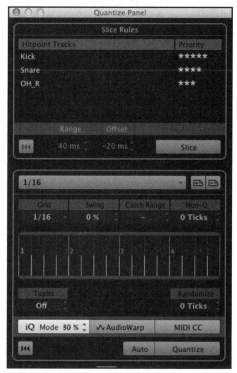

Figure 13.9. The Quantize Panel with Slice Rules (Group Editing only).

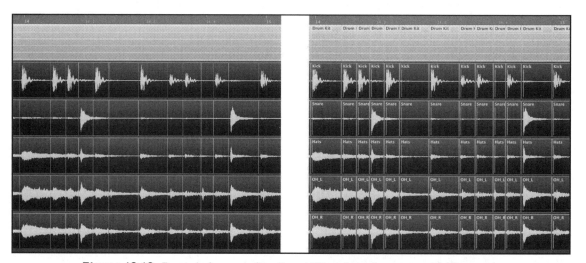

Figure 13.10. Events before and after slice at Hitpoint locations, measure 14.

If you audition the playback now, you won't notice any audible difference, because you haven't altered the timing yet. The Slice command only creates individual events for every Hitpoint across all the events. But the actual slices are not made directly at the Hitpoints. Instead, the Offset control on the Slice Rules is set at its default of -20 ms (milliseconds). That way, the initial attack of the drum note is retained, and you won't get popping or clicking due to slices made inside of the waveform. The Offset amount ensures that slices are made at quiescent parts of the event. But if you'd rather adjust where the slices are made, you can customize the amount of Offset.

Similarly, the Range control has a default of 40 ms, which ensures that the slices will be a minimum of 40 ms apart. For this example, I found that a Range setting of 80 ms garnered the best results. This was because of a few flams (notes played very close together) that created some clumsy-sounding results if they were sliced into individual events. Therefore, hit Undo (Ctrl/Command + Z), change the Range to 80 ms, and click the Slice button again.

Another tip is to consider how busy the drum performance is. Events with a lot of Hitpoints (such as sixteenth-notes or 32nd-notes) might require a shorter Range, while events with sparse Hitpoints might require a longer Range.

QUANTIZING THE SLICES

The Quantize section of the Quantize Panel (see Figure 13.9) is identical to that of MIDI Quantize. Basically you'll need to determine an appropriate Quantize Preset based on the shortest note that was played in the recording. The shortest note in the "Drum Audio Quantize" project is a sixteenth-note. Therefore, the 1/16 preset is the best choice. Then you can also enable iQ (Iterative Quantize) to retain a percentage of the original timing. In this example, the default of 60 percent will not garner a tight timing. This is because of how far offbeat the drumming was at certain sections. I would recommend using iQ whenever possible, but in this case, you'll need to set the percentage to around 80 percent. Then click the Quantize button, and your events should resemble the right side of Figure 13.11.

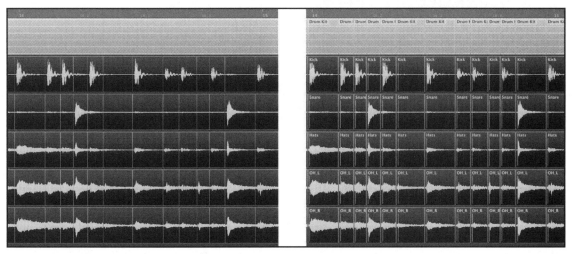

Figure 13.11. Events prior to and after quantization resulting in gaps, measure 14.

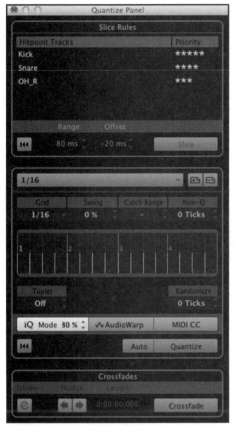

Figure 13.12. The Crossfades controls.

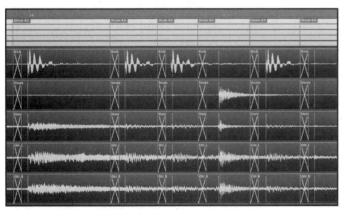

Figure 13.13. Crossfades added to all events and tracks.

When you audition the playback now, the events land very closely, but not precisely, to the nearest sixteenth-note. That's due to the iQ retaining some of the human timing element. However, you'll also notice that audible and visible gaps have appeared between many of the events. That's because the quantization process moved the events forward or backward in time. Those gaps reveal the degree to which the events have been moved. So while the timing has been improved, the silence created by the gaps makes the playback sound choppy and stuttering. Fortunately, there's an easy remedy for this problem.

CROSSFADING THE SLICES

You may not have noticed that the Quantize Panel had some controls added to it when you clicked the Slice button. However, there's now a Crossfades section at the bottom of the Quantize Panel, as shown in Figure 13.12.

When you click the Crossfade button, you'll notice that a small crossfade will be applied across all of the events. And since Group Editing is on, the crossfades are applied to all of the tracks and shown in Figure 13.13, which has been zoomed in to show more crossfade detail.

Now that the crossfades have removed the audible gaps from between the events, when you audition the playback, it's void of that choppy, stuttering feel, and the timing is dramatically improved. If longer or shorter crossfades are desired, you can now adjust the Length setting from the default of 0.22 PPQN (Pulses Per Quarter Note) or even click the Nudge buttons to reposition the crossfades. If you want to further customize the crossfades, you can click the "e" button to open the Crossfade Editor. But in this example, I'm sure you'll agree that the quantization of this drum performance was a vast improvement over the original. To hear the difference, hit Undo (Ctrl/Command + Z) a few times until you return to a presliced or prequantized state, and listen to the unquantized original performance. You'll certainly prefer the quantized version.

If for any reason you got results that didn't sound good, you can load the "Drum Audio Quantize Complete" project to listen to my results and compare the Hitpoint detection results.

TEMPO DETECTION

Cubase (the full level) has a feature called Tempo Detection. It's similar to multitrack Audio Quantize in that it uses Hitpoint detection to determine where percussive notes occur. However, it doesn't quantize the audio. Rather, it quantizes the tempo of Cubase to an audio file. This is extraordinarily useful when you receive drum tracks from another studio that were not recorded to a click track. In that case, the Tempo Detection can line up your Cubase measures, bars, and beats to the audio files. You can even try this on an audio file of a complete mix, as long as it has consistent drum transients that Tempo Detection can "see" and convert into tempo information. In fact, I love to do that by importing audio CDs of my favorite drummers into Cubase and then using Tempo Detection to see just how tightly they really play. Tempo Detection will also introduce you to two new track types: Tempo and Signature.

Tempo Detection on a Multitrack Project

If you ever find yourself getting worse results from drummers when they're trying to follow the click track, you may just need to let them record their performances using their own freestyle timing. But that can cause problems later when trying to reference the project timing to measures, bars, and beats. For an example, load the "Tempo Detection.cpr" project from the disc that came with this book. (See Appendix A: "Using the Included Disc.") This is a recording of a drum set, and we don't know what the tempo of the song is. To see what I mean, make sure that Metronome in Play is enabled in the Metronome Setup window (Transport menu), and listen to the playback. You'll notice that the Click and the tempo of the Audio tracks are not synchronous. And since these tracks weren't recorded to a click track, the timing would drift if you were to try and guess what the correct tempo might be.

CHOOSING A TRACK FOR TEMPO DETECTION

As you can see in Figure 13.14, there is a project with ten tracks: Kick, Snare, Hi-Hats, four Tom Toms, and two Overheads.

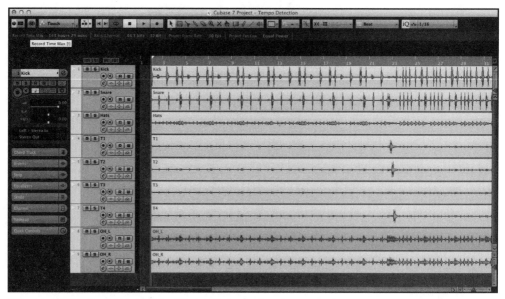

Figure 13.14. Track layout of the "Tempo Detection" project.

For Tempo Detection to work properly, it needs lots of percussive transients. The track in the project that fits the bill is one of the overhead tracks, such as OH_L (Overhead Left) or OH_R (Overhead Right). Since those microphones pick up the entire drum kit, they contain the most drum notes. Select the OH_L event (which I have colorized green rather than yellow to make it easier to identify), then click the Project menu and select Tempo Detection.

ANALYZING THE TEMPO

The Tempo Detection panel has one large Analyze button along with some additional options, as shown in Figure 13.15.

The first step is to click the Analyze button. A progress bar will appear, and gives you an idea of how long the analysis will take. When it is complete, two new tracks will be added around the OH_L track. (See Figure 13.16.) I'll discuss the Signature track at the top in a moment. For now, look at the new track underneath called the Tempo track.

THE TEMPO TRACK

When you look at the data contained on the Tempo track, you will see a series of little boxes on a horizontal string. The string is the Project tempo, while the little boxes are

Figure 13.15. The Tempo Detection panel.

where the Tempo Detection analysis determined the tempo changes occurred. In other words, and in a similar way to Hitpoint detection in the Sample Editor, a strong transient (such as a drum note) is identified as a Hitpoint. Then Cubase places a tempo change along the tempo line at those locations. The Tempo track is also where you can customize the tempo of your project to create tempo changes. You do this by adding a Tempo track to the project, then using the Draw tool to add your own little boxes (or, as some like to call them, donuts on a rope) across the tempo line. However, let's get back to Tempo Detection.

Now when you play back the project, you'll hear that the Click and the Audio tracks are perfectly in sync. The Tempo Detection process does not alter the audio files in any way, only the Tempo track. However, you may also have noticed a few other changes, which appear in Figure 13.16.

Figure 13.16. Additional features of the Tempo Detection process.

The Time Ruler at the top of the Event Display is now rust colored rather than blue. That's because the Time Warp tool has been selected automatically, and when you hover your mouse over an event, it will appear as a mechanical metronome (the kind that might be sitting on your piano right now) with horizontal arrows at the top. Using that tool, you could reposition the Warp markers located in the Time Ruler to fine-tune the tempo. You won't need to do that in this example, because the Tempo Detection was nearly perfect.

Another thing to consider is the placement of the Audio tracks inside the Event Display. I put the strongest downbeat right on measure 2. This helped Cubase determine where the first Warp marker (and therefore the first Tempo change) should be placed.

THE DIVIDE AND MULTIPLY BUTTONS

When you listen to the playback, you'll notice that the Click sounds as though it's in double-time compared to the Audio tracks. This is a very common occurrence and very easy to fix using either the Multiply or Divide buttons on the Tempo Detection panel. (See Figure 13.15.) If the Click sounds double-time, click the Divide button. When you do, the tempo changes are divided in half from roughly 180 BPM to 90 BPM. However, if the resulting Tempo Detection sounds half-time, you can click the Multiply button to double the tempo changes.

THE TIME SIGNATURE TRACK

The Signature track contains any changes to the time signature. You'll notice that at measure 1, there's an establishing time signature of 4/4. (See Figure 13.16.) However, at measure 2, there's a change to 1/4. This is because the Tempo Detection places the Warp markers at what it has determined (or what it thinks) are quarter-note positions, but it doesn't know what the true time signature is. You may have also noticed that, during playback, all the Clicks are high-pitched beeps. That's another reminder that you'll need to edit the Signature track to establish the proper time signature.

Before you can edit the time signatures, you will need to close the Tempo Detection dialog. Then, since these tracks are 4/4, you'll have to switch to the Object Selection tool and double-click the 1/4 value at measure 2 and type in "4/4." (See Figure 13.17 for more detail.)

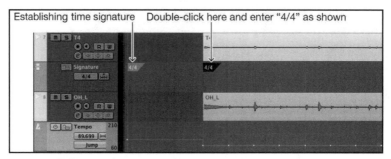

Figure 13.17. Editing the time signature.

Now that the project has the proper tempo and time signatures, you'll notice that the Click and the audio playback are solidly synchronized. This will allow you to more easily edit the tracks and events, and you can reference the current position to measures, bars, and beats.

THE CHORD TRACK

The Chord track is a very useful tool with which to create chord progressions and can even make suggestions regarding what chords might work well with the chords you've already added to your project. It can also be used in conjunction with the VariAudio 2.0 editor to create vocal harmony Audio tracks, and I'll explore those possibilities in the next section. For now, it's time to learn how to use the Chord track with MIDI and Instrument tracks.

Preparing the Project

To begin with, create a simple new project to work with. Go to the File menu and select New Project. The Steinberg Hub will appear, from where you can click on the More tab at the upper left-hand corner and then double-click on the Empty template. (For more detailed instructions for creating a new project, see "Cubasic No. 1: Using Proper Media Management" in Chapter 3.) Save this project with the name "Chord Track R01." You'll now have an empty project, as shown in Figure 13.18.

Figure 13.18. A blank empty project.

Next you'll need to add an Instrument track to this project. While you can use the Chord track with MIDI tracks with which to address external synthesizers, stick with the Cubase sound palette for now. Go to the Project menu, select Add Track, and then choose Instrument from the submenu. When the Add Instrument Track window appears, make sure the Browser is visible by clicking the Browse button on the right, and then click the criteria shown in Figure 13.19.

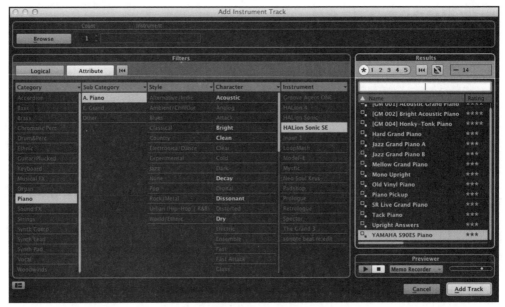

Figure 13.19. Choosing the YAMAHA S90ES Piano instrument.

Notice how the selections in the left-hand Filters columns narrows our selections in the Results column. When you click (from left to right) Piano category, A. Piano sub category, and then HALion Sonic SE instrument, all the instruments in Cubase that meet those criteria appear in the Results column. You could choose any of the piano, but the really nice-sounding YAMAHA S90ES Piano is found at the bottom of the Results column. Click that sound, then click the Add Track button at the lower right-hand corner of the window. When the Instrument track appears in your Track Column, make sure the track is record enabled and play some notes on your MIDI keyboard to audition the sound. (Don't worry if you don't have a MIDI keyboard, because the Chord track can be used without one.)

Adding a Chord Track

Repeat the Add Track procedure, but choose Chord from the submenu. The Chord track will be added to your Track Column directly beneath the Instrument track. Take a quick look at Figure 13.20, and change the Set Track for Auditioning setting on the Chord track from the default of Use Monitored Tracks to YAMAHA S90ES Piano.

Figure 13.20. The newly added Chord track.

Notice that the Chord track is enabled by default, in that the Audition Chords button is active (the button on the track with the speaker icon) and while it's not entirely necessary, the Monitor on the Instrument track (a slightly different Small Speaker icon) is enabled. Now if you play notes on your MIDI keyboard, you'll hear the Instrument track.

From this point, if you want to follow along with me, I'm going to change the tempo and time signature of the project. The reason for this will become apparent later on. To do this, look at the Transport Panel and set the Tempo to Fixed, then double-click the time signature and set it to 3/4, then double-click the default tempo of 120.000 and change it to 91.000.

Programming the Chord Track

Programming the Chord track can be done by MIDI or manually with the mouse. However, before you can start programming, you must first create some empty Chord events. Confirm that your Snap is enabled (see "Cubasic No. 5: Snap" in chapter 5), and set to Bar. Then select the Draw tool from the Toolbar and move your pointer to the Event Display of the Chord track. Your pointer will resemble a pencil, indicating that the Draw tool is selected. Notice that the Chord track is divided into an upper half (for Chord events) and a lower half (for Scale events) and separated by a light blue strip that runs across the length of the Event Display. (See Figure 13.21 starting on the Chord track from measure 1.) So to enter Chord events, you'll need to click on the upper half of the Event Display of the Chord track. Click on measures 2, 3, 4, and 5. The results should look like Figure 13.21.

Figure 13.21. Adding Chord events with the Draw tool.

The Chord events will snap directly to the measures and resemble small squares with "X"s inside. Those Xs represent empty Chord events. If you were to start playback now, you wouldn't hear anything. That's because the Chord events need to be programmed with (yup, you guessed it) chords. Select the Object Selection tool and double-click on the Chord event at measure 2 to reveal the Chord editor, as shown in Figure 13.22.

Notice the two tabs at the top of the Chord Editor: Editor and Chord Assistant. For now, make sure you're on the Editor,

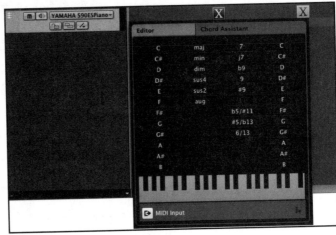

Figure 13.22. The Chord editor.

and then take a look at the four columns. They are (from left to right) the root note, chord type, tension, and bass note. Now you can start programming the selected Chord event.

MANUAL CHORD EVENT PROGRAMMING

You can enter chords manually by clicking the root note in the first column. Go ahead and click C. You'll hear a C major triad with a C in the bass. That's confirmed by the other default settings in the other three columns. If you were to then click on a different chord type, such as min or sus4, you'd hear the results. Try clicking different tensions in the third column, and notice that unlike in any other column, you can select multiple tensions, such as 9 and #5/b13. You can also click a note in the bass-note column for even more complexity.

Now that you've programmed your first event, pay attention to the Chord event in the Event Display, and notice that the chord has been entered where the X used to be. Also notice that the keyboard in the bottom of the editor is depicting the chord, as seen in Figure 13.23.

MIDI CHORD EVENT PROGRAMMING

In the lower right-hand corner of the Chord Editor, you'll find the MIDI Input button. It's enabled by default, which allows you to play the desired chord from your MIDI controller. Try playing a C major triad, and notice that all the columns reflect the chord you've played. I'm going to leave mine set to C major.

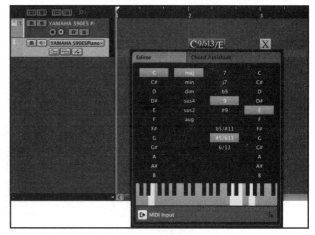

Figure 13.23. A programmed Chord event.

ADVANCING TO THE NEXT CHORD

With the Chord Editor still visible, you can type the Right Arrow key on your computer keyboard to advance to the next Chord event. (Conversely, the Left Arrow key advances to the previous events, if any.) Or if you've accidentally closed the Editor, simply double-click on the next Chord event you wish to program. I'm going to make the event at measure 3 a C major. Even though the event before it is also a C major, I want that chord to play at measures 2 and 3. Then at measure 4, I want an F major, followed by a C major at measure 5.

ADDING MORE CHORD EVENTS

In the lower left-hand corner of the Chord Editor, you will see the Add Chord Event button. That button was not available until now because we have no Chord events past measure 5. Clicking the button will create a new Chord event at measure 6. Using that button and your preferred programming method, create a C major at measure 6, an A minor at measure 7, a G major at measure 8, and a G major 7 at measure 9. Click anywhere outside the Chord Editor to close the window, and now the results will appear as they do in Figure 13.24.

Figure 13.24. Completed Chord event programming.

Now start playback of the project, and you'll hear the programmed chords played by the piano sound on the Instrument track.

ADDING MORE TRACKS

You can add as many Instrument or MIDI tracks to the project as you wish and have them all follow the Chord track. Try adding a guitar sound with an automated picking pattern. Add another Instrument track, but this time, in the Browser, click the Guitar/Plucked category and type "picking" into the search field, as shown in Figure 13.25.

Figure 13.25. Using the Search field.

Only one instrument with that criteria will appear in the Results column, and its name is "Nylon Finger Picking." Double-click that sound, and it will be placed onto a new Instrument track that appears in your Track Column. Now enable the monitor on both the piano and guitar tracks, and set the Select Track for Auditioning setting on the Chord track back to Use Monitored Tracks, as shown in Figure 13.26.

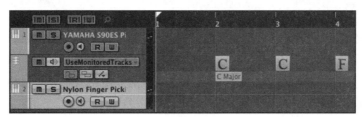

Figure 13.26. Monitor buttons enabled and Chord track Auditioning setting changed.

Now when you start playback on the project, you'll hear an arpeggiated nylon string guitar added to the accompaniment. Both Instrument tracks will stop playing at measure 10.

USING THE CHORD TAB

Looking in the Inspector, you'll notice that every MIDI and Instrument track has a Chord Track tab. The settings contained within can allow prerecorded tracks to follow the Chord track. To see how this feature works, add another Instrument track to the project, and record some triads that do not match those found in the Chord track. If you'd rather load a preconfigured project, I've provided one for you called "Chord Track R01 before chord follow.cpr" that can be found on the disc that comes with this book. (See Appendix A: "Using the Included Disc.") If you play my preconfigured project, you'll notice that the "Ahh Choir & Strings" track is a cacophony of dissonance. What you'll do now is allow the Chord track to update the voicing of the MIDI information. Take a look at the Chord Track tab in the Inspector on the left-hand side of Figure 13.27.

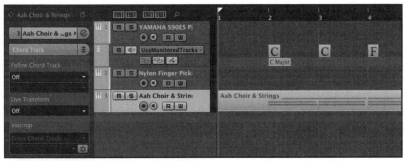

Figure 13.27. The Chord Track tab.

There are three settings in the Chord Track tab: Follow Chord Track, Live Transform, and Voicings. To allow this new Instrument track to be rechorded to the programmed Chord track, switch the Follow Chord Track setting from Off to Chords. You will then see the Follow Chord Track dialog box, as shown in Figure 13.28.

There are two main settings: Follow Directly (for MIDI data that was recorded with a programmed Chord track in mind) or Synchronize Track Data with Chord Track First (for freestyle MIDI data that was recorded without following a Chord track.) Since the chords in this Instrument event have nothing to do with the Chord track, choose the second

Figure 13.28. The Follow Chord Track dialog box

option along with the Analyze Chords option, then click the OK button. Now take a look at the before and after of the MIDI data, as shown in Figure 13.29.

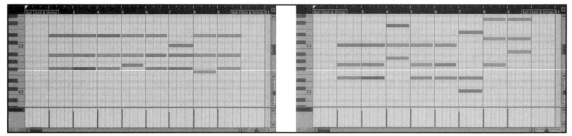

Figure 13.29. Before (left) and after (right) of the MIDI data.

You can see that the MIDI data has had its voicing updated to follow the Chord track. Now when you play the project, the new Instrument track sounds complementary to the others.

VARIAUDIO 2.0 AND VOCAL HARMONY GENERATION (CUBASE ONLY)

VariAudio is only available in the full level of Cubase. I've already discussed how to use VariAudio to pitch correct vocal performances. Now VariAudio 2.0 offers several enhanced new features, including the creation of up to four-part harmony. You can try this on one of your own projects, or if you'd like to follow along with me, load the project "Chord Track R02.cpr" from the disc that comes with this book. (See Appendix A: "Using the Included Disc.")

Listening to the "Chord Track R02" Project

After you load the project, you'll notice that it's the same version of the Chord Track project I used in the previous section, with the addition of a vocal track and vocal recording. The project will resemble Figure 13.30.

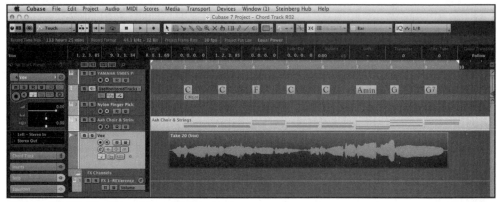

Figure 13.30. The "Chord Track R02" project.

You will see the Instrument tracks that are being played or had their voicings changed by the Chord track, along with a newly recorded vocal track. Remember that VariAudio works with monophonic (single note) recordings only. Any recordings that contain more than one note at a time are not eligible for VariAudio editing.

Now you're going to generate vocal harmonies from the vocal (Vox) track with the help of the Chord track.

GENERATING HARMONY VOICES

Select the Vox event ("Take 20 [Vox]"), then click on the Audio menu and select Generate Harmony Voices. The corresponding dialog box will appear, as shown in Figure 13.31.

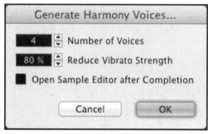

Figure 13.31. The Generate Harmony Voices dialog box.

You can create up to four-part harmony by changing the Number of Voices setting. A setting of 1 will generate the soprano voice, 2 will add the alto, 3 the tenor, and 4 the bass. If you want nonsequential voices (like the alto and bass), you should select 4 voices and then delete or mute the other generated voices. Go ahead and choose 4 voices.

Solo vocals can contain a wide range of vibrato, which is something the harmony voices should not, at least not as much. So change the Reduce Vibrato Strength control to 80 percent, and make sure the Open Sample Editor after Completion setting is unchecked. (I'll go over that in a moment.) The generation process will vary depending on the speed of your computer and the length of the audio file. When finished, you will see that four additional Audio tracks have been added underneath the Vox track, as shown in Figure 13.32.

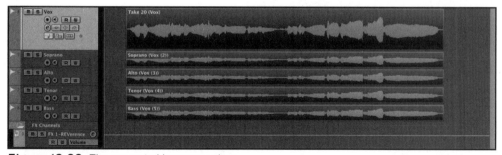

Figure 13.32. The generated harmony voices.

Each track and event have been given the corresponding voice name (Soprano, Alto, etc.) Because the level of each new track is equal to that of the source track, it's a good idea to turn them down a little bit. Use the Object Selection tool to select the four harmony Audio events (without choosing the source track), double-click on the Volume setting in the Info Line, and enter a value of -4. Then start playback and listen to the harmonies in context with the Instrument and Vox tracks.

The generation of the harmony voices was accomplished from the VariAudio processor analyzing the pitch of the source track and comparing the results to the Chord track. It then placed the newly created voices on their own Audio track. It's important to point out that I did have a reverb effect and some compression and EQ on the source track (which I'll discuss more in Chapter 15), and those settings were duplicated on the harmony tracks.

CHOOSING THE VOICES

Since all of the harmony events have been placed onto Audio tracks, you can use the track Mute button to render one or more tracks temporarily inaudible. You can also use the Mute tool to make certain events inaudible, or if you know you'll never use one of the voices, you can right/Ctrl-click on the unwanted track and choose Remove Selected Tracks from the submenu.

EDITING THE HARMONIES

One of the new features of VariAudio 2.0 is allowing you to edit multiple audio events simultaneously. Using the Object Selection tool, select all the harmony events and include the source event ("Take 20 [Vox]"), then double-click on any event to open the VariAudio editor, as shown in Figure 13.33.

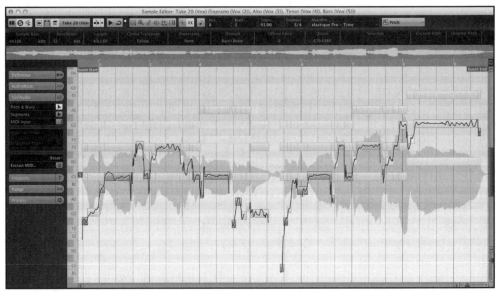

Figure 13.33. The VariAudio editor in harmony voices.

Notice that the VariAudio Segment Colors in the upper right-hand corner is set to Pitch, and that the Pitch & Warp button in the VariAudio tab (left-hand side) is selected. This will allow you to see all the pitch segments colorized and easier to edit. The bass voice is located at the bottom of the editor and not shown in Figure 13.33. However, all of the voices, including the source event, can now be edited. In the upper right-hand corner of Figure 13.33, you will see the Currently Edited Audio Event setting, which is currently showing "Take 20 (Vox)." That's the source event. Clicking on that setting will allow you to choose a different voice, as shown in Figure 13.34.

Since all of the harmony voices were selected prior to opening the VariAudio editor, they're all selectable in the list. Before choosing an event, find the button to the right that resembles a stack of three books. That's the Edit Active Audio Event Only button. When it's activated, only the voice you're currently editing will be heard during playback.

Figure 13.34. The Currently Edited Audio Event setting.

Now select the Soprano event from the list in Figure 13.34. You'll now see the highest pitches displayed in the editor. Go ahead and retune the last note at measure 8. Type your Tab key on your computer keyboard to switch to the Segments tool, and click the bottom of that last note at measure 5, as shown in Figure 13.35.

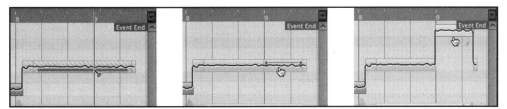

Figure 13.35. Editing a harmony voice.

The left frame of Figure 13.35 shows the edit with the Segments tool. Type the Tab key on your computer keyboard, and hover over the new segment you've created at measure 9, as shown in the middle frame of Figure 13.35. Finally, click and drag that segment up to D4, as shown in the right frame of Figure 13.35. You can now monitor the results and all the harmony voices by closing the VariAudio editor and playing through the project. The completed version of this edit is "Chord Track R03.cpr," which can be found on the disc that came with this book. (See Appendix A: "Using the Included Disc.")

GETTING INTO THE MIX

Now that you've added a bunch of new skills to your Cubase editing repertoire, you can start mixing and adding effects and EQ, and editing a mixdown of a project. Now might be a good time to go pour yourself a tall, refreshing beverage, because the next series of chapters are going to get intense.

The Art of Mixing

Mixing music is, indeed, an art form. Hopefully you're not intimidated by that fact. You see, there are many types of art and different levels of artistic expression. The masters of the visual arts did not create their most famous masterpieces on their first day. It took Vermeer nearly a decade of work before he painted Girl with a Pearl Earring, and Rodin sculpted The Thinker late in his career. Whether you're a sculptor, painter, or music maker, you have to start your art somewhere. And believe it or not, making professional-sounding mixes is easier than you think. In this chapter, you will learn:

- The "Big Three" actions for a professional mix.
- How to use the Cubase MixConsole.
- How to adjust volumes and use Group tracks.
- How to make a more spacious mix with the Pan controls.
- How to make tracks more audibly legible with EQ (equalization).
- The concept and importance of the Stereo Output Channel.

A WORD ABOUT BUFFER SETTINGS

When you get to the mixing phase of your project, it means you're done recording new tracks. So the buffer settings that control your latency don't need to be as low. In fact, low buffer settings can be problematic at this point. That's because the mixing process usually involves adding components such as EQ and effects that require more processing power to create. Low buffer settings may not allow enough time for the computer to generate these processor-intensive effects. The results will usually be manifested as pops, clicks, dropouts, and distortion. To prevent those anomalies and distractions, make sure to increase your buffer settings. See Appendix C: "Managing Audio Interface Buffer Settings" for detailed instructions.

THE "BIG THREE" ACTIONS FOR A PROFESSIONAL MIX

When I said that mixing is easier than you think, you might have thought that too bold a statement. Certainly the art of mixing requires a multifaceted approach developed through years of training and experience. But the basic goal of mixing is this: to ensure that every recorded sound is audible. Granted, that task can be a very challenging one, especially when you start adding a lot of tracks to a project. In other words, it's usually easier to mix one singer and one piano than it is to mix an entire pop band. However, regardless of the track count, musical genre, or instrumentation, there are three basic actions required to make a balanced professional mix: loudness, direction, and focus. Translated into Cubase terms, I'm talking about volume, pan, and EQ (equalization or tonal control).

Action No. 1: Controlling Loudness with Volume

Regardless of how much mixing you've done, you're probably familiar with the Channel Fader, either in Cubase or on a physical mixer. The Fader controls the volume of whatever is plugged into that channel. In the case of Cubase, the Channel Fader controls the volume of the MIDI, Instrument, or Audio track you've recorded. (Group Channels, FX Channels, ReWire Channels, and Output Channels also have Channel Faders.) In the early days of audio mixers, the Faders were usually knobs or levers and resembled the laboratory set from the 1931 film Frankenstein. They weren't very elegant looking, but they did what they were designed to do: make volume adjustments.

The same is true for the Channel Faders in Cubase. If a track is too quiet, turn up the Fader. If it's too loud, turn the Fader down. It's important to realize that Faders go down as well as up. Therefore, turning some Faders down can make other tracks more audible.

Action No. 2: Controlling Direction with Pan

Early audio recordings were done in mono. That is, the sound was recorded with one microphone and played back through one speaker. But humans have two ears, one on each side of our heads, which allows us to hear in stereo. To make that possible, our brains process the sounds coming through our left ears separately from the sounds coming through our right ears. This gives us an idea of where the sounds are coming from. Early humans used their stereoscopic auditory senses to determine where the sounds of a ferocious and hungry animal were coming from. Today, we use them to avoid being hit by a passing automobile. (That is, unless we have our earbuds cranked to 110 dB as we walk obliviously down the sidewalk.)

But we also listen to music stereoscopically. Even before there was any recording equipment, humans went to musical performances and enjoyed being able to hear every instrument of a full orchestra. The layout of the instrumentation onstage made it much easier for human ears and brains to process all the different sounds. The violins and violas sat stage right and were perceived by the left ear, while the celli and basses sat stage left and were perceived by the right ear. If all of the musicians were placed at center stage, the sound would essentially be monophonic, and it would be much more difficult to hear the individual instruments. (I'm sure that would also violate some union rules, but I digress.)

When stereo recording became possible, it meant that stereo pairs of microphones were placed in front of the orchestra and then played through separate left and right speakers. As pop music hit the scene, a full band was recorded in much the same way. But then multitracking allowed every instrument to be recorded onto its own discrete track. So how do you simulate a natural stereophonic environment with a series of monophonic tracks?

The answer is the Pan control. Pan is short for panorama, or the perception of sounds from different directions. By taking a track and panning it to the left or the right, you're able to send the signal to the listener's left or right ear. The result is a much more pleasing and spatial mix. In fact, you'll find that if you can't adequately balance a series of tracks with volume control, spreading them across the stereo audio landscape with the Pan control can instantly create audibility. Whether we know it or not, the direction from which the sound is coming is constantly being analyzed by our ears and brains.

IDEAS FOR PAN CONTROL SETTINGS

I work with a lot of recordings from people who hire me to mix their music. Many of them have given it their best effort, but they usually tell me, "We tried, but we just can't make it sound right." Believe it or not, many of the Cubase or Nuendo (Steinberg's audio-post DAW program) projects I receive have the tracks all panned center. That renders the mix monophonic, and it's no wonder the results to that point have been dissatisfying. So let me share with you some ideas on where tracks should be panned.

If you're recording a symphony orchestra in a multitrack fashion (separate instruments or sections on separate tracks), the positions of the Pan controls are pretty easy. Basically, you'd be replicating the layout of instrumentation on the stage. But solo instruments are quite different. For example, when a piano is played, the performer hears the low strings in his or her left ear, middle notes in both ears, and high strings in his or her right ear. But when we hear the piano played at a concert or recital, we don't perceive the instrument in the same way, because the piano is usually turned perpendicular to the audience. The best way to handle this situation is to listen carefully to a wide pan (player perspective) or a narrow pan (audience perspective) and decide which sounds better. You can also ask the performers which method they prefer.

Things get even more challenging with pop bands. What I mean by "pop" is a band with combo-style instrumentation such as drums, guitars, piano, brass, turntables and/or vocals. This could be a country, rock, hip-hop, or jazz band. If the band has a drum set, you'd simply pan each drum microphone to the listener's perspective. In other words, for a right-handed drummer, the bass drum would be center, the high tom would be panned toward the right, the floor tom would be panned toward the left, and so on. However, I have found some drummers who prefer to have their mix panned player-perspective rather than audience-perspective. It's a good idea to ask them which they like. But the other instrumentation is almost as easy to determine if you ask the question "Which side of the stage do you stand on during a performance?"

For example, let's say I was recording a rock band like AC/DC. (I reserve the right to dream at any time.) We already know how the drums will be panned. Then Brian Johnson (vocals) stands mostly center stage. Cliff Williams (bass guitar) stands slightly to audience right of Phil Rudd (drums). Then Malcolm Young (rhythm guitar) stands on audience left, while Angus Young (lead guitar) stands (rather, flails) on audience right. If you have any AC/DC in your music library, take a listen to it. You'll find that their stage layout is precisely re-created in their studio recordings. If you have trouble hearing what I'm talking about, use headphones and only put one cup (or ear bud) on at a time.

Of course, the "Where do you stand" method should not be treated as a rule but rather a guideline. There are plenty of recorded examples where this method wasn't employed. Take any Van Halen album, especially the early ones. Even though Eddie Van Halen stood on audience right, his guitars (except for most solos and intros) are panned hard audience left. It's really strange to listen to "Runnin' with the Devil" with only the right headphone on, because you won't hear any guitar (except for the reverb) until the solo. I still don't know why (producer) Ted Templeman did it that way. I can only assume that Eddie wanted to be heard more from the driver's side of a car stereo. (And since Van Halen fans like me never had a date to sit in the passenger seat…Oh, never mind.)

Action No. 3: Controlling Focus with EQ

Focus is a little hard to describe in audio terms. Instead, I'll use the metaphor of photography. Imagine you're trying to photograph a bear at some distance from you in the woods. You'll need a long telephoto lens to increase the size of the bear for the proper photographic composition. Long lenses have a much deeper range of focal points. Because of this, let's pretend that the foreground is filled with trees, which the camera autofocus is mistakenly presuming to be the subject of your photograph. In other words, the nearby trees are in focus, while the distant bear is out of focus. To solve this problem and get the shot, you'd turn off autofocus and manually move the focus past the trees and toward the bear instead.

Now let's explore this metaphor in audio terms. If you have a lot of foreground tracks, especially instruments that compete for the same tonal space (such as vocals and rock guitars), it becomes very challenging to make all the tracks heard by using volume or pan alone. Background instrumentation can be just as important as foreground tracks. So in situations like these, you'll need tonal control, which Cubase refers to as equalization and I refer to as EQ. Either way, they're synonymous.

I'll be going through some practical examples of EQ later in this chapter. But I want to leave you with this concept: EQ is a specialized volume control. A Channel Fader adjusts the overall track volume; however, an EQ adjusts the volume of certain frequencies. With EQ, you can accentuate the signature "voice" of a track, which might include emphasizing the volume of certain frequencies or deemphasizing the volume of others. The result is that you can use EQ to bring both foreground and background instrumentation into proper audio focus.

INTRODUCTION TO THE CUBASE MIXCONSOLE CONTROLS

Before you start using the MixConsole, you need to understand its controls and the myriad of different places you can find them. You also need to understand the identical natures of a physical mixer and the Cubase MixConsole. They both collect a series of audio signals and blend them together to create something rich and wonderful for other humans to listen to.

In an analog or digital tape–based studio, an example of which can be seen in Figure 14.1, the physical mixer, more than the tape machines, is the centerpiece of the control room.

Figure 14.1. A tape-based digital recording studio, circa 1999.

For the perspective client, the supposition was: the bigger the mixer, the more "pro" the studio. Therefore, it was common for studio owners to purchase not only the mixer they needed, but as much mixer as they could afford. The size of the mixer was a critical component of the recording studio and also a great marketing tool.

Now that DAW software is the de facto standard for audio recording, the physical mixer has been reproduced in software. The MixConsole in Cubase largely replaces a physical mixer, but it can also do things that physical mixers cannot, regardless of cost. Features such as fader automation, multiple aux sends, multiple effect returns, and 4-band equalizers on every channel were usually only found on the most expensive of mixers (literally tens, if not hundreds, of thousands of dollars). Today, the Cubase MixConsole has all of those features and more.

Before I can get into the details of the MixConsole, you will have to load an existing project, or start a new empty project and add at least one Audio track.

The MixConsole and the Inspector

I know that sounds like an early '70s British comedy, but what I'm talking about is the basic mixing functionality found in the Inspector. For every Instrument, Audio, ReWire, Input Channel, Output Channel, Group, and FX Channel track (the latter two of which I'll discuss later), there are Inserts, Strip, Equalizers, Sends, and Channel tabs, as shown in Figure 14.2. (Note: MIDI tracks have MIDI Inserts, which are different from the Inserts found on other tracks. MIDI tracks also do not have Strip, Equalizers, or Sends tabs.)

Basically, the Inspector can display the most commonly used mixing controls on any selected track. That means that a lot of the controls can be accessed directly from the Project window without having to go to the Cubase MixConsole. I'll discuss what all of these MixConsole features are used for as I go along, but first take a look at other ways to access them.

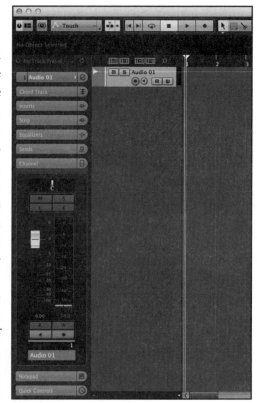

Figure 14.2. Inspector tabs for mixing.

The Channel Settings

To the upper left of the Fader shown in Figure 14.2, you will see a button labeled "E." That's the Edit button. Clicking the Edit button will open the Channel Settings window for the selected track. It contains the same MixConsole controls as the Inspector tabs, but it displays them all simultaneously, as shown in Figure 14.3.

Figure 14.3. The Channel Settings window.

The Channel Settings window gives you access to the entire signal path of a single channel. Before going any further, now is a good time to notice the many tabs at the top of the window, including Inserts, Strip, Channel Strip, Equalizer, Sends, and Cue Sends; and at the bottom you'll find the Plug-ins, Routing, Destinations, and Panning tabs. I'll go over many of these in a moment, but it's important to know that clicking these tabs is how you gain access to the controls contained within.

Here's how the Channel Settings relate to a physical mixer: If you've ever used a physical mixer, the controls closest to you are the Faders. Then, usually above the Faders, are a series of knobs for EQ (equalization), aux (auxiliary) sends, and input gain. That tall row of controls from each Fader to the input knob is known as a mixer channel strip, and the signal flows from top to bottom. However, Cubase does not display all those controls in the same way. If it did, you'd need a computer screen that's about three times as tall as the one you have. Instead, Cubase arranges the controls from left to right, and instead of the signal flowing from top to bottom, it usually flows from left to right. In other words, the sound from the track flows through the Inserts, then into the Strip and Channel Strip, next to the Equalizers, then to the Sends, and finally to the Channel Fader. This signal flow is very important to understand, and I'll discuss why later. But bear in mind that while the signal flow in Cubase is identical to that of a traditional analog mixer, it can also be customized for your specific needs.

The Cubase MixConsole

The Cubase MixConsole is used nearly as much as the Project window, especially once you start the mixing process. It's so important that many Cubase users (myself included) invest in a second computer monitor display upon which to permanently place the MixConsole. (If you want to add another monitor display, make sure its screen resolution is at least

1280 X 768 pixels [WXGA], and remember that there's no such thing as having too much resolution.)

GETTING AROUND THE MIXCONSOLE

Go to the Devices menu and select MixConsole, or type F3 on your computer keyboard. Be aware that the appearance and controls found in the MixConsole can be easily customized, but your MixConsole should resemble the one shown in Figure 14.4.

Figure 14.4. The Cubase MixConsole.

The MixConsole allows you to see and adjust all the Faders of all channels from a centralized window while you're listening to some or all of the tracks. Since this project only has one Audio track, the MixConsole isn't displaying a lot of channels. Now configure your MixConsole by customizing the settings in the upper left-hand corner of the MixConsole, as shown in Figure 14.5.

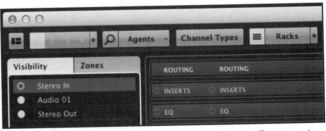

Figure 14.5. The Window Layout, Agents, Channel Types, and Racks buttons.

All of these buttons control what you see on your MixConsole. The Windows Layout button is similar to the one found on the Project Window. Click on that button to reveal the following settings shown in Figure 14.6.

Make sure that you match the settings for your Window Layout to the ones in Figure 14.6. The Channel Selector is located on the left-hand side of the MixConsole and controls the channel

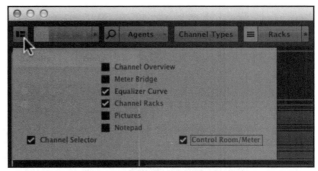

Figure 14.6. The MixConsole Window Layout settings.

visibility. The center column of checkboxes lets you add those features in the area of the MixConsole above the Faders, in which you'll make the Equalizer Curve and Channel Racks visible. Lastly, the Control Room/Meter is located on the far right of the MixConsole and provides access to the Control Room features and complex volume and loudness metering. Click anywhere outside the Windows Layout window to return to the MixConsole, then click the Agents button and select Show All Channels. Next click the Channel Types button and make sure All Channel Types is selected at the top of the submenu. (Note: With the submenu still open, pay attention to the color coding of each Channel Type. Those colors will also be depicted on the Fader knobs to help differentiate the Channel Types on the MixConsole.) Then click the Racks button and make the settings shown in Figure 14.7.

Figure 14.7. The Racks settings.

Make sure all six of the topmost radio buttons are enabled, then click anywhere outside the Racks settings to close the window. Now refer back to Figure 14.5 and disable the radio button next to Stereo In (along with any additional input channels you might see.) This is because you won't need to adjust any input channels during the mix; therefore, they won't need to be visible. Then next to the Visibility tab (see Figure 14.5), click on the Zones tab. You'll notice that each channel has two disabled radio buttons. The left button will force the selected channel to the left side of the MixConsole, whereas the right button forces the channel to the right side. Personally, I like the Stereo Output channel to be on the right side of the MixConsole, so click the right Radio button. When finished, your MixConsole should now appear as it does in Figure 14.7.

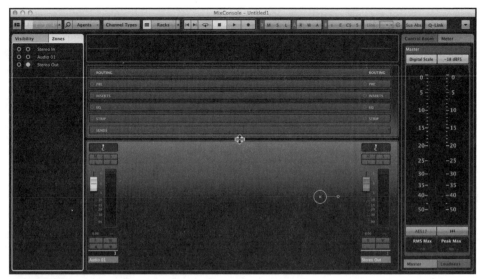

Figure 14.8. The reconfigured MixConsole.

It's possible that your Faders are covering part of your Racks. Notice the mouse pointer in the center of Figure 14.8. When you hover your mouse over the border between the Faders and Racks, your mouse turns into that icon, and clicking and dragging will allow you to modify how much of either MixConsole section you see.

GOING FULL SCREEN WITH THE MIXCONSOLE

Even though the MixConsole has customizable width and height, you can also put it into Full Screen mode if you are using more than one monitor. That way you can keep the Project window and MixConsole visible simultaneously, and Full Screen mode allows every pixel of a secondary monitor to be used by the MixConsole. An example of this is shown in Figure 14.9.

Figure 14.9. Project window and MixConsole on two 1920 X 1200 displays.

To enable Full Screen mode, right/Ctrl-click anywhere on the MixConsole (except for the Channel Selector on the left-hand side) to reveal the submenu in Figure 14.10.

Notice that I can choose Monitor 1 (my MacBook Pro built-in display) or Monitor 2 (a Dell monitor connected via HDMI), either of which will allow the MixConsole to occupy the entire monitor.

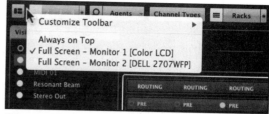

Figure 14.10. The Full Screen submenu.

TRACK ORDER AND APPEARANCE IN THE MIXCONSOLE

In the Track column of the Project window, you may have noticed that all the tracks are numbered from top to bottom. That numbering is identical to the left-to-right track order in the MixConsole. For example, in Figure 14.11, you see one Audio, one MIDI, and one Instrument track.

Since the Audio track is first in the Track Column, it is numbered 1 and is the left-most track in the MixConsole. The MIDI and Instrument tracks 2 and 3 follow

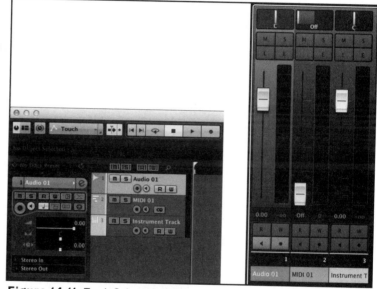

Figure 14.11. Track Column (left) and corresponding MixConsole channels (right).

down the Track Column and across the MixConsole. Therefore, when you rearrange the tracks in the Track Column, both their numbering and placement in the MixConsole will be adjusted accordingly.

TRACK TYPES AND THE RACKS

It's important to recognize that different track types will offer different options in the Racks. For example, the MixConsole in Figure 14.11 has one Audio, one MIDI, and one Instrument track. The Inserts Rack of a MIDI track will have different options compared to the Instrument and Audio tracks. That's because MIDI tracks don't make sound, but there are MIDI-specific Inserts you can use (such as arpeggiators and the Beat Designer) to modify the MIDI data in real-time. However, MIDI Inserts are quite different from the Audio Inserts used on Instrument and Audio tracks. Audio Inserts actually process the audio generated by the track in real-time. Basically, MIDI tracks don't have certain MixConsole controls, such as Audio Inserts, EQ, the Strip, or Sends.

You may have also noticed that the Fader and Pan control of the MIDI tracks are turned all the way down by default. (See Figure 14.11.) It may seem counterproductive to turn a newly created track all the way down before you've even used it. But there's an important reason for this. Since the MIDI Fader and Pan controls are actually transmitting MIDI continuous controllers (7 [volume] and 10 [pan] respectively), any default setting might adversely affect the loudness of that sound coming from either a VST Instrument or an external MIDI synthesizer (or other sound-generating device). Therefore, a MIDI Fader and Pan control are designed to transmit nothing upon their creation, which is why they're turned all the way down. Then if you determine that the track volume or pan needs to be adjusted, you can move the controls accordingly.

CHANNEL CONTROLS

At the bottom of the MixConsole, you will see the channel controls for each and every channel. Take a look at what each control does by looking at your Audio channel, as shown in Figure 14.12.

At the top of the Figure 14.12, you'll find the Pan control, which is currently in the center position, as indicated by the "C." Moving the horizontal Fader from left to right will place the sound of the channel at the corresponding position in the Stereo field.

Below the Pan control are the Mute (M) and Solo (S) buttons. Clicking the Mute button will prevent sound from coming through the channel, whereas clicking the Solo button will allow only the sound from that channel (or any other soloed channels) to be heard.

Next are the Listen (L) and Edit (E) buttons. The Listen button is similar to the Solo button, but is reserved for the engineer or producer who is using the Control Room to monitor the channel without affecting the current mix. Clicking the Edit button will reveal the Channel Settings (see Figure 14.3) for that particular channel. For Instrument tracks, clicking and holding the Edit button (or using an Alt/Option-click) will open the control panel of the VST Instrument to which the track is assigned.

Figure 14.12.
The channel controls.

The Fader and VU (volume unit) Meter are side by side. Adjusting the Fader up and down will alter the volume of the channel, while the VU Meter will display a visual representation of the channel volume.

Below the Fader and VU Meter are the automation buttons. There's a Read (R) button and a Write (W) button. (See Appendix B: "A Primer on Automation.") Below the automation buttons are the Record Enable and Monitor Enable buttons that are identical to those found on the Track Controls in the Project window, followed by the Track number and Track name.

THE CUBASE SIGNAL FLOW

After you've made Instrument or audio recordings, it's important to understand the journey that audio signal takes through Cubase. That journey is known as signal flow. Signal flow is a lot like a road map, which, when used properly, can help you arrive at your desired destination. The same is true for the destinations of your tracks, because if you don't know the signal flow, the sound from your tracks can easily get lost. In a tape-based studio, it was easier to see the signal flow, because you could just trace the wires leading from one audio component to another. (The MixConsole in Cubase makes this process even less transparent, because DAW software has no cables.) But once it hit the MixConsole, you had to know how the signal flowed through it to determine the destination of the audio.

Classic MixConsole Signal Flow

Based on tried-and-true methodology, the producers, engineers, and mixer-designers developed a signal flow that would deliver consistent and predictable audio results: Input > Inserts > EQ > Prefader Sends > Fader. (The Cubase Sends are usually postfader and used for effects such as reverb and delay. I'll explore Sends in the next chapter.) This is known as the classic signal flow, and most contemporary mixers use this to move audio from one point to another. Cubase uses this same signal flow; however, it can be customized and includes even more mixing features.

SIGNAL FLOW IN THE MIXCONSOLE

The way the signal flows through the MixConsole is basically top to bottom. Here's a look at an Audio channel in Figure 14.13.

You'll notice the Racks (which I'll go over in a moment) appear from top to bottom: Routing, Pre, Inserts, EQ, Strip, Sends, then finally to the Fader. Baring the Cubase-specific Routing, Pre, and Strip Racks, you'll see how Cubase adheres to the classic signal flow.

Figure 14.13. The signal flow of an Audio channel.

SIGNAL FLOW OF THE CHANNEL SETTINGS WINDOW

Click the Edit button (see Figure 14.12) on any Instrument or Audio track to reveal the Channel Settings window, and refer back to Figure 14.3. You'll see that all of the Racks in Figure 14.13 are also represented in the Channel Settings window. However, due to the horizontal orientation, the signal takes a more roundabout path. For example, the Routing is located in the Toolbar at the top of the window, and then the Pre settings are in the lower part of the EQ window. The Inserts, Strip and Channel Strip (they're actually the same thing), and Equalizer flow are shown from left to right, followed by the Sends and the Fader. Even though the Channel Settings window might have you believing differently, the signal flow is identical to that depicted in the MixConsole.

WHEN THE SIGNAL FLOW ISN'T CLASSIC

You should be aware of a couple of detours on the signal path. First, while there are eight Inserts on every channel, only the first six are part of the classic signal flow. Inserts 7 and 8 are postfader Inserts, meaning that they are fed after the signal passes through the Fader. Some effect plug-ins, such as limiters, ditherers, and sample-rate converters, should be placed at the very end of the signal flow. That's why Inserts 7 and 8 are placed after the Fader.

Next, the position of the EQ can be modified from within the Strip Rack, which I'll discuss in a moment. That's so that you can reposition the EQ before or after certain Strip effects.

The Method and Madness of the Classic Signal Flow

When you start mixing, you'll start applying the three actions I discussed earlier: loudness, direction, and focus. But first I'll discuss why the signal flows through the Racks and Faders the way it does. (Note: Racks will be discussed a little later.)

INSERTS

After signal leaves the Pre and Routing Racks, it flows into the Inserts Rack. The eight Insert slots are empty by default, and into them you can install VST effect plug-ins. Inserts are very similar to guitar pedals, in that the signal flows from one pedal into the next. Also, the processed sound travels from one Insert to the other. Therefore, the types of plug-ins you can use on Inserts are generally any volume-oriented effect. Plug-ins such as compressors, de-essers, expanders, noise gates, and EQs will function properly when assigned to Inserts rather than Sends. (See "Plug-in Effects on Inserts and Sends" in chapter 15.)

But the order in which the effects are assigned has a lot to do with how they'll interact with one another in the signal flow. For example, let's say you install an EQ plug-in first, followed by a compressor. In this case, any changes you make to the EQ will alter the response of the compressor. That's usually not a desirable situation. Instead, EQs should come after compressors, which is the reason that the Inserts come before the Cubase EQ. You'll learn more about using Inserts in chapter 15.

CHANNEL STRIP AND EQ

After the signal passes through Insert 6 (or the last populated prefader Insert slot), the signal flows into the Channel Strip and EQ Racks. As I mentioned before, EQ allows you to focus on certain frequencies to be emphasized or deemphasized. But why not place the EQ after the Fader? You could certainly do this by adding a separate EQ plug-in into Inserts 7 or 8. But it's better to have the Fader be in control of the loudness, so that it has the final determination of the channel volume. Plus, if the Cubase EQ came after the Fader, the Sends (see chapter 15) would not receive the same tonally focused signal. And since the Fader is available to you in so many places, it's easy to adjust.

CHANNEL FADER AND PAN CONTROL

These are the most essential controls for mixing. They each operate on the channel in its entirety, meaning that all of the processing that happens with Inserts and EQ is going to arrive at the Fader and the Pan control. (See Figure 14.12 and/or 14.13.) This gives them the "final say" as to how loud or soft the channel is (loudness) as well as in which ear (direction) the listener will be able to hear most, if not all, of the signal.

The Racks

The Racks are located above the Faders, and you've made six of the nine Racks visible. Each Rack has a variety of features and controls contained within. Currently, all of your Racks are closed. To open a Rack, click on its name. For example, in Figure 14.14, you'll see the Routing Rack in its closed and opened conditions.

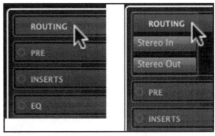

With the Rack open, you can modify the settings within. To close the Rack, click on the Rack name again. Notice that opening any Rack on any channel will open all the Racks on every channel. Now you can learn about the controls found in each Rack.

Figure 14.14. The Routing Rack, closed (left) and open (right).

THE ROUTING RACK

The controls in the Routing Rack are identical to those found in the top Inspector tab in the Project window. The controls will differ depending on the type of track it's associated with. For example, I've added one MIDI and one Instrument track to this project, so now take a look at the routing differences in Figure 14.15.

Clicking on any of the controls will allow you to choose a different setting. The Audio track Routing controls (left side of Figure 14.15) allow you to choose the source input for the track (and its associated channel), along with the output

Figure 14.15. The Routing controls for different track types.

destination. In this case, the input is set to Stereo In and the output is set to Stereo Out, as defined in the VST Connections window.

The MIDI track Routing controls (middle of Figure 14.15) are a bit different. The Routing controls here allow you to choose which MIDI input the track (and its associated channel) is receiving from, which MIDI output the data is being sent to, and on which MIDI channel the data will be transmitted. In this case, the track is receiving from All MIDI Inputs and being sent to the Taurus-3 built-in USB MIDI interface and on MIDI channel 1. (See Chapter 4: "The Ins and Outs of Cubase…Literally.")

The Instrument track Routing controls are different still. Remember that Instrument tracks start as MIDI data, which is then converted to Audio information when the MIDI data is received by a VST (virtual) Instrument inside of Cubase. Therefore, the Routing controls allow you to select a MIDI input and an Audio output. In this case, the track is receiving from All MIDI Inputs and the audio is being sent to the Stereo Output.

THE PRE RACK

Underneath the Routing Rack, you will find the Pre Rack, as shown in Figure 14.16.

The MIDI channel in the middle of Figure 14.16 allows you to add Input Transformers to the Pre Rack, whereas the Audio and Instrument channels will have the following controls from top to bottom. First, there are High-Cut (HC) and Low-Cut (LC) filters that can be adjusted to limit the amount of high or low frequencies allowed through the channel. For example, the Audio channel on the left side of Figure 14.16 has no Pre controls enabled or adjusted, but the Instrument channel on the right shows the small (green) HC control dragged from its default Off position on the right to a setting of 2.17 kHz. (Notice the mouse pointer is hovering over the

Figure 14.16. The Pre Rack for Audio, MIDI, and Instrument tracks (left to right).

HD control to reveal the numeric value and the HC Power button to the left.) The LC control is also set to filter low frequencies, as depicted by the small (green) control, which is adjusted from left to right. Double-clicking on either control will allow you to enter a specific numeric frequency value.

Underneath the HC and LC filters, you'll find the Pre-Gain control (labeled Gain) that can adjust the overall level of the signal coming into the channel. This is another advantage to recording in 32-bit, because you can dramatically increase the signal without clipping the audio engine of Cubase. You can click and drag the Gain control from left (to decrease), to right (to increase), or you can double-click the numeric display and type in the desired increase or decrease. For values below the default of 0.0 dB, you must enter a "-" followed by the integers.

Underneath the Gain, you'll find a phase switch that can be enabled if you need to correct for phase cancellation (two tracks out of phase will cancel each other out), or for Mid-Side miking configurations. When disabled, it will read 0 degrees and be gray; when enabled, it will read 180 degrees and be orange.

THE INSERTS RACK

Under The Pre Rack you'll find the Inserts Rack. This is where you can assign all of your volume-based plug-in effects. There are eight Insert slots, the first six of which are prefader and the last two of which are postfader. Refer to Figure 14.17 to see the Inserts Rack.

Figure 14.17. The Inserts Rack.

Notice that the Audio channel on the left has the AutoPan, DeEsser, and Phaser plug-ins assigned to slots 1, 2, and 3 respectively. To assign a plug-in, click in an empty slot, as has been done on the Instrument channel slot 1. Notice the list of plug-ins on the right, particularly No Effect at the top of the list. Selecting No Effect will unload any plug-in from the selected slot. The rest of the plug-ins are in categories such as Delay, Distortion, and the like. Click a category to reveal the plug-ins contained within, and click the desired plug-in to load it into the slot. You can also type the name of the plug-in in the search window at the top of the list.

When you load a plug-in, its control panel will appear on the screen. Notice the control panel at the far right of Figure 14.17. That's the control panel for the AutoPan plug-in on the Audio channel. If you close the control panel and need to reveal it again, double-click on the corresponding populated Insert slot.

The MIDI channel does have slots for Inserts; these are for MIDI plug-ins only. Because MIDI is not sound, no audio plug-ins will appear in the list.

THE EQ RACK

Under the Inserts Rack you'll find the EQ Rack. Due to the large number of controls, the EQ Rack is much taller than the others you've looked at so far. You may need to use the vertical scroll bar at the far right of the Racks to reveal the settings for all four EQ controls, which are shown in Figure 14.18.

Each EQ is labeled 1, 2, 3, or 4, and typically control the low, low-mid, high-mid, and high frequencies respectively. Notice that the Audio channel on the left has no EQs enabled, while the Instrument channel on the right has all four EQs enabled. Hovering above EQ 4 you will see a Mouse cursor, which will reveal the Power button and the EQ type setting for that particular EQ. Click on the EQ type to select a different setting, such as Low Pass I or Parametric II. (EQs 1 through 4 will each have different EQ types.) Inside of each EQ are three controls. They are (from top to bottom) the Gain, Frequency, and Q-Factor. Clicking and dragging on one of the (green) horizontal controls will adjust the setting. You can also double-click on a control to enter a specific value. This is a great way to make specific EQ edits. However, notice that at the top of Figure 14.18, you can see the Equalizer Curve, which you enabled in the Window Layout settings. This offers a really fun way to edit EQ settings. Click on the Equalizer Curve to reveal the EQ controls and the real-time Spectrum Analyzer window, shown in Figure 14.19.

Figure 14.18. The EQ Rack.

There is a lot of information displayed in the Equalizer Curve window. First, if you've already made some EQ, you can see as many as four numbered points

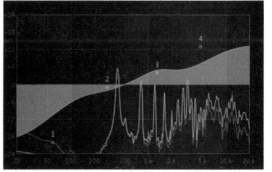

Figure 14.19. The Equalizer Curve with spectrum analyzer.

that represent each of the four EQs. If you don't have any EQs edited, you can click on the center line to create a point, then drag the newly created point to make gain and frequency adjustments. The position of each point from left to right will show the frequency of the associated EQ, while the top to bottom position will show the gain of each EQ. The Equalizer Curve is shown in solid green.

There is a real-time spectrum analyzer in the Equalizer Curve window as well, represented by the waveformlike thread that runs from left to right. This displays the frequency content of the audio that is currently playing through the channel. (For the spectrum analyzer to be visible, playback must be engaged and there must be audio currently passing through the channel.) The spectrum analyzer allows you to adjust the EQ controls while you're looking at the frequency content of the audio. The spectrum analyzer has two threads shown in dark green (the original spectrum) and bright green (the spectrum after the EQ treatment). The Equalizer Curve window also allows you to edit the EQ without opening any additional windows or controls, such as the EQ Rack or Channel Settings window. Click anywhere outside the Equalizer Curve to close the window.

THE STRIP (CHANNEL STRIP) RACK

Under the EQ Rack you'll find the Strip Rack. The Strip is synonymous with the Channel Strip and provides many commonly used effects. While the Strip offers many of the same plug-ins that you could assign to the Inserts, using the Strip effects allows you to keep those six (or eight) precious Insert slots open for additional or third-party plug-ins. Using the Strip effects also allows you to edit the effects without opening any additional control panel windows that tend to clutter your display. That's because all of the Strip effect controls are located right on the MixConsole. Take a look at an empty Strip Rack in Figure 14.20.

MIDI channels will not have any Strip effects. But the Audio (left) and Instrument (right) channels both have Strip effects, including Gate, Comp (Compressor) EQ Position, Trans (Transient), Sat (Saturation), and Limit (Limiter). The only effect that will not have associated controls is the EQ Position. As I mentioned earlier, the EQ can be repositioned in the signal flow. This is accomplished by clicking and dragging the EQ Position above or below the other Strip effects. In other words, there may be times when you want the EQ before the Compressor effects.

Figure 14.20. An empty Strip Rack.

Figure 14.21. The noise gate

Click on a Strip effect to reveal a list of plug-ins. In the case of the Gate, there's only one: Noise Gate, which is shown in Figure 14.21.

The Noise Gate allows quiet signals to be blocked, while louder signals pass through. It's a little like a window that can be set to open only when the wind blows hard enough. The Noise Gate can prevent quiet passages that don't contain any significant audio to be removed from the signal path. Adjust the Threshold control, and watch the three-segment lights underneath to monitor when the Noise Gate is open (green), near the Threshold (amber), or closed (red). Next is the Compressor effect, as shown in Figure 14.22.

Figure 14.22. The Compressor effect (Tube Compressor selected).

There are three compressors to choose from: Standard, Tube, and Vintage, and the controls for each will vary slightly. The controls for the Tube Compressor are shown in Figure 14.22. A compressor will narrow the dynamic range of the audio signal, thereby making quiet passages sound louder, while making loud passages quieter. Adjust the Input control and monitor the Gain Reduction meter as it moves (somewhat antithetically) from right to left. If the gain is reduced by too much, use the Output control to make up for the difference. The Attack and Release control how long it takes for the compressor to "grab" and "let go" of the signal, and the Drive control adjusts how much signal is fed to the virtual tube.

I mentioned the EQ Position earlier, so next in the Strip is the Trans effect. There is only one effect for this particular slot, and it's the EnvelopeShaper, shown in Figure 14.23.

The EnvelopeShaper controls the attack and release of percussive signals, which is perfect to make mushy drums sound more snappy and punchy. It's similar to the ADSR (attack-decay-sustain-release) envelope of a synthesizer, except that it can be applied to any audio signal. Increase the Attack control to add sharpness and punch, or reduce the control to create a more washed-out feel. Increase the Release control to bring out the room ambience, or decrease the control to tighten the sound, especially for drums that were recorded with distant microphone placement.

Figure 14.23. The EnvelopeShaper.

Figure 14.24. The Tape Saturation effect.

The Sat section is next and has two saturation effects: Tape and Tube. Both effects emulate the musically pleasing properties of either magnetic tape or vacuum tubes, and offer identical controls, as shown in Figure 14.24.

Increase the Drive control to feed more signal to the virtual tape or tube. High Drive settings might require a decrease in the Output control to match the original volume. The LF (low frequency) and HF (high frequency) controls offer broad tonal treatments.

The Limit section is last and offers three different effects: Brickwall Limiter, Maximizer, and Standard Limiter. Limiters are basically a very aggressive form of a compressor. For instance, take a look at the Brickwall Limiter, shown in Figure 14.25.

The Threshold control can be adjusted to a maximum permissible volume level. Any signal above that level will be immediately restricted to the Threshold setting, thereby running into the proverbial "brick wall." For instance, if the Threshold were set at -3 dB below zero, any audio exceeding that volume would be reduced to the Threshold setting. The Standard Limiter is a bit more gentle, but is not a true brick wall limiter. Neither is the Maximizer, but it can increase the average loudness of a channel, thereby increasing the perceived loudness of the recorded audio.

Figure 14.25. The Brickwall Limiter effect.

BYPASSING THE RACKS

To the right of every Rack, you will find a small Radio button. This is the Bypass button for each Rack in each channel, as shown in Figure 14.26.

The Bypass buttons have three different states: off (no settings for effects loaded), enabled (all settings and effects enabled), or bypassed (all settings or effects bypassed). Notice the right side of Figure 14.26. This particular channel has no altered settings or effects loaded; therefore, all of the Rack Bypass buttons are off and appear as black Radio buttons. Conversely, the middle channel has settings and effects loaded into all the Racks, which are currently all enabled, and the Radio button is blue. The right channel has all the settings and effects bypassed in all the Racks, and the Radio button is a light yellow. The Rack Bypass button takes an "all or none" approach to all the effects in the Rack: you can click on a Power button of an individual setting or effect to bypass it separately from the others.

Figure 14.26. The Rack Bypass buttons.

GETTING INTO THE MIX

Now that you know about the Cubase MixConsole, its settings and signal flow, and the three actions of mixing, it's time to start applying what you've learned. For the rest of this section, go ahead and load the "The Right Track Matt R07.cpr" project from the disc that came with this book. (See Appendix A: "Using the Included Disc.") The project contains several MIDI, Instrument, and Audio tracks and is in desperate need of mixing. Therefore, get ready to apply the three actions of mixing.

Taking a Listen

This is a fairly simple project with only nine audible tracks, but it will still present you with some challenges. Some will be easier to solve than others. Go ahead and take a listen to the R07 version. You'll notice that you can hear plenty of drums, bass, and tambourine, and the synth pad (Comp Pad), but the vocals are a little buried, and the acoustic guitar (Q-Stick) is only clearly audible when it's being played loudly. You've got some work to do.

CREATING A GROUP CHANNEL TRACK

Notice that there are three drum tracks: Kick, Snare, and Hats. This is because the original drum track (SR Alta Kit) was separated into separate channels using the Dissolve Part command. That makes it really easy to adjust the loudness, direction, and focus of each individual drum sound.

However, it also means that if you find yourself needing to adjust the volume of all the drums equally, you'll have to move three separate Faders rather than one. Plus, if you wanted to apply an Insert plug-in or EQ the entire drum set, you'd have to make identical adjustments to three different tracks. Fortunately, you can make all of those tasks easier by creating a Group Channel track. Click the Project menu, select Add Track, and then select Group Channel. A dialog box will ask you how many Group Channels you'd like and in what configuration. For your purposes, create two stereo Group Channels. (Only on rare occasions would you want to create mono Group Channels.) The Group Channels are added to the bottom of the Track Column and appear at the far right of the MixConsole, as shown in Figure 14.27.

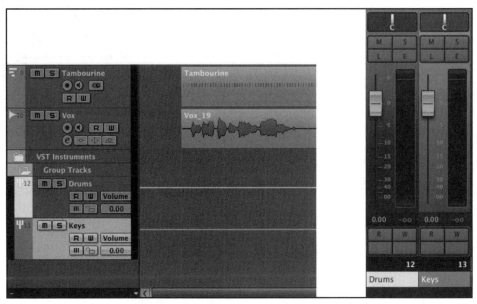

Figure 14.27. Group Channels in the Project window (left) and MixConsole (right), names changed.

You can double-click on the Group Channel name on either the Project window or MixConsole to change the name. Change Group 1 to Drums and Group 2 to Keys. (See Figure 14.27.) Then type and hold the Shift key on your computer keyboard, and click on the first and last of the three Drum channels in the MixConsole, as shown in Figure 14.28.

All three channels on the right are now a light gray, indicating that they've been selected. (Notice that the SR Alta Kit channel on the left is unselected and a darker gray.) Then open the Routing Rack, type and hold the Shift and Alt/Option keys, and click on the audio Output setting of any selected track, as shown in Figure 14.29.

Figure 14.28. Selecting the three Drum channels.

Figure 14.29. Channel Output settings.

Normally a channel's Output Routing is assigned to the Stereo Out by default, meaning that the signal will flow to the Stereo Output channel. (See chapter 16.) But now you can interrupt that signal flow and send the signal from all three Drum channels into the Drums Group channel. Doing so will make it possible to adjust the overall volume of all three tracks, simply by adjusting the Drums Group Channel Fader. (The Channel Faders won't move when you adjust the Group Fader, but the volume will adjust based on the position of the Group Fader.)

You might think that since you created a Keys Group, you can repeat this process for the Comp Pad and Rhodes channels. Don't do this quite yet, because you'll need to discuss how to add Output Channels to VST Instruments in a moment.

Applying the "Big Three" Mixing Actions

Now you're going to really start mixing this project by applying the "Big Three" actions of volume, pan, and EQ. But before you do, I think it's important to stress that mixing has a lot to do with personal taste. There can be tens or even hundreds of different iterations of a mix, and all of them can be good for different reasons. For example, when Prince mixes a song, he usually does several different versions, only one of which makes it to the CD or MP3 release. One producer would mix a song one way, while ten others would mix it ten different ways, and they might all sound wonderful for different reasons. With that in mind, you can use the mix settings I'm about to describe, but don't be afraid to go with what your ears are telling you to do. Everyone's ears are different, but you can still create a mix that meets the expectations of the client, the listener, and you.

ADJUSTING LOUDNESS WITH CHANNEL FADERS
Adjusting volume is done by clicking and dragging the Channel Faders up and down. We already know the drums are a little loud, so I'm going to have you reduce the volume of the Drums group to -5.5. When you do, the Bass channel becomes a little loud, so turn that down to -6.5. Both of those Fader moves have helped the vocals become more present in the mix. However, the Comp Pad and Rhodes channels are too loud. Both of those channels (including the Tambourine channel) are coming from the same VST Instrument (HALion Sonic SE) on separate MIDI channels. Right now, all of the audio coming out of that VST Instrument is being premixed together by HALion Sonic SE (hereby known

as HSSE) and delivered to the MixConsole on the HSSE Main channel. You could adjust the corresponding MIDI Channel Faders, but it would be better if you had the full mixing capabilities of all three HSSE sounds. To do that, you'll need to activate more Output Channels for HSSE.

ACTIVATING MORE VST INSTRUMENT OUTPUT CHANNELS

Every VST Instrument has a different numbers of discrete audio outputs. In the case of HSSE, there are up to sixteen stereo Output Channels. But by default, only one is activated when the plug-in is added to the VST Instruments rack. To activate more Output Channels, you'll need to click the Devices menu and select VST Instruments, or just type F11 on your computer keyboard. The VST Instruments rack and the Output Activate button are shown in Figure 14.30.

Notice the mouse pointer on the left of Figure 14.30. It is pointing at the Active Outputs button for VST Instrument slot 1. When you click it,

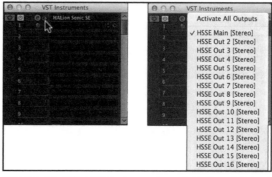

Figure 14.30. VST Instruments rack (left) and Output Activate menu (right).

the Activate Output menu will appear and show you the active and inactive outputs. At the top of the menu, there's an option for Activate All Outputs. You could select that, but the result would be fifteen additional HSSE channels added to the MixConsole. This is why only one stereo pair is activated by default. Otherwise, you could really fill up the MixConsole by adding a lot of outputs. Since you only need three, go ahead and activate HSSE Out 2 (Stereo) and HSSE Out 3 (Stereo). HSSE Main (Stereo) was already activated by default, indicated by the check to the left of the output name. Now when you look at the MixConsole, you will see the newly activated VST Instrument outputs, as shown in Figure 14.31.

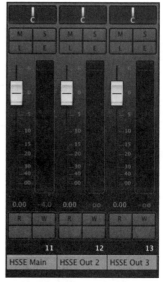

Figure 14.31. Newly activated VST Instruments Output Channels.

Now click the Edit button on the first VST Instruments rack slot (it's the "E" button just to the left of the mouse pointer on the left side of Figure 14.30) to reveal the HSSE control panel, as shown in Figure 14.32. (You can also Alt/Option-click the Edit button on any of the newly created HSSE Output Channels.)

Figure 14.32. HSSE control panel, Mix tab, and output assignments.

On the left side of the control panel, notice that the Comp Syn, Rhodes, and Tambourine sounds are on parts 1, 2, and 3, respectively. Click on the Mix tab at the top center to reveal the Output column at the far right side of the control panel. Set the second part to Out 2 and the third part to Out 3. Then close the HSSE control panel and the VST Instruments rack, and locate the newly activated channels on the mixer. Now is a good time to route all three channels into the Keys Group you created earlier. (See "Creating a Group Channel Track" earlier in this chapter.)

Next, turn the three HSSE channels down to -6.0, -3.5, and -2, respectively. (If you'd like to rename the new channels, double-click on their names and enter the desired text.) Now you should be starting to hear a better mix with more balanced volumes.

ADJUSTING DIRECTION WITH THE PAN CONTROLS

Since you haven't adjusted any Pan controls, the mix will be sounding decidedly monophonic. Certain sounds, such as the drums and keyboard, already have a little stereo direction, because they've been programmed that way. But individual instruments and tracks are hard to pick out in the mix. Therefore, it's time to start adding some direction with Pan.

I want the guitar channel (Q-Stick) to have a strong presence in this mix, but it's getting lost in the center position. So try adjusting the Pan control (see Figure 14.12) to R25. It should suddenly become much easier to hear. Now since you moved the guitar to the right, move the keyboard channels (HSSE Main and HSSE Out 2) to the left at about L50. This will help the channels in the center position (most notably the vocals) be more easily heard. But the tambourine (HSSE Out 3) is also center, so try pushing it to the left at about L75. Even though you've panned the keyboard sound to the left, the tambourine is clearer when it's on the opposite side of the hi-hats of the drum set. Those are usually panned to the right for a right-handed drummer with audience-perspective panning.

ADJUSTING FOCUS WITH EQ

Now that the Vocal channel (Vox) has been made more present by the Fader and Pan adjustments to the other channels, you'll need to craft some EQ to help bring it out of the mix. It's probably loud enough, but it sounds a little boxy and muddy. Click the Edit button on the Vox channel to open the Channel Settings window, as shown in Figure 14.33.

EQ1 and EQ2 are still powered off, as indicated by their Power buttons. Since this vocal recording doesn't have a lot of low or low-mid frequencies, they can remain off, as they are the EQs that normally focus those frequencies. However, EQ3 focuses high-mid frequencies, and some focus here will help immensely. EQ3 has been powered up, which made the small dot with a "3" on the EQ line visible. I dragged that little dot upward until I liked the sound. If you'd rather type in the Gain, Frequency, and Q-Factor settings as they're shown in Figure 14.33, just double-click on each numeric value, and enter 5.2, 2330, and 0.7, respectively.

But after I added that high-mid focus, I felt as though putting a little shine on the high frequencies with EQ4 would help. See Figure 14.32 for the proper placement of the "4" dot, or enter the values using the same procedure as editing EQ3 in the previous paragraph. Afterward, you'll

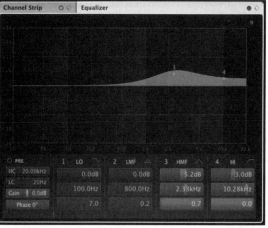

Figure 14.33. Channel Settings window of Vox channel with adjusted EQ focus.

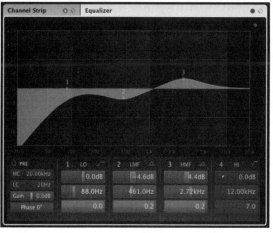

Figure 14.34. Channel Settings window of Q-Stick channel with adjusted EQ focus.

notice the vocals have been made a bit shinier and more noticeable by the high-mid and high EQ focus.

Now listen to the Q-Stick Acoustic Guitar channel. It also sounds a little boxy, but it has a few other characteristics you can improve upon. Click the Q-Stick channel Edit button to reveal the Channel Settings window, as shown in Figure 14.34.

I really wanted to hear more of the pick noise—that is, the sound of the pick as it comes across the strings—and it is found in the high-mid frequencies. Therefore, I edited EQ3 to focus more on those frequencies. But then the low-mids sounded a little throaty, so I used EQ2 to defocus the frequencies around 461.0 Hz. (Notice that the 2 dot has been moved below the EQ line, and the Gain value is a negative value of -4.6.) Lastly, there's some low-frequency thumping caused when the player's arm (my arm) bounced off the guitar body. To reduce that unwanted sound, I set the EQ1 Q-Factor to High Pass 1 and changed the frequency to 88 Hz. That means that any frequencies below 88 Hz will be dramatically reduced. A visualization of that is the steep drop of the left curve past the 1 dot for EQ1. Now when you listen to the guitar in context, you can hear it more clearly with plenty of pick noise. The volume of the guitar (and the vocal) is still somewhat inconsistent, but you can fix that in the next chapter.

MIX ON, D'ARTAGNAN

Now that you've used the "Big Three" mixing actions of loudness, direction, and focus (or volume, pan, and EQ), your project will have a much more improved and balanced mix. If you'd like to listen to the results of this chapter, you can load the "The Right Track Matt R08.cpr" project from the disc that came with this book. (See Appendix A: "Using the Included Disc.") But you still have a ways to go. You still need to add effects in the Inserts and Sends. But which effects and which plug-ins will you use? Proceed to chapter 15 to find out.

Effects: Inserts,
Sends, and
FX Channels

In the early days of audio recording, there were no electronic special effects (also known as effects or FX). If the engineer or producer decided that the recording should include reverb or other time-based or spatial effects, then the instrumentation had to be placed within a suitable acoustic environment during the recording. That way, the sound of the concert hall, recital room, or sound stage would become part of the recording. Later, engineers found ways to simulate acoustic environments by running microphones into separate acoustically suitable rooms and recording the sound of a speaker as it filled the room with the recorded tracks. Then came early reverbs based on plates or springs. Then electronic effects such as digital reverbs added wonderful spatial effects for the studios that could afford them. (Since I couldn't afford the Lexicon 224XL at $7,900, my first digital reverb was the $950 Yamaha SPX90.) Today, Cubase comes with a variety of reverbs, including the fantastic REVerence convolution reverb. (Living in this era has spoiled us rotten.)

But the earliest effects were not special, per se. Rather, dynamic effects such as compressors and limiters helped tame and limit the dynamic range of acoustic instrument recordings. For example, the human voice can go from a whisper to a roar, making it possible for the recording to become either too soft or too loud. Early compressors were based on tubes, transistors, and even optical sensors. Today, the compressors (and the other dynamic processors) that come with DAW software are digital and offer precise control of the dynamics of the recorded tracks. Before proceeding, make sure that you've read chapter 14 to understand the concepts of signal flow, Inserts, and Sends. In this chapter, you will learn:

- The differences between Inserts and Sends.
- How to properly use the signal flow through the Inserts.
- How to use some of the most common effects.
- The concept of the FX Channel track.

THE CONCEPT AND HISTORY OF PLUG-INS

In 1996, Steinberg (the creator of Cubase) designed a plug-in technology called VST, or Virtual Studio Technology. The concept of plug-ins was not new. Other creative software programs (such as the photo-editing program Photoshop from Adobe) had plug-in capabilities. Plug-ins are specialized software programs that plug into and expand upon the capabilities of the host program.

What was new about VST was that it defined a standard upon which anyone (even you) could construct his or her own plug-ins. And since Steinberg provided the VST Software Developers Kit (SDK) for free, no one needed to pay Steinberg to create and market a plug-in. The result was a firestorm of development that continues to this day, and we are all the beneficiaries of a wealth of incredible plug-ins that either come with or can be purchased for use in Cubase.

All of the real-time effects in Cubase are based on plug-ins. That real-time capability is the most profound advantage of VST plug-ins. By tapping into the processing power of your computer's CPU (Central Processing Unit), all of the effects of instrument plug-ins can be applied instantly. This makes them behave just like hardware processors such as rack-mounted compressors and reverbs. Prior to VST plug-ins, those types of effects had to be rendered (processed offline) onto the audio file. That took time and tried the patience of many an artist, engineer, and producer. Plus, if you didn't like the result, you had to undo and render the effect all over again. The advantages of VST plug-ins, both in terms of price and creative freedom, are clear. (Did I mention we're spoiled rotten?)

EFFECT AND PLUG-IN PLACEMENT AND CLASSIFICATION

Studios used to have only a few varieties of effects—usually compressors and delays, perhaps a modulation effect such as a flanger or chorus, and a reverb. Guitarists have always had a plethora of stomp-boxes, including distortion, phaser, and wah-wah effects. But today, there are so many effect plug-ins that come with Cubase that they've been organized into different classifications. For the rest of this chapter, go ahead and load the "The Right Track Matt R08.cpr" project from the disc that came with this book. (See Appendix A: "Using the Included Disc.")

The Differences Between Dry and Wet Signals

I know this sounds like a weather forecast, but when you're using any effect (hardware or software), you have to understand the difference between dry and wet signals. Dry signal is the original unprocessed sound that remains uncolored as it passes through the plug-in. Wet signal is the processed sound after it passes to the output of the plug-in. Some effect classifications require that only wet (processed) signal appear at the plug-in output. But others require a mix of dry (unprocessed) and wet (processed) signals. To that end, you'll notice that some effect control panels include a mix or balance control with which to blend the wet and dry signal. As you will see in a moment, the presence of that mix control has a lot to do with whether the plug-in is used on an Insert or a Send.

Plug-in Effects on Inserts and Sends

There are very few rules in recording that you cannot break. However, determining the proper placement of plug-ins into the signal flow, either on the Inserts or Sends, is paramount for the effect to function properly. Therefore, here are a few guidelines that will help you make the initial determination.

- Plug-ins that alter the volume (such as compressors, limiters, and gates) should go on an Insert.
- Plug-ins that provide spatial effects should be used with a combination of Sends and FX Channel tracks.
- If the control panel of the plug-in has a mix or balance control, it might work best when used with a combination of Sends and FX Channel tracks.
- If the plug-in has a mix control and is being used on a Send, the control must be set to 100 percent wet.

EXAMPLES OF INSERT EFFECTS

For guitarists or any other musicians that use stomp-boxes or guitar pedals, the Inserts are very easy to understand. By referring to Figure 14.17 in the previous chapter, you can see that signal flows from Insert slot 1 (AutoPan) to slot 2 (DeEsser) through slot 3 (Phaser) and all the way through slot 6 if populated with plug-ins. This is identical to stomp-boxes, in that the sound from the first pedal flows into the next, to the next, and so on. An example of this can be seen in Figure 15.1.

All of the stomp-boxes pictured in Figure 15.1 are types of effects you will find in Cubase. Let's see how the effects are listed in Cubase. Click the Edit button on the Q-Stick channel to reveal the Channel Settings window as shown in Figure 15.2, then click the first Insert slot to reveal the plug-in list. (Figure 15.2 is shown with slot 2 selected.)

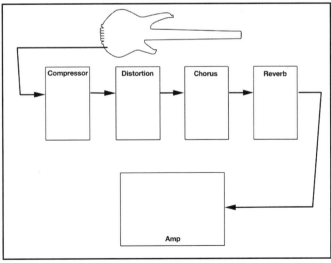

Figure 15.1. Signal flow of guitar stomp-boxes.

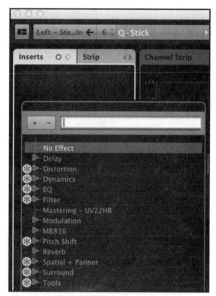

Figure 15.2. Plug-in list.

Figure 15.3. StudioChorus plug-in left and right mix controls.

I've added an asterisk in front of all the effect categories that work best as Inserts. None of the effects in these categories will have a mix control, so any sound present at the input will be processed and sent to the output without any of the dry (original) signal. (You'll notice that the Mastering—UV22HR is not circled. This must be used on an Insert but is a very specialized plug-in that I will discuss in the next chapter.)

MODULATION EFFECTS

In Figure 15.2, you'll notice that Modulation has no asterisk. That's because modulation effects can be used either as Inserts or as Sends. Most of the modulation plug-in control panels will have a mix control like the ones found on the StudioChorus, shown in Figure 15.3.

The presence of a mix control on any plug-in control panel means that it can be used on an Insert or a Send. If used on an Insert, the mix control would be adjusted somewhere between wet and dry. However, if it's being used on a Send, the mix control must be 100 percent wet. That's because the dry signal will come from the track itself, and the wet signal will come through the FX Channel track, which I'll discuss in a moment.

EXAMPLES OF SEND EFFECTS

If you look at the plug-in list in Figure 15.2, you'll see that Delay, Modulation, and Reverb have no asterisks. These plug-ins also have mix controls, which means they will work on Inserts. But delay and reverb effects work best when used as Sends. This is because Sends allow you to share the plug-in processing among several tracks. This provides the advantage of putting multiple tracks through one effect, which makes them sound complementary. You also only need to use one plug-in to process several if not all tracks, which saves on computer processing power. Many new DAW users are under the impression that for every track that needs reverb, they must apply it separately. But by using Sends and FX Channel tracks, all of the tracks can be processed using only one plug-in.

Reverbs, delays, and most modulation plug-ins are time-based effects. In other words, they all have some sort of time control. Modulation effects have times in the milliseconds, where delays and reverbs can offer multiple seconds of time.

ASSIGNING PLUG-INS TO INSERTS

Now that you know what kinds of effects work best on Inserts, you can start to apply some to your song. (Note: While you could use the effects in the Strip Rack, use the Insert slots for all of the plug-ins you'll be using.) Start with the Q-Stick channel. Click that channel's Edit button to reveal the Channel Settings window, then click the Solo button so that you're only hearing that track. Now start playback and listen to the guitar. You'll notice that at the end of measures 4 and 12, there are some very loud sixteenth-note strums. The rest of the track has a pretty balanced dynamic range. So use a dynamic plug-in to tame the loudness of this track.

Assigning a Compressor to the Q-Stick Channel

A compressor is one of the most useful tools for dynamic control, and the Q-Stick channel is a perfect example of a track that needs some compression. It's useful to have playback engaged while making the following settings, so that you can hear the difference as you go. Click on the first Insert slot, select Dynamics (see Figure 15.2), and then select Compressor from the plug-in list. The Compressor plug-in control panel will appear. At the top of the control panel, click the Preset field (see the top of Figure 15.4), which then displays a Preset list. Double-click the Strummed Acoustic Guitar preset from the list. The control panel should now be loaded with the settings shown in Figure 15.4.

Figure 15.4. The Compressor control panel and Preset settings.

Don't be confused by the preset name. I know it sounds like you might be calling up a guitar sound for a VST Instrument. But instead, you're calling up preset values for all of the Compressor controls. If you're still listening to playback, you'll notice that the track doesn't have as wide a dynamic range.

A PRIMER ON COMPRESSORS

What the Compressor is doing is reducing the loudness (as indicated in the GR or Gain Reduction meter) during the loud spots. The Threshold control is set at -19.1 dB, which means that any sound louder than -19.1 dB will be compressed. The Ratio control of 2.18 means that every time the Threshold is exceeded by 2.18 dB, only 1 dB of volume will be added to the signal. So if you exceeded the Threshold by 6.54 dB, only 3 dB of volume would be added.

But if the volume is being reduced, why does the track sound louder? That's because the Make-Up control is set to Auto, which means that the plug-in is monitoring how much gain is being reduced, and increasing the output of the plug-in accordingly to make up for it. If the result was too much gain reduction, you could disable the Auto button and adjust the Make-Up knob manually.

AUDITIONING THE "BEFORE AND AFTER"

Hardware processors have Bypass buttons that allow you to hear the dry versus wet signal for a "before and after" comparison. You can do the same thing using the Power button on the Plug-in control panel (at the upper left-hand corner of Figure 15.4) or by using the Power button on the Insert slot, as shown in Figure 15.5.

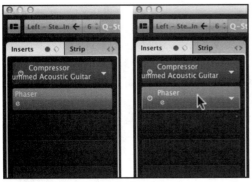

Figure 15.5. Insert slot Power buttons.

To illustrate where the Power buttons are and how they're sometimes not visible, I've added a Phaser plug-in to Insert slot 2. (I won't be using it in this mix.) Notice on the left side of Figure 15.5 that the Compressor Power button is visible, but that slot 1 is darker than slot 2. That's because slot 1 has its Power button off. So when the power of an Insert effect is off, the Power button will always be visible and will not have a lighter (blue) background.

Now look at the Phaser plug-in in slot 2 and notice its lighter (blue) background. That means the plug-in is powered up, but the Power button is nowhere to be found. Now look at the right side of Figure 15.5, and notice the mouse pointer hovering over slot 2. Only when you hover your mouse over a plug-in that's powered up will the Power button be visible. When the Power button is missing and the background is light (blue), you can hear the processing of the plug-in. When the Power button is visible and the background dark, the wet signal is removed, leaving only the dry, unprocessed signal.

RECALLING THE PLUG-IN CONTROL PANEL

Clicking the Edit button (the "e" seen on the Phaser in Figure 15.5) will reveal the control panel. However, sometimes you won't see the Edit button, but all you need to do is double-click the Insert slot of the effect you wish to edit, and the Plug-in control panel will appear. (Note: Before moving on, if you did load an effect into slot 2, remove it by clicking the slot and choosing No Effect from the top of the list.)

Assigning a Compressor to the Vox Channel

Repeat the process of assigning the Compressor, but this time do so on the Vox track and choose the Tube Compressor. (The Tube Compressor is identical to the one found in the Strip; however, the Insert version has the full control panel.) When you listen to the project, the vocals have started overpowering the rest of the tracks. But they're not constantly overpowering, so the Tube Compressor will be very useful. Click on the Preset window of the Tube Compressor plug-in you just added to the Vox channel, and select the AM Male Vocal 2 preset, as shown in Figure 15.6.

Figure 15.6. The Tube Compressor with AM Male Vocal 2 preset (modified).

Make sure the channel isn't soloed, so that you can hear the Compressor in context with the other tracks. You'll notice that the Vox channel has become louder, so I compensated by adjusting the Output control from 3.0 dB to 1.0 dB. Then I set the Input control to 19.9 so that the Compressor has to work a little harder, and I set the Drive control to 4.5 to "heat up" the virtual tube (shown behind the grill in the lower left-hand corner of the control panel.) Lastly I set the Release to 10 so that it "lets go" of the compressed sound when the vocals pause.

Assigning a Chorus to the Bass Channel

Now that you know how to assign plug-ins to an Insert, go ahead and add a chorus effect to the Bass channel. A light amount of chorus can add spatial depth to any instrument, but the effect is more obvious when the track is monophonic to begin with. That's why you're going to use the Bass track for this example. It's not in dire need of an effect, but a little choru s will add a nice finishing touch. Repeat the process outlined in "Assigning a Compressor to the Q-Stick Channel," but this time use the Bass channel, and select Chorus from the Modulation category (see Figure 15.2) in the plug-in list. Then click the Preset window from the Chorus control panel, and select the Flying Bass preset, as shown in Figure 15.7.

The Chorus does not add a profound effect, but rather a very subtle pitch modulation mixed with the original dry signal. The Flying Bass preset adds only a small amount of effect and retains

Figure 15.7. Chorus with the Flying Bass preset.

the low end of the bass guitar. That's because the low filter is set to 495 Hz, which means that the bass frequencies below that point will be unaffected by the Chorus and therefore maintain the rich low end. If you want a more pronounced effect, you could increase either the Rate or Width controls. Since the Chorus plug-in is used on an Insert, the Mix knob is set in the middle at 58 percent, indicating a balance of 42 percent dry and 58 percent wet.

Reordering the Inserts

Now that you have a Chorus in Insert slot 1 of the Bass channel, you might feel the need to add Compressor to the signal flow. However, all compressors should usually come before any spatial effects. Fortunately, Cubase has a very easy way to modify the order of the Inserts. You can do it from any screen that shows all the Insert slots (i.e., Insert slots in the Inspector, Channel Settings window, or MixConsole Inserts Rack). Simply click and drag the plug-in to the desired empty slot, as shown in Figure 15.8.

Figure 15.8. Reordering slot 1 to slot 2.

When you click and drag on the plug-in, it will turn amber, and the other slots will turn green. With your mouse over slot 2, release the mouse button, and the Chorus will now appear in slot 2, leaving you to assign the VintageCompressor into slot 1. (The VintageCompressor is identical to that found in the Strip, but the Insert version has the full control panel.) This time I didn't load a preset. Instead, I pressed the +4 Ratio button, and set the Input to +12 and the Release to 10 ms, as shown in Figure 15.9.

Figure 15.9. The VintageCompressor on the Bass channel, default preset modified.

REORDERING AND COPYING
INSERTS IN THE MIXCONSOLE VIEW

When you are in the MixConsole with the Inserts Rack open, you can click and drag Insert plug-ins to the slots of other like channels. In other words, you can drag MIDI Inserts to other MIDI or Instrument channels, or Audio Inserts to other Audio, Instrument, Group Channel, or Output Channels. This process is shown in Figure 15.10.

Figure 15.10. Dragging and moving an Insert plug-in to a different channel.

The colors (green and amber) of empty and the slot currently being dragged is identical to that of reordering Inserts in the Channel Settings or Inspector. If you'd rather duplicate the plug-in and its settings to another channel, repeat the process while holding the Alt/ Option key on your computer keyboard at any time during the drag and prior to releasing the mouse button. You'll notice a small "+" sign under the mouse that indicates that you are making a copy. When you release the mouse button, the plug-in will be present on both channels, as shown in Figure 15.11.

Figure 15.11. Dragging and duplicating an Insert plug-in to another channel.

Now both channels will have their own discrete Chorus effects with identical settings. Altering the settings of one copied plug-in will have no effect on the plug-in from which it was copied. Personally, I didn't like the Chorus on the Q-Stick channel, because it made the guitar sound too processed and unnatural. So I clicked on the right side of the Chorus slot and chose No Effect to remove the plug-in.

USING SENDS AND FX CHANNEL TRACKS

As I've previously mentioned, time-based effects such as reverb and delay work best when assigned to Sends and FX Channel tracks. This allows several channels to share one plug-in, and also saves on computer processing power. For this example, you're going to add a reverb and delay effect to your project by adding FX Channel tracks. Then you'll be able to use the Sends to add those effects across multiple channels. (Note: I'm going to show you the long way first so that you see the entire process, and then I'll show you a short cut.)

Creating an FX Channel Track

FX Channel tracks are added to the Project and MixConsole windows. They are similar to Audio, Instrument, and Group Channel tracks, because they process audio signals. However, FX Channel tracks do not carry the signals of tracks or files. Instead, they are specialized tracks that return the signals from plug-ins back into the signal flow of the MixConsole. Click the Project menu, select Add Track, and select FX Channel. The Add FX Channel Track dialog box will appear, as shown in Figure 15.12.

Figure 15.12. The Add FX Channel Track dialog box.

The default configuration is Stereo. Only under rare circumstances would you ever use a mono configuration for an FX Channel track. Now click on the effect drop-down box, select the Reverb category, and select REVerence. When you click the Add Track button on the lower right of the dialog box, the REVerence control panel will appear, as shown in Figure 15.13.

Figure 15.13. The REVerence control panel.

Click the Preset field, and choose the Music Academy preset. This is a very gentle reverb without a lot of decay, so it will work well on your mid-tempo project. Notice also that the default mix is set to 100 percent. This setting is critical when using any effect on an FX Channel track. For now, close the REVerence control panel, and take a look at both the Project window and MixConsole. You'll notice that FX Channels have been added to the Track Column and MixConsole respectively, as shown in Figure 15.14.

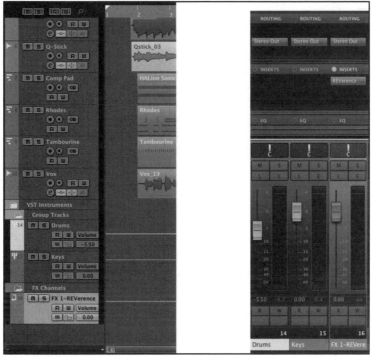

Figure 15.14. FX Channel track in the Track Column and MixConsole.

Notice that in the MixConsole view with Inserts showing, the REVerence reverb plug-in you just added is on Insert slot 1. The FX Channel itself looks very similar to any other channel. It even has the same Racks as the other Audio channels. But instead of routing tracks to the channel, its sole purpose is to route the output of the inserted plug-in into the MixConsole. But how do you get signal into the REVerence? You do that with the Sends of other Audio channels.

Assigning Sends to FX Channel Tracks

Start by assigning the REVerence Reverb you just made to the Vox (vocal) channel. You can do this by selecting the Vox track in the Track Column, the Channel Settings window, or the MixConsole Sends Rack. I prefer to use the latter method, because this allows me to see all of the Sends on all of the tracks simultaneously. To do this, click on the Sends Rack of the Vox channel, and in the same fashion you would with an Insert plug-in, click on Send slot 1, choose FX 1-REVerence, enable the Send Power button, and adjust the Send Fader. This step-by-step procedure is shown in Figure 15.15; pay special attention to the mouse pointer.

Figure 15.15. The channel Send assignment procedure.

The Send Fader is a small, blue line that moves from left to right. By default, the Fader is turned all the way down at the far left of the slot. Click and drag the Fader to the right to send some signal from the Vox channel into the REVerence FX Channel track. The further you drag the Fader to the right, the more reverb you will hear on the vocals. If you need finer control, you can adjust the Fader either in the Sends tab of the Inspector or the Channel Settings window Sends. Those methods have larger Send Faders as well as the numeric readout. The adjustment of the Fader is really a "season to taste" setting. I found that on this particular vocal track, a setting of -8 dB sounds about right.

If you'd like to customize any of the settings on the control panel assigned to a Send, simply double-click on the Send (much like you would an Insert plug-in), or you can also double-click the Insert slot of the associated FX Channel. (See the right side of Figure 15.14.)

ASSIGNING AND ADJUSTING SENDS ON SOLOED TRACKS

I make the following confusing mistake on a regular basis and want you to be aware of it. I sometimes have the Solo button enabled on the channel on which I want to use a Send before going through the procedure in Figure 15.15. But when I start adjusting the Send Fader, I don't hear any effect being added to the signal. That's because the channel was soloed prior to turning on the Send Power button, which results in the muting of all other channels, including the FX Channel. If this happens to you, just disable and reenable the Solo button on the channel upon which you're adjusting the Send. Now that the power is enabled on the Send, the FX Channel track will also have its Solo enabled, which allows you to listen to the effect of the plug-in while you're adjusting the Send Fader.

Assigning Other Channels to the FX Channel Track

Now you can repeat the procedure outlined in Figure 15.15 for any Instrument or Audio channel. To that end, I'm going to add a little of the REVerence reverb to the Kick, Snare, and Q-Stick channels, as shown in Figure 15.16.

You can see the advantages of doing this from the MixConsole, because you can assign and adjust the Sends and Faders across multiple channels. Notice that the Kick and Snare channels have lower Send Faders, while the Q-Stick channel has more. All of this is a "season to taste" setting decided upon by you and/or the client.

Creating Another FX Channel Track and Plug-in

Cubase is very flexible in its use of Sends and FX Channel tracks. You can create as many FX Channel tracks as you need, and you can assign any eight of those tracks to the eight sends of any channel. In

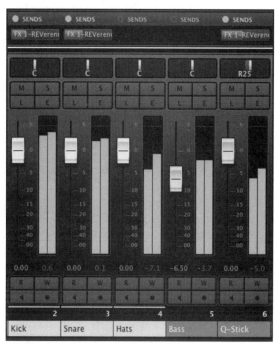

Figure 15.16. Multiple channels assigned to the FX 1-REVerence FX Channel track.

a little while, I'll have you explore this concept by creating a delay effect on another FX Channel track, but now I'm going to show you a shortcut. Open the MixConsole and click on the Vox channel number (10) below the Fader, then right/Ctrl-click the Fader knob and choose Add FX Channel to "Vox" from the menu. This will save you the step of going to the Sends Rack and assigning the effect to the channel. When you see the Add FX Channel Track dialog box, choose the Delay category and the StereoDelay effect. Then choose the Alternating preset, and modify the settings as shown in Figure 15.17.

Figure 15.17. Modified settings for the Alternating preset, StereoDelay plug-in.

Set the left and right Delay times to 1/8 and 1/4, respectively. Notice that the Sync buttons are enabled on the StereoDelay control panel. That will match the Delay settings to the tempo of the Cubase Project. Then turn the left Pan control to -100 (full left) and the right Pan control to 100 (full right). Notice that the Mix controls are both set to 100 percent wet, as is necessary with plug-ins on FX Channel tracks.

Now as you increase the Send 2 Fader, you will hear some stereo delay (repeats bouncing from left to right) added to the vocals. I used a very low setting of -16 dB. Too high a setting and it will sound as though you're mixing at the Grand Canyon. (Not that this would be a bad thing, as the scenery might inspire you.)

Figure 15.18. The MixConsole Functions menu.

STARTING ALL OVER AGAIN

Sometimes you'll get into a mix and feel like a fresh start might be in order. If you've used my method of adding revisions as you go, this task is easier. However, you can also just reset the MixConsole. This is especially useful if you're going to perform a Channel Batch Export without adding effects, EQs, and so forth. In the upper right-hand corner of the MixConsole, you'll see the Functions Menu button indicated by a black triangle, as shown in Figure 15.18.

Selecting Reset MixConsoles will present you with a dialog box that will ask if you want to Reset Selected channels or Reset All channels; the former would require you to have selected at least one channel prior to selecting this command. The result will be that selected or all channels will have the Rack effects and settings removed, and all the Pan and Fader controls will be set to their default positions.

TAKING A MOMENT TO LOOK (LISTEN) BACK

If you want to hear my version of the mix, you can load "The Right Track Matt R09.cpr" project from the disc that came with this book. (See Appendix A: "Using the Included Disc.") But you should also load and listen to the project in its remixed state by loading "The Right Track Matt R07.cpr" project. This version had no mixing, EQ, or effects added. When you compare the R07 version to the R09 version, the difference is very noticeable. R07 sounds pretty flat and lifeless, while R09 sounds more open, balanced, and polished. When a project gets to point where you're happy with the mix, it's time to master it and share it with the world, which you'll do in the next chapter.

Mastering and Audio Mixdown

Now that your project is sounding properly mixed, it's time to share it with the world by performing an Audio Mixdown. That process will create a stereo audio file, herein referred to as a "mixdown," and usually in WAV (Microsoft Wave Format), AIFF (Audio Interleaved File Format), or MP3 (MPEG-1 Layer 3) format. Once your Cubase Project has been exported, you can burn it to audio CD; publish it to your website, SoundCloud, or Facebook page; or make it available for purchase on iTunes, cdbaby.com, or any of a number of sites for distributing independent music. But Cubase has not only great mixing capabilities but also some really cool tools for audio mastering. I'm going to show you how to avail your projects of the mastering tools Cubase provides. In this chapter, I'm going to describe mastering in detail, but I'll also be discussing:

- The goals of mastering.
- My three-adjective approach to mastering.
- The Loudness War.
- Statistical analysis of various CD audio file examples.
- Audio Mixdown of multiple audio file formats.

THE DARK ART OF MASTERING

Have you ever looked at the album credits and seen "Mastering by Bob Clearmountain" or "Mastering by Bob Ludwig"? Ever wonder what "mastering" is? The good news is that your name doesn't need to be Bob before you can master a mix, and that Cubase comes with great mastering tools. But that doesn't answer the question of what mastering is.

The Definition of Mastering

Because mastering is something of an ambiguous dark art, it has no easy definition. However, I've narrowed the long list down to the three basic goals of mastering:

1. Your last chance to add broad treatments to your mix.
2. Matching your mix to other commercial recordings in the same genre.
3. Matching all of your mixes prior to distribution as a collection.

Now I'll explore what each of these goals mean in an audio context.

BROAD TREATMENTS

By now you should be really happy with the sound of each track within the project. However, when you listen to the mix of all those tracks, you will invariably determine that some overall improvements could be made. Are the overall bass frequencies of a project overbearing, or are they lacking? Is the overall volume of the project too low or too high? Does the mix of the project sound tinny or boxy, or does it lack definition? These are all questions that engineers are constantly analyzing during the mastering process.

But you'll notice that the questions are being asked of the project, not the individual tracks. This is a very important aspect of mastering. In other words, you may have applied individual EQ to the bass guitar and the bass drum to make each track sound tonally balanced. But now, how do those tracks sound when played together in the mix? The bottom line about this goal of mastering is that you're listening to the project as a whole rather than track by track. After listening to and analyzing the sound of the project, the mastering treatments you determine it needs are applied broadly to the entire mix.

MATCHING TO OTHER MIXES OF THE SAME GENRE

In the world of rap and hip-hop, it's totally appropriate to lay in copious amounts of thunderous bass frequencies. However, it would probably be a mistake to apply the same mastering treatment to country or jazz projects. Similarly, jazz and orchestral projects have a much wider range of dynamics than heavy metal or punk projects. But who determines the appropriateness of any mastering treatment? Well, the artists, bands, producers, and mastering engineers certainly have a lot to do with it. But ultimately, it's the end-listener that has the final say. Basically, if you were mastering a project of a specific genre, it would behoove you to listen to a lot of commercial releases of music in the same genre.

MASTERING YOUR MIXES AS A COLLECTION

If you produce nothing but singles, then you needn't worry about this aspect of mastering. But if you combine your own music or that of a client into a collection (CD, LP, Digipak, etc.), then making all the songs within that collection sound evenly balanced is critical. For example, the overall volumes of all the projects should be about the same. If they're not, the end-listener will be reaching for his or her volume control at the start of every song.

Or if one song sounds much brighter (contains more high frequencies) than the others, the experience of listening to the album in its entirety would be disrupted. For example, if you were listening to Pink Floyd's Dark Side of the Moon and the song "Money" were noticeably quieter and contained more high frequencies than the rest of the songs, you'd certainly notice the difference. Essentially, if the song doesn't sound like the others on the record, you or the end-listener might just skip listening to the song. (Even though "Money," like the other songs, is expertly mixed and mastered, I usually skip it.) That's why all the songs in a collection need to have similar tonalities and volume levels. Without that cohesion, the album will come across as a haphazardly slapped-together bunch of songs (like a "greatest hits" album of several bands) rather than a methodical approach that injects the signature sound of the band or artist on every song. Addressing the overall listening experience of the artist and end-listener alike is the most mature approach to mastering.

What to Expect from This Section

The finite size of this book will limit your ability to master a collection of songs. Therefore, I'm going to concentrate on the first two mastering goals: broad treatments and genre matching.

Matt's Three-Adjective Approach to Mastering

I've mastered hundreds of songs for different clients. One of the first things I ask a client is, "How do you want the song (album, record, etc.) to sound?" Only on the rarest of occasions do I get answers like "Tame the high frequencies between 2.2 kHz and 6.6 kHz, and make the average volume -10 dB below zero." Instead, they usually provide a list of general adjectives, such as "Just make it punchy, shiny, and LOUD!" With those adjectives in mind, let's talk about the Cubase plug-ins that will produce what the client wants to hear.

PUNCHY EQUALS COMPRESSION

As you learned in the previous chapter, compression can decrease the dynamic range of an audio signal, thereby smoothing the loudness by minimizing the difference between loud and quiet passages. A fringe benefit of compression is that it can make the audio sound punchier. Cubase has a fantastic plug-in called the MultibandCompressor that applies different amounts of compression to different frequency bands.

SHINY EQUALS EQ

EQ, or tonal control, is a critical component of mastering. So when a client says "shiny," it usually means adding some high-mid or high frequencies, but it can refer to the overall tonal clarity as well. Cubase comes with several different EQ plug-ins, or you can use the built-in 4-band EQ I've used on the Audio and Instrument tracks. As you'll see in a moment, the Output Channel Fader has its own EQ, or you can choose a different EQ plug-in.

LOUD EQUALS LIMITING

A limiter is similar to a compressor, except that it provides a ceiling past which the peak volumes will not exceed. This allows the average volume, known as the perceived loudness, to be increased. The result is a much narrower dynamic range and a louder-sounding master. Cubase has a very capable mastering limiter called the Maximizer.

Contemporary Mastering and the Loudness War

The "loud" adjective in the mastering equation is the subject of much debate. Over the past few decades, the availability and use (or overuse) of software-based mastering limiters have succeeded in completely removing the dynamics from popular music. The phenomenon has become so pervasive that it's been added to the English lexicon. It's known as the Loudness War. To illustrate this phenomenon, I'm going to load some CD tracks into Cubase and analyze their average or perceived loudness. You can do the same thing by importing an audio CD track into Cubase by clicking the File menu, selecting Import, and then selecting Audio CD. After the track is imported, you can click on the Audio event, and select Statistics from the Audio menu.

(Note: Copyright, not to mention karma, prevents me from including any of the source material on the disc that comes with this book. You'll have to use music from your library for your own analyses.)

COMPARING THE EVOLUTION OF LOUDNESS

In Figure 16.1, I've imported four CD tracks from different musical eras. Take a look at the differences in volume as depicted by their event waveform displays.

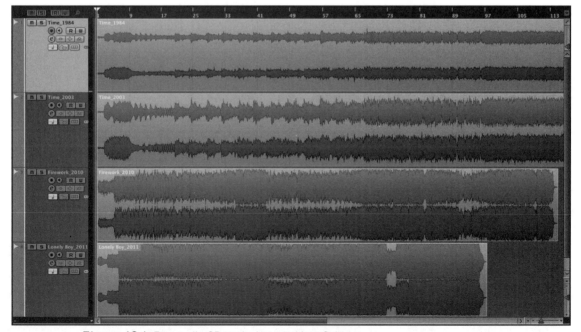

Figure 16.1. Four audio CD tracks imported into Cubase.

The top two tracks are different masters of Pink Floyd's "Time" from Dark Side of the Moon. The top track is from the original 1984 CD release and is virtually identical to the original LP release from 1973. The next track is the same song, but comes from the 2003 thirtieth-anniversary remaster. They certainly look different, don't they? Track 3 has the 2010 release of Katy Perry's "Firework," and track 4 is the Black Keys' "Lonely Boy" from 2011. Do you see how the volume has increased over the decades? But to what degree? To find out, I'm going to select the "Time_1984" event and choose Statistics from the Audio menu. The results are in Figure 16.2.

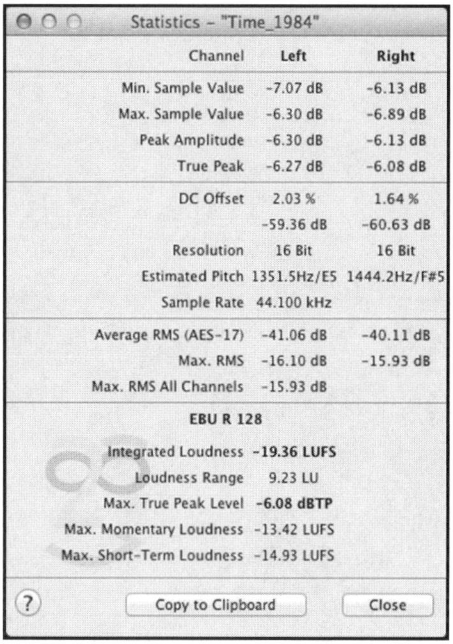

Cubase supports the EBU R 128 (European Broadcast Union Recommendation R 128) standard for measuring loudness. Instead of measuring in decibels, EBU R 128 uses LUFS (Loudness Unit Full Scale) to depict the perceived loudness of audio. Cubase can analyze the loudness of a piece of audio and display the integrated loudness in LUFS. Like decibels, LUFS values are always depicted in negative numbers, with 0 being the absolute loudest possible measurement.

At the bottom of Figure 16.2, you will find the EBU R 128 section. Notice that the integrated loudness is -19.36 LUFS, which means that there's just under 20 LUFS of total dynamic range. LUFS values take into account all of the left and right sides of a stereo audio file to produce one value, rather than the dB values in the top half of the Statistics window that shows separate values for the left and right channels.

When "Time" was remastered in 2003, the integrated loudness increased. Figure 16.3 shows the statistics from the "Time_2003" event.

Now the integrated loudness has jumped from -19.36 to -12.58 LUFS, an increase in perceived loudness of almost 7 LUFS and a reduction of over one third of the dynamic range. It's the same song but with different mastering outcomes, particularly in integrated loudness. Now take a look at Figure 16.4, which shows the statistics for "Firework."

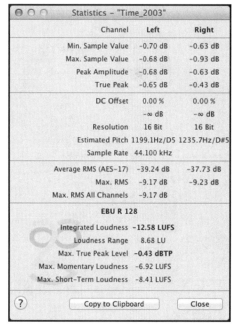

Figure 16.2. Statistical analysis of "Time" from 1984.

Figure 16.3. Statistical analysis of "Time" from 2003.

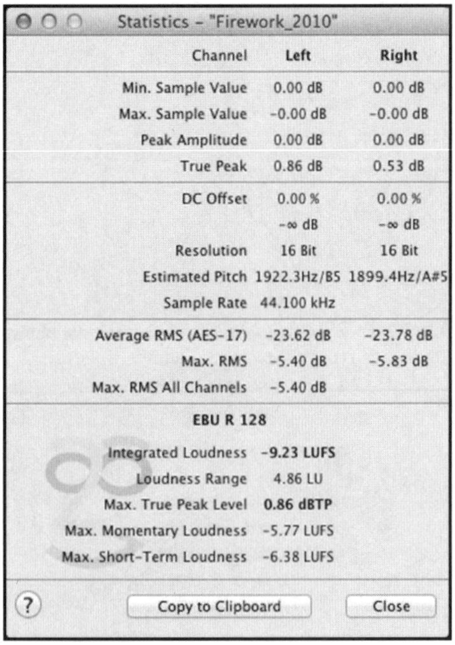

Statistics - "Firework_2010"

Channel	Left	Right
Min. Sample Value	0.00 dB	0.00 dB
Max. Sample Value	-0.00 dB	-0.00 dB
Peak Amplitude	0.00 dB	0.00 dB
True Peak	0.86 dB	0.53 dB
DC Offset	0.00 %	0.00 %
	-∞ dB	-∞ dB
Resolution	16 Bit	16 Bit
Estimated Pitch	1922.3Hz/B5	1899.4Hz/A#5
Sample Rate	44.100 kHz	
Average RMS (AES-17)	-23.62 dB	-23.78 dB
Max. RMS	-5.40 dB	-5.83 dB
Max. RMS All Channels	-5.40 dB	
EBU R 128		
Integrated Loudness	-9.23 LUFS	
Loudness Range	4.86 LU	
Max. True Peak Level	0.86 dBTP	
Max. Momentary Loudness	-5.77 LUFS	
Max. Short-Term Loudness	-6.38 LUFS	

Figure 16.4. Statistical analysis of "Firework" from 2010.

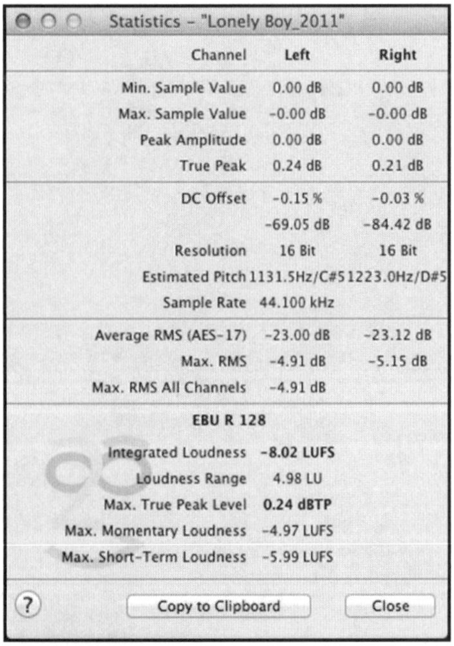

Statistics - "Lonely Boy_2011"

Channel	Left	Right
Min. Sample Value	0.00 dB	0.00 dB
Max. Sample Value	-0.00 dB	-0.00 dB
Peak Amplitude	0.00 dB	0.00 dB
True Peak	0.24 dB	0.21 dB
DC Offset	-0.15 %	-0.03 %
	-69.05 dB	-84.42 dB
Resolution	16 Bit	16 Bit
Estimated Pitch	1131.5Hz/C#5	1223.0Hz/D#5
Sample Rate	44.100 kHz	
Average RMS (AES-17)	-23.00 dB	-23.12 dB
Max. RMS	-4.91 dB	-5.15 dB
Max. RMS All Channels	-4.91 dB	
EBU R 128		
Integrated Loudness	-8.02 LUFS	
Loudness Range	4.98 LU	
Max. True Peak Level	0.24 dBTP	
Max. Momentary Loudness	-4.97 LUFS	
Max. Short-Term Loudness	-5.99 LUFS	

Figure 16.5. Statistical analysis of "Lonely Boy" from 2011.

The integrated loudness jumps up to -9.23 LUFS, which means "Firework," like many popular songs of today, doesn't have a wide dynamic range. Finally, look at Figure 16.5, which shows the statistics for "Lonely Boy."

"Lonely Boy" was the No. 1 song on the Billboard Rock Song chart. It's a great song by a great band. But as you can see, the average is up to -8.02 LUFS. Suffice it to say that the integrated loudness of pop music has been increasing year by year.

Daring to Be Different

I like a lot of different genres of music. I especially enjoy going to live performances of symphony orchestras, particularly if they're performing Mahler, Bach, Orff, or Holst. But no matter what is on the program, I'm sure to experience a wide dynamic range, from triple pianissimo to triple forte.

Well, it appears that contemporary pop music is all triple forte. That doesn't leave much room for the dynamics to be as useful as the melody, lyrics, chord progression, or beat. But humans actually do enjoy wide dynamic range. If we didn't, we wouldn't go to firework shows. Can you imagine how boring it would be to have the explosions be roughly the same volume as the background noise of cars and conversation?

With that in mind, I'm going to dare you to be different when mastering your music or that of your clients. Figure 16.3 shows an integrated loudness of -12.58 LUFS. That's about the average level I try to achieve when mastering music for my own personal enjoyment. However, I usually master another version that gets closer to -11 or even -9 LUFS. This is because my song may end up played on the radio or on someone's MP3 player with a bunch of other music, and I don't want listeners to be constantly adjusting their volume control. Of course, if clients request that their music approach the average volume of -9 LUFS or even higher, I will do as they ask. But if I really like their music, I may make some private mixes with a wider dynamic range for myself.

Now consider this: Throughout history, every audio device has had a volume control incorporated into the design. That volume control is what the end-listener uses to set the desired listening volume. Recognizing that fact throws the idea of the Loudness War into irrelevance. It may take some time, but I hope that, in the future, the listening public will demand a wider dynamic range. Since car stereos, home entertainment systems, and MP3 players all have their own volume controls with which to control the volume level, maybe we should trust the end-listeners to have the loudness their way.

Note: Different audio software programs (such as Cubase and WaveLab) will analyze and report the average volumes in different ways and using different loudness scales. Therefore, when making your own analyses, always use the same program and don't mix results with those from a different program.

THE MARCH TOWARD THE OUTPUT CHANNEL FADER

For the rest of this chapter, you could certainly apply mastering processes to your own Cubase Project. However, if you'd like to follow along with me, make sure you load "The Right Track Matt R09.cpr" project from the disc that came with this book. (See Appendix A: "Using the Included Disc.") Since you've used that project throughout this book, you may have noticed that the signal flows through the mixer from left to right. In other words, Audio and Instrument channels come first, followed by Group channels, and finally FX Channel tracks. An example of this can be seen in Figure 16.6.

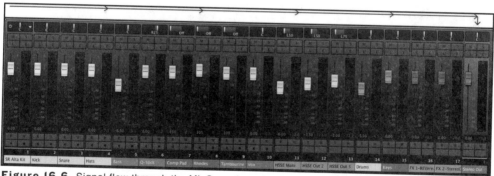

Figure 16.6. Signal flow through the MixConsole to the Output Channel Fader.

The concept is that every audio-generating channel in the MixConsole will eventually be routed to the Output Channel Fader. And whatever you are monitoring from the Output Channel Fader is what will eventually be delivered to the ears of the end-listener.

Examining the Output Channel Fader

Output Channels (and Input Channels) are color-coded red, which makes them easier to find in the MixConsole. The Output Channel is the right-most channel. This requires you to scroll across the MixConsole to locate it. I prefer to enable the right Zone button (see chapter 14, Figure 14.8) in the Channel Selector so that the Output Channel is always visible, regardless of how many tracks and channels the MixConsole has.

A closer look at the Output Channel in the MixConsole will reveal how similar it is to an Audio, Instrument, Group, or FX channel. However, there is one item that is better illustrated by clicking the Output Channel Edit button to open the Channel Settings window, as shown in Figure 16.7.

Figure 16.7. Channel Settings window of the Output Channel.

Notice that there are Sends on the right-hand side of the window. Be aware that you cannot assign any Sends here, because the Output Channel Fader is the final destination for every Output Channel, including FX Channels used with Sends. However, many of the other controls with which you're already familiar are present. The Inserts are where you'll apply certain mastering plug-ins, the EQ is what you'll use to craft the overall tonality of the project, and since Inserts 7 and 8 come after the Output Channel, that's where you'll install a mastering limiter and a dithering plug-in. (More on dithering later.)

Adjusting the Output Channel Fader Level

The Output Channel Fader also controls the volume of the mixdown. If it's set too low, the mixdown will be quieter than it should be. However, if it's set too high, the Output Channel, and therefore the mixdown, can become clipped. Whether you're mixing to audio file, audio CD, or MP3, clipping will compromise, if not ruin, your mixdown. Cubase has several facilities with which to monitor and adjust the Output Channel Fader for the loudest clipping-free mixdown level.

PEAK METER VALUE

There are two numeric values that appear at the bottom of the Output Channel. The value at the bottom with a larger font is the Channel Level that shows the position of the Output Channel Fader. But above the Channel Level is the Peak Meter value in a slightly smaller font. Both of these values are shown in Figure 16.8.

The Peak Meter value is constantly monitoring the peak output level of your Cubase Project. The value depicts the loudest peak that was encountered during playback. Figure 16.8 shows the peak value of the R09 version of your project. That value is 2.0 dB above zero. Zero, as you probably already know, is the maximum output level. Therefore, any value above zero indicates clipping. Similarly, a negative value might indicate that the Output Channel Fader is set too low. For example, a value of -1.0 would indicate an appropriate Output Channel Fader setting, but -10.0 would result in a very quiet mixdown. The best way to use the Peak Meter value is to click it to reset it to -∞ (infinity, or absolute silence). Then start playback from the beginning of the project and continue through to the end of

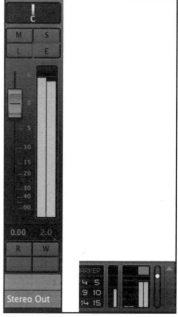

Figure 16.8. Output Channel and Transport Panel peak lights and controls.

the project. The Peak Meter value displays the loudest volume encountered during project playback. Whether the value is positive or negative will determine the appropriate action. (More on that in a moment.)

CLIP INDICATORS

Clipping results in audible distortion and occurs when the maximum output level is pushed beyond the maximum limit of 0 dB. Recording in 32-bit floating point gives your Cubase Project an astronomically wide internal dynamic range, and also makes it impossible to clip the signal flow within Cubase. That is, until the signal reaches the Output Channel Fader; when it clips, your mixdown will also be clipped.

Cubase has a clipping indicator that is shown in two different locations: the bottom of the Output Channel and the right side of the Transport Panel. (See Figure 16.8.) When the Peak Meter value has exceeded 0 dB, the clip indicators glow red. You can reset the clip indicators by clicking on them, which will also reset the Peak Meter value to -∞ dB. If you've followed the procedure of determining the maximum Peak Meter value and the clip indicator has turned red, it means you need to make an Output Channel Fader adjustment.

ADJUSTING THE OUTPUT CHANNEL FADER
FOR OPTIMAL AUDIO MIXDOWN LEVEL

There are two different ways to adjust the output level of the Output Channel Fader. The first one is easy: just move the Fader up or down, or type the desired value into the Channel Level. (See Figure 16.8.) But I prefer using the Gain (also known as the Pre-gain) control in the Pre Rack, either on the MixConsole or in the Channel Settings window. (See lower left-hand corner of Figure 16.7.) You can do so by adjusting the Gain slider (EQ tab) or Pre-Gain knob (Control Strip tab), or you can double-click the control and type in the desired value. I prefer this method because of the mastering process you're about to undertake. By adjusting the Gain, you're also optimizing the signal level as it passes through the Insert slots, and that's where most of the mastering plug-ins will be installed. Therefore, prior to mastering, I'll set the Output Channel Fader to its default 0.00 dB position and then play the project from start to finish. When the Peak Meter Value has been determined, I enter the opposite of that value into the Gain value. In other words, if the Peak Meter value is 2.0 (a positive value), I'll enter -2.1 or -2.2 (negative values) into the Gain value. That way, I'll have a few tenths of a decibel (undetectable by the human ear) for a safety margin.

THE IMPORTANCE OF SETTING THE OUTPUT
CHANNEL FADER PRIOR TO MASTERING

You may have asked yourself why you needed to set the Output Channel Fader before you started applying mastering plug-ins. The first reason is to set an optimal signal flow through the Insert slots, Strip, and EQ Racks, and then to the Output Channel Fader. But the main reason is that if someone else is going to be doing your mastering (or if you plan to do the mastering in a different program, such as WaveLab), you'll want a premastered mixdown in WAV or AIFF format. That mixdown should be void of any effects on the Output Channel Fader and should also be set to the optimal output level. I'll explore this more when I discuss exporting mixdowns later in this chapter.

APPLYING THE MASTERING PLUG-INS

Now that you've optimized your Output Channel Fader output level, it's time to experiment with some mastering plug-ins and associated settings. It's critical during the mastering process to be constantly listening to the playback. Unlike some other programs, Cubase allows you to assign plug-ins during playback, but you will notice a slight audio dropout. That shouldn't concern you, as it is normal, and it sure beats having to repeatedly hit Stop and Play. For the following example, you're going to use my "punchy, shiny, and LOUD" method for mastering. That will mean using the Output Channel section for the application of the MultibandCompressor, EQ, and Maximizer.

Keeping Your Ears Honest

Before proceeding, you should know a few important rules that will help you achieve great mastering results no matter what the end-listener is using for playback. First and foremost, do not allow your monitor speaker volume to exceed an average output level of 85 dB. We all like to hear the music nice and loud. However, levels above 85 dB, even for a short amount of time, will color the way our ears hear the music. But levels below 85 dB will not allow us to hear enough audio detail. Do yourself a favor and get an SPL (Sound Pressure Level) meter to determine your monitor speaker volume. Or if you have an iPod touch, iPhone, or iPad, go to the App Store and check out the Audio Tool from Performance Audio. It's only a few bucks, looks really cool, and among its other tools, it has a great SPL meter called Decibel Meter Pro 2.

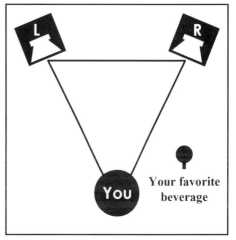

Figure 16.9. Overhead view of proper speaker/head arrangement.

And speaking of speakers, you'll also need a good pair of studio monitors. The prices for these specialized speakers have come down considerably, making them affordable as well as indispensable. Don't try to use headphones, the speakers that came with your computer, or any consumer-grade speakers such as those of a home stereo system. They don't sound very accurate and will lie to your ears. Also make sure the speakers are placed at ear level (not above or below your eye line) and arranged in an equilateral triangle, as shown in Figure 16.9.

Finally, grab some commercially released music from bands and/or genres that match the music you're mastering. In other words, if you're mastering a country project, grab some Brad Paisley or Shania Twain CDs. Basically, grab the best-sounding CDs from a like genre and keep them handy for comparison. That way you can compare the mastering of a popular band or artist to your own.

A WORD ABOUT HEADPHONES

When you try to mix or master using headphones, you'll lose one of the most important aspects of stereo sound: proper phase alignment. Because headphones place the speakers so close to your eardrum, they don't allow you to discern how the sound travels through the air to both ears, making it impossible to hear phase problems. Therefore, you should not use headphones as your only speakers during the mixing or mastering processes.

However, as I mentioned in chapter 2, I will make one exception: "i" device earbuds. I'm talking about the white earbuds that come with every Apple iPod and iPhone. If you're like me, you listened to them and upgraded to a better pair, or you were already aware of how unspectacular they sound and never unwrapped them. If you still have them, they might serve a useful purpose here. At the end of a mastering session and before I perform the mixdown, I'll listen to how it sounds on the earbuds. That's because many end-listeners out there still use their original earbuds. This allows me to hear how the mastered mixdown will sound to the joggers, dog-walkers, and pedestrians I see with their ubiquitous white cables dangling from their ears. The theory is: if you can make a master sound nicely balanced on studio monitors as well as earbuds, it will sound good on any audio system.

Using the MultibandCompressor

The "punchy" adjective is achieved by using the MultibandCompressor plug-in. But as you will see, you'll gain more than punch from this powerful plug-in. From the Output Channel Inserts of the Channel Settings window, click on Insert slot 1, select the Dynamics category, and then choose MulitbandCompressor. The MultibandCompressor control panel will appear, as shown in Figure 16.10.

Figure 16.10. The MultibandCompressor control panel, Rock Master 2 preset (modified).

By default, there is no preset visible in the Preset field. However, you should be aware that the MultibandCompressor is processing the signal and the sound. Therefore, it's normal to hear the volume level jump up when you first load the plug-in. If you ever need to return to this default setting, load the preset named "Reset."

THE OPERATION OF THE MULTIBANDCOMPRESSOR

An ordinary compressor operates on all audio frequencies simultaneously and equally, whereas the MultibandCompressor operates as four separate frequency-based compressors. This allows you to compress each frequency band differently, which prevents a preponderance of certain frequencies from adversely affecting the volumes of others. To get a better idea of how the frequency bands are divided, click on the Solo Band button just above the Ratio knob on any of the four bands. What you'll hear are the frequencies being compressed by the associated band. The low frequencies will be mostly the rumble of bass drum and bass guitar. The low-mids will contain the fundamental frequencies of the vocals, keyboards, snare drum, and acoustic guitar. The high-mids will contain the brightness of the instruments in the low-mid band, and the tambourine becomes audible. Finally, the highs contain guitar-pick noise, the tambourine jangles, the hi-hat cymbals, and the sibilance of the vocals.

AUDITIONING MULTIBANDCOMPRESSOR PRESETS

Now listen to some of the MultibandCompressor presets. Click the Presets field (see Figure 16.10), and choose Rock Master. To my ears, the low band has a nice response, but the low and high-mid bands become too deficient, and the high band becomes too thin and bright. Now try the Rock Master 2 preset. Suddenly the lows are nice and punchy, plus the acoustic guitar and the vocals (low-mid band) become more pronounced. The highs are also nicely tamed. I like this preset, so go with that. However, you'll notice that the Output Level on the control panel is set to 2.2 dB. That has increased the overall volume level, and the clip indicators are lit because of it. Therefore, enter a value of 0.0. (See Figure 16.10.) The volume will drop a bit, but don't worry, because you'll be adjusting the "LOUD" a little later.

Now click the Bypass button at the top of the control panel to audition the before and after of the MultibandCompressor. The before sounds kind of vague and undefined, whereas the after has more definition, and the mix is punching through your speakers to your ears. As you can see, the MultibandCompressor is more than punchy low frequencies. It can be used to craft a smoother volume response across all the frequency bands. That makes your EQ task quite a bit easier.

Using the Output Channel Fader EQ

After the signal flows out of the MultibandCompressor (or the last plug-in installed in Inserts 1 through 6), it goes into the Output Channel EQ. This is the same 4-band, fully parametric EQ you've used on Audio, Instrument, Group, and FX channels, so you're already familiar with how it works. In the context of mastering, EQ is where you can craft the tonality, not of a single channel, but of the entire mix. Since the EQ is part of the Output Channel, you don't need to assign an EQ plug-in.

ADJUSTING THE EQ PARAMETERS

This is where you can add the "shiny" quality to the master. After some careful listening and comparison to other commercial masters, I came up with the EQ curve shown in Figure 16.11.

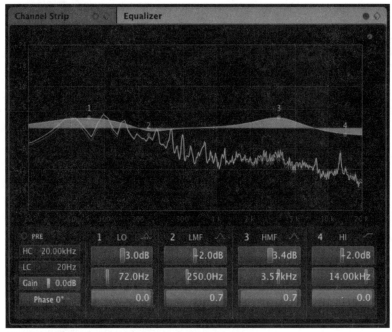

Figure 16.11. Mastering EQ curve using four bands.

The first thing I wanted to hear was a few more high-mids, so I increased EQ 3 to 3.5 dB at 3,570 Hz. Then I noticed a little throatiness in the low-mids, so I decreased EQ 2 to -2.0 dB at 250 Hz. But I wanted a little more low end, so I switched EQ 1 to the Parametric II filter and added 3.0 dB at 72 Hz. Then I compared that to some like genres and determined that the whole mix sounded a little too shiny. So I set the highs of EQ 4 to a High Shelf I filter type and decreased the frequencies above 14,000 Hz by 2.0 dB. That also helped add a little analoglike warmth. But your results may vary; feel free to try your own settings.

Using the Maximizer

This is how you add the "LOUD" quality to your master. While the Maximizer mastering limiter that comes with Cubase is technically not a "brick wall" limiter, it still does a nice job of increasing the average volumes. This is also where you utilize Insert 7, because it comes after the Output Channel Fader. (You're saving Insert 8 for later.) Click on Insert slot 7 and choose Maximizer from the Dynamics category. Compared to the other mastering treatments, the Maximizer has a very simple control panel, as shown in Figure 16.12.

Up until you installed the Maximizer, the Output Channel was the final destination of your mixdown. But now the output-level control of the Maximizer serves that purpose. Notice in Figure 16.12 that I've set the output to -0.2 dB below zero. That sets a safety that limits the total output of the mixdown to two-tenths of a decibel below zero, and ensures that CD players and other audio devices don't distort when decoding audio signals above -0.1 or 0.0 dB. (I've found a few commercial CDs that will distort certain CD players yet sound fine when played in others. One example is the Rush album Vapor Trails.) The Soft Clip button is on by default, which provides a more gentle type of limiting. However, if you're mastering loud, edgy music, such as industrial metal or dub step, you might want to disable Soft Clip. All that leaves is adjusting the Optimize control, which determines the perceived loudness of the mixdown. Or another way to look at it is by asking, "To what degree shall I fight in the Loudness War?" The default is 25.0, but if the master were for me, I'd set it to 0.0 (which will still lightly limit the output and leave the maximum at -0.2 dB). But if I needed the mix to compete with contemporary music, I'd go for as high as possible without the sound becoming too crushed. In this example, I found that 29.0 was an appropriate setting.

Figure 16.12. The Maximizer control panel.

OPTIONAL: ADDING TAPE SATURATION

Magnetic analog tape has some very musically pleasing qualities, and Cubase has a physical model that emulates the nuances of tape. The Tape Saturation effect is located in the Strip Rack in the Sat effect. If you already have the Channel Settings window open, click the Channel Strip tab to the left of the Equalizer tab to reveal the Sat effects, as shown in Figure 16.3.

The Drive control doesn't need to be adjusted very high because the plug-in adds the tape nuance even when the control is set to zero. I turned it up to 1.0 dB and left the rest of the controls at their default positions.

Figure 16.13. The Tape Saturation effect in the Channel Strip.

Take a Moment to Listen and Save

Now that your mix is a punchy, shiny, and LOUD master, listen to the before and after of the mastering processes. The easiest way to do this is to use the Inserts, Channel Strip, and EQ Bypass buttons, as shown in Figure 16.14.

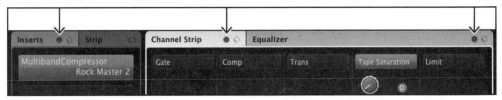

Figure 16.14. The Inserts, Channel Strip, and EQ Bypass buttons.

When they are bypassed, you're hearing the original mix. When enabled, you're hearing the mastered version. The difference can be a little startling. The mixed version, while sounding fine, definitely lacks some of the refinement and impact of the mastered version. Now is a good time to save this version of the project, which I've already done as version R10. But since R10 is already in your Project Folder, I'm going to have you save it as R11.

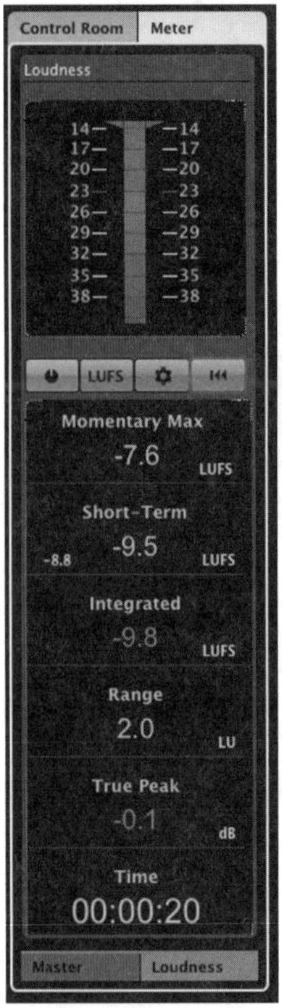

ANALYZING LOUDNESS PRIOR TO MIXDOWN

So, how'd you do pertaining to the Loudness War? It's time to find out. Click the Window Layout button at the upper left-hand corner of the MixConsole, and make sure Control Room/Mixer is enabled, which will reveal the Control Room/Meter on the right side of the MixConsole. Then click the Meter tab (top of meter) and the Loudness tab (bottom of meter) to reveal the Loudness Meter, as shown in Figure 16.15.

The Loudness Meter will give you the EBU R 128 loudness analysis statistics like you saw in the Statistics windows. (See Figures 16.2 through 16.5.) The difference is that the Loudness Meter works in real-time as the project is playing. Take a look at the buttons located about a third of the way down Figure 16.15. On the left, you'll see the Power button, so make sure the power is on. Then on the right, you'll see the Reset button, which is used to start the analysis all over again. Underneath those buttons, you'll find the real-time analysis. Take a look at the Integrated value, which is the same as the integrated loudness in the Statistics window. This project has a loudness of -9.8 LUFS. That's perfect if you want the loudness of this song to compete with contemporary pop songs on the radio.

You can conduct an analysis by hitting the Reset button and then playing your project from beginning to end. Notice that the Time value at the bottom of the meter will show you how long the analysis has been taking place. The Time will stop when you stop playback on your project.

If you found that the loudness was too low or too high, you could adjust the Optimize control on the Maximizer (see Figure 16.12), then perform another analysis.

Figure 16.15. The Loudness Meter.

EXPORTING THE AUDIO MIXDOWN, TIMES THREE

Now that you've mixed and mastered your project, it's time to export it as a mixdown that you can share with the world. But to do it right, you'll need to save three different versions. This is because you should always execute your mixdown for three contingencies.

First, you'll want a high-bit-rate version that matches the Bit Resolution (Project menu, Project Setup window) of your recorded tracks. In other words, if you recorded your Audio tracks in 32-bit float, you'll want a 32-bit-float mixdown. This version should also be void of all mastering plug-ins and EQ. This will provide you with a "future proof" mixdown that you can give to another mastering engineer—or the ability to remaster the original mix at any later date. Without this file, you'd have to remix and remaster the same project in Cubase, and there's no guarantee that future versions of Cubase, the plug-ins, the operating system, or the computer will be able to load this Cubase Project file.

Second, you'll want an audio CD–compatible file that you can burn onto an audio CD. This version should include the mastering processes but needs to be 16-bit resolution. If the project was originally recorded in 24- or 32-bit, you'll need to dither the mixdown to 16-bit for audio CD. It's a very easy process that I'll discuss in a moment. (Note: If you recorded your tracks at a higher sample rate than 44.1 kHz, you'll need to convert it to 44.1 before it can be burned to an audio CD.)

Lastly, you'll want an MP3 version for e-mail, Internet, and e-commerce purposes. These are much smaller than the WAV or AIFF versions but don't sound quite the same because of data compression (not to be confused with audio compression). That data compression does alter the sound characteristics, but MP3 files can be easily shared via e-mail, uploaded to websites, or submitted for sale to cdbaby.com, iTunes, and so forth. With that in mind, it's time to make some mixdowns.

Setting the Left and Right Locators

The Locators are used for a myriad of different purposes during the recording and mixing processes. But for mixdown, they're used to determine, along the Time Ruler, the project starts and ends. Let me show you an easy way to set the Locators for mixdown. From the Project window, I'm going to type Ctrl/Command + A, which will select all of the events in the Event Display. Then I'm going to type "P" (Locators to Selection) on my computer keyboard, which will place the Left Locator at the earliest Event Boundary and the Right Locator at the latest Event Boundary, as shown in Figure 16.16.

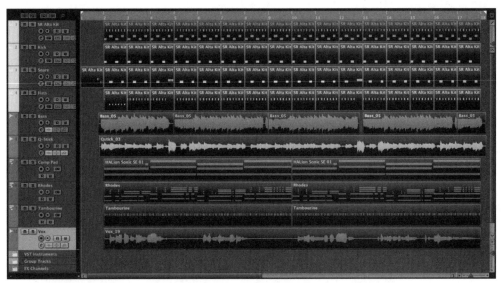

Figure 16.16. Results of the Locators to Selection command.

You could perform the audio export now, but you'd have a couple of problems. The first of which is that there would be quite a bit of silence before the song started. The left Event Boundary does not have any notes until the fourth beat of measure 1. It would be better to move the Left Locator (with Snap off) slightly to the left of that first note. Similarly, since you're using a delay and reverb in this project, it's conceivable that the audio produced by those time-based effects will continue past the Right Locator. To that end, move the Right Locator a few more beats to the right. In the case of this project, the downbeat of measure 19 would do nicely.

Mixdown No. 1: High Bit Rate with No Mastering

Before proceeding, determine the bit resolution of the project. Click the Project menu, and choose Project Setup. Look for the Bit Resolution setting. In this case, it's 32-Bit Float. Now you know that your high-bit-rate version should also be in 32-Bit-Float format. Then click the Inserts, Channel Strip, and EQ Bypass buttons on the Output Channel. (See Figure 16.14.) Then click the File menu, select Export, and choose Audio Mixdown. The Export Audio Mixdown dialog box will appear, as shown in Figure 16.17.

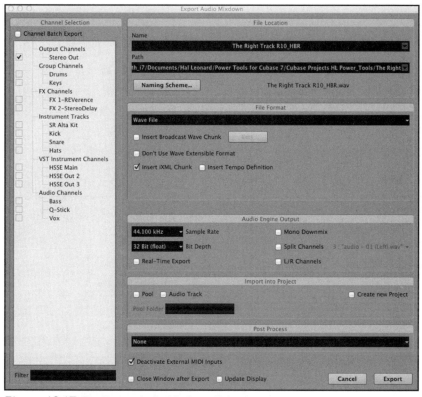

Figure 16.17. The Export Audio Mixdown dialog box.

Make sure that the Stereo Out is enabled under the Channel Selection column on the left-hand side. Then set the Sample Rate to 44.100 kHz (or the sample rate of the project as shown in the Project Setup window) and the Bit Depth to 32-Bit (float) (or the bit resolution in the Project Setup window). Next, type in the desired file name at the top of the window. I include the revision number of the project, then an underscore, then HBR to indicate this as the high-bit-rate mixdown. Then click the Path button and select Choose. A standard file navigation box will appear. I recommend choosing the Project Folder you created when you started the project, then creating a new folder called "Mixes." I set the File Format to Wave File (WAV or Microsoft Wave Format) and then verify that all of the checkboxes (other than Stereo Out) are disabled. Notice that the Deactivate External MIDI Inputs checkbox is enabled. This is to prevent any MIDI notes played from your MIDI controller during the export from being recorded into your mixdown file. Finally, hit the Export button. The mixdown will usually proceed in faster than real-time speed, but that depends largely on the complexity of the project and the speed of your computer. (If you want to hear the project in real-time during the export, enable the Real-Time Export checkbox.) When the export is complete, the window will stay open, allowing you to export your next mixdown.

Mixdown No. 2: Audio CD—Compatible with Mastering

Return to the mixer, and enable the Inserts and EQ buttons. (See Figure 16.14.) But if the project bit resolution was higher than 16-bit (and in the case of this example project, it was), you'd need to dither down to 16-bit. As weird as that might sound, it's much easier than you think.

USING THE APOGEE UV22HR DITHERING PLUG-IN

The more digital bits you use, the wider your dynamic range. That's why at 32-bit, Cubase has a huge dynamic range of 1,536 dB. But audio CDs are 16-bit with a dynamic range of 96 dB. If you don't dither the mixdown, Cubase will unceremoniously lop off half the bits. But with the Apogee UV22HR (the dithering plug-in that comes with Cubase), the dithering process will analyze which of the 16-bits most accurately represent the original dynamic range and use them to export the audio. All you need to do is click on Output Channel Insert slot 8 (see Figure 16.7) and select UV22HR from the Mastering category. The control panel will appear, as shown in Figure 16.18.

There are only two buttons to click: 16 and hi. Believe it or not, that's it. However, if you're sending your mixdowns to another mastering engineer, it would be wise to ask him or her what bit-resolution he or she wants the file in. Not all audio programs are capable of recognizing 32-bit files.

Figure 16.18. The UV22HR dithering plug-in with audio CD–compatible settings.

Therefore, you might need to use the UV22HR output bits set to 24 or even 16 depending on his or her answer, but the Inserts and EQ would also need to be disabled to allow for proper second-party mastering.

PROCEEDING WITH THE MIXDOWN

All you need to do now is change the file name and bit depth (and possibly the sample rate to 44.1 kHz) in the Export Audio Mixdown window. (See Figure 16.17.) I used the same naming convention as before, except this time I changed "HBR" to "16" to indicate that this is a 16-bit version ("The Right Track R10_16"). Then set the bit depth to 16-bit, and click the Export button.

Mixdown No. 3: MP3 Version

For this version, you'll need to leave the UV22HR on. But you'll need to change the name to include only the name of the song, and you'll need to change the File Format from Wave File (see Figure 16.17) to MPEG 1 Layer 3 File, as shown in Figure 16.19.

Figure 16.19. MPEG 1 Layer 3 File Format.

The settings in the File Format section will change to include MP3 specific settings, the most important of which is the Bit Rate slider. This is used to balance the file size to the audio quality. Increasing the slider will provide a higher-quality sound but with increased file size. Lowering the slider will make the file smaller and easier to download over slow Internet connections but will also degrade the sound quality. With the continual increase in Internet speeds, I would recommend a bit rate of no lower than 256 kBit. That will create a good-sounding file with a manageable file size. (Note: Sometimes the slider won't let you select 256 kBit, which is why I double-click in that field and type in 256.)

You can disable the High Quality mode, although I can't think of a good reason to do so. While not compulsory, I would recommend enabling the Insert ID3 tag option and then clicking the Edit ID3 Tab button. The ID3 Tag window will appear, as shown in Figure 16.20.

If you've used a program such as iTunes or Windows Media Player, you'll certainly recognize these fields. The ID3 tags are what appear in the information section of a media player program. So it's a good idea to fill in the appropriate fields. For example, the File Name does not necessarily equal the Title field. This allows you to reference the song by title name or file name. The other fields should be filled in accordingly, and you can see the examples I've used for this project in Figure 16.20. When finished, click OK, and click the Export button on the Export Audio Mixdown window.

Figure 16.20. The ID3 Tag window.

Examining the Results

Now that your project has been mixed to the three file formats, you can close Cubase and view the contents of your Project Folder, as shown in Figure 16.21.

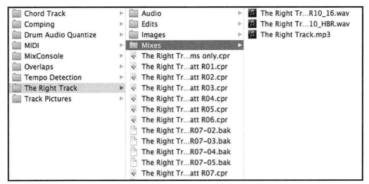

Figure 16.21. The Project Folder with Mixes folder and mixdown files.

The look of the Project Folder will be different on Mac or PC, but the file hierarchy is identical to that of Figure 16.21. It's a good idea to listen to each file before certifying it finished. That will prevent you from delivering versions with errors or glitches. It's rare, but you've already listened to the song about a million times, so three more won't hurt you. It's also a good idea to load the MP3 version into iTunes or any other program that reads ID3 tags to verify the information, spelling, and so forth.

Finally, make sure you listen to each mixdown file and make sure they all sound the same way they did in Cubase. I don't remember the last time I found an error in a mixdown file, but it's still critical to make sure there aren't any problems that might affect how they sound to the end-listener.

Optional Mixdown No. 4: High Bit Rate with Mastering

It's not a bad idea to create a high-bit-rate version that includes all the mastering plug-ins. However, I've found that if I get the urge to do any remastering, I'll load the original HBR file into a new Cubase Project (or a mastering program such as WaveLab) and start the mastering from scratch. There's a possibility that listening to the song after few months or years, I'll want to start the mastering from scratch and try some different treatments or even new plug-ins. That's why I choose not to perform this type of mixdown.

BACKING UP YOUR WORK

You're done, right? Wrong! It is critical that you take a moment to back up your project. And since I've taught you the proper Cubase media-management model, it's incredibly easy to do. Simply drag the Project Folder to your backup hard drive. You could also use optical media such as DVDs for backup purposes, but they're much more fragile than hard drives, which are getting cheaper by the minute. In fact, because I have had hard drives crash before I'm finished with a project, I regularly back up the Project Folder to a backup hard disk during the recording, editing, mixing, and mastering processes. Why take a chance?

The Concept of Onsite and Offsite Backup

Once you've backed up your Cubase Project(s), that's good but not good enough. Unfortunately, disasters happen, and I could recite from a long list of client tragedies that have eaten irreplaceable data, including hard-disk failures, robberies, fires, floods, and even vengeful spouses. (Now is a good time to knock on wood.) Since I've learned my lesson (more than once), I keep one hard disk (usually an external USB, FireWire, or eSATA version) at my studio and another hard disk with the same data at home. That way, if disaster strikes at one location, I still have another backup. The moral of the story is: back it up or pack it up. Consider this my urgent plea for your promise to back up your Cubase Projects. I would hate to learn that you've lost your hard work for any reason. This is your final warning. (Cue ominous music, then back that up too.)

MOVING FORWARD

Are you ready for some good news? Now that you're at the end of this book, you'll never have to listen to "The Right Track Matt" ever again. (Don't let me see your look of relief.) This does mean that you're on your own, but hopefully I've enriched you with knowledge that will make the process of creating music easier. It has been my distinct honor to show you how to use Cubase. It is a fantastic program, and I hope you use it to create wonderful music for the world to hear. Cubase is also a very deep program, and content limits prevented me from going over all of its many facets. In fact, each one of these chapters could have been a book unto itself had I the room to make it so. Alas, however, our time together has come to an end. But please keep trying other Cubase features on your own. It's software, and you can't break it, so go for broke.

Appendix A: Using the Included Disc

On the enclosed disc, you will find the Cubase Projects I used throughout the book. The project you'll be using the most is "The Right Track Matt RXX.cpr." I have no doubt you will grow intensely bored of that song. (I sure have.) But the sooner you learn the techniques for editing and mixing that and the other projects on the disc, the sooner you can move on to your own material. There are detailed references to all these projects throughout the book, but let me explain a little bit more about them here.

COPYING THE FILES TO YOUR COMPUTER

When you put the disc into your computer's optical drive and view its directory, you will see a folder called Cubase Projects HL. This is to differentiate it from the default Cubase Projects Folder that is created on your computer hard disk during the installation of Cubase. I would recommend copying the folder to your computer. The total size of the folder content is less than 360 MB, so it won't take much space. While you could load and play the Cubase Projects HL folder from the disc, the slow speed of an optical drive will be a problem. Take a moment to copy the folder to a location on your computer where you can easily find it.

Cubase Projects

Inside the Cubase Projects HL folder, you will find seven Project Folders. Loading the projects contained within each Project Folder will allow you to see the features in Cubase that I was using while I was writing the book. Some Project Folders will contain multiple Project files (.cpr) with different revision numbers at the ends of their file names (R01, R02, etc.). These are to differentiate the progress of each project. I use this as my standard methodology while working on any Cubase Project so that I can always refer to an earlier version. All of the MIDI or Instrument tracks are using HALion Sonic SE, which is one of the Cubase built-in virtual synthesizers.

A Word About the Audio Tracks

I had a dilemma when deciding how to record the Audio tracks for this book. Part of me wanted to hire studio musicians to come to my studio and lay down some truly wonderful tracks. But the editors reminded me that we needed to stay within budget and keep the book affordable. I also realized the benefit of providing you with tracks that are not—how shall I say it—Grammy winners. Therefore, I recorded all the tracks myself at my home studio using only one entry-level microphone: an AKG C3000S. This was to provide you with the same types of recordings you're creating in your home-studio environment.

The guitar and bass tracks were recorded direct (instrument plugged directly into the input) to a Steinberg MR816CSX audio interface without any additional processing between the source and the audio interface. The bass was a Status S2 Classic with EMG 40TW pickups, and the guitar was a Rainsong WS1000 acoustic guitar with a Fishman pickup.

I have no doubt that you will be able to create recordings and mixes that will equal or surpass the quality of those found in these projects. But I also don't want you to fall into the trap of thinking, "I won't record Audio tracks until I get a [insert expensive audio product here]." It's better to record everything and record often, no matter what microphones, processors, or instruments you have at your disposal.

Appendix B:
A Primer on Automation

When I started to tally up the page totals of this book, it became apparent that I had gone overboard. I had fully intended to provide a chapter dedicated to automation, but I just ran out of space. While I didn't use any in the projects you'll be using (see Appendix A: "Using the Included Disc"), I do feel it necessary to cover the basics of automation with this primer.

THE CONCEPT OF AUTOMATION

When I say automation, what I'm referring to is programming the movement of the buttons, sliders, switches, and knobs in Cubase. Automation allows you to create virtual hands that can manipulate Cubase controls over the timeline of a project. The automation in Cubase is much more powerful and effective than the traditional method, which usually involved all band members hovering over the mixer and tweaking the controls during the mixdown. Modern DAW automation also reduces the animosity between band members when one forgot to move his or her assigned slider at the right time. I've even seen a few mix sessions devolve into all-out fist fights. I'd like to reduce the possibility of that by exploring the benefits of automation.

The Read and Write Enable Buttons

Once you've seen the Read and Write Enable buttons, you'll start seeing them everywhere in Cubase. Sometimes they're on the MixConsole, while other times they're on the control panel of a VST plug-in. Many Read and Write buttons are shown in Figure B.1.

When Write is enabled, it means that any knob, button, slider, or parameter that gets moved during playback (you needn't be in Record mode or recording for automation programming) will be written into the corresponding Automation track. (More on Automation tracks in a moment.) The controls will then reenact the movement during playback, but only when Read is enabled.

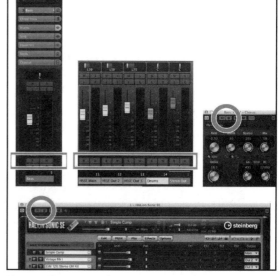

Figure B.1. The ubiquitous Read and Write Automation Enable buttons.

The Automation Tracks

All tracks (MIDI, Instrument, Audio, Group, and FX Channel) and the Output Channels have their own Automation tracks. By default, they're hidden to prevent an inordinate number of additional tracks being visible in the Track Column. To reveal the Automation Lanes, hover your mouse over the lower-left corner of a track. The normally invisible Show/Hide Automation button will appear, as shown in Figure B.2.

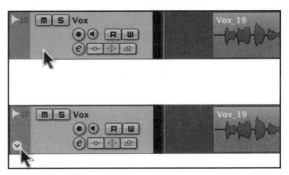

Figure B.2. Revealing the Show/Hide Automation button.

When you click on the Show/Hide Automation button, the Automation track (or tracks) will appear directly beneath the Source track, as shown in Figure B.3.

By default, the volume data will be shown first and appear as a horizontal line. If no automation data has been programmed, the vertical position of the data line will not vary. Note also that every Automation track has its own Read and Write buttons. They allow you to disable one specific track without affecting others. Automation

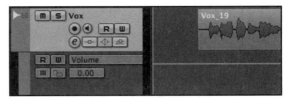

Figure B.3. The Automation track displaying volume data (default).

tracks can also be resized for more precise editing. You can open additional Automation tracks by clicking on the Show/Hide Automation button of any visible Automation track. Another great method is right/Ctrl-clicking any track and choosing Show All Used Automation from the submenu.

Using the Data Selector

Clicking on the data selector (labeled as Volume in Figure B.3) will allow you to choose what automation data you'd like to edit or program. Data types that have been automated will appear with an asterisk, as shown in Figure B.4.

You'll notice that volume and pan have asterisks, while the other data types don't. The most commonly

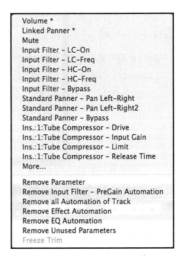

Figure B.4. The automation data selector list.

automated data appear in the list, but you can also select More (see Figure B.4) to select any automatable data type.

CREATING AND EDITING AUTOMATION DATA

There are two ways to create automation data: manipulating the controls during playback (with Write Automation button enabled) or drawing the data into an Automation Lane. The latter method is preferred, as it allows you to visualize and edit the data in context with the track upon which the automation data does or will exist. To that end, it's time to create some automation data.

Creating Simple Automation Data

With the volume data selected and the Automation track set to Read enable, you can use your mouse in Object Selection mode to click on the horizontal automation data line. For example, in Figure B.5, I've clicked once on measure 3 and again on measure 4.

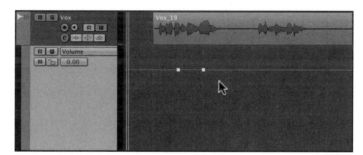

Figure B.5. Creating two automation points.

Two automation points will appear as small squares on the data line. Those automation points are only visible when the mouse is hovering within the Automation track. Now you can click and drag the vertical and horizontal position of either point to automate the Volume Fader. Bear in mind that the horizontal placement of the point will be governed by the Snap setting. You can disable Snap by typing "J" on your computer keyboard.

Creating Complex Automation with the Draw and Line Tools

The Draw tool can be selected by clicking on it in the Toolbox (see Figure B.6) or by typing "8" on the upper row of number keys on your computer keyboard.

With the Draw tool selected, you can click and drag across the Automation Lane to create complex

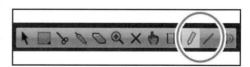

Figure B.6. The Draw and Line tools in the Toolbox, top of Project window Toolbar.

automation data. Similarly, you can click and hold on the Line tool to choose from five curves: Line, Parabola, Sine, Triangle, and Square. Clicking and dragging in the Automation Lane will create automation data based on the shape of the selected Line tool curve. After the data has been created, you can switch back to your Object Select tool by typing "1" on the upper row of number keys on your computer keyboard and adjusting the placement of the automation points.

EXPERIMENTING WITH AUTOMATION

In this primer, I've provided you with only a smattering of automation possibilities. I would urge you to experiment with different automation data on different tracks. Automation data is not permanent and can always be edited or erased. You can do this by right/Ctrl-clicking the Automation track and choosing Select All Events from the submenu, then hitting the Backspace to erase all the data on the track. You can also turn off the Read enable for the track to ignore the automation, or you can click the Mute Automation button (the lower left Automation Track button resembling a Roman numeral III, see Figure B.5) to temporarily or permanently disable the Automation track.

Appendix C: Managing Audio Interface Buffer Settings

Managing the buffer size of your audio interface is critical. If you don't, both the recording and mixing processes can be severely hampered, because there's either too much latency or too small a buffer to play back all the components of your project simultaneously. As the track count of your project gets higher and higher, you'll want to regularly increase the buffer size. This is because you'll be creating more processor-intensive virtual components during the mix, such as reverbs, delays, compressors, and other effects. The more of those you add, the larger the buffer will need to be. If the buffer is set too low, you can end up with pops, clicks, and other distortion. In this appendix, I'll show you how to adjust the buffer settings.

THE SIMPLE RULE FOR DETERMINING BUFFER SIZE

Determining the proper buffer size is simple if you follow this rule: Recording = smaller buffer sizes, while mixing and mastering = larger buffer sizes. To adjust the buffer size, click the Devices menu and select Device Setup. The Device Setup window will appear, as shown in Figure C.1.

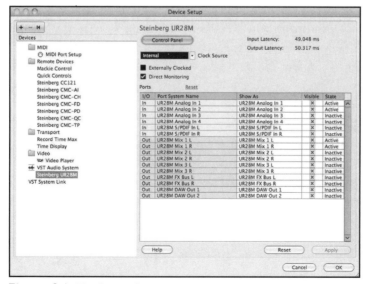

Figure C.1. The Device Setup window.

You'll first need to click on the VST Audio System on the left side of the Device Setup window. Next, click on whatever appears below the VST Audio System heading. This is the make and model of your audio interface, so what is shown in Figure C.1 will be different from what you see on your window (unless you too are using a Steinberg UR28M). Then click on the Control Panel button.

Control Panel Settings (Including Latency)

Clicking on the Control Panel button will reveal another window. However, the appearance of the window and the settings themselves will be specific to your audio interface and will be different on Mac and PC, as shown in Figure C.2.

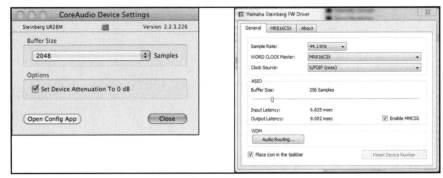

Figure C.2. Control panels: Mac (left) and Windows (right).

Since different manufacturers will design their control panels differently, I cannot speak about all the settings you might find on yours, save one: buffer size. The buffer size is what controls your audio interface latency. Latency is how long it takes for your computer to receive an audio signal at the interface In port, and then send it to the interface Out port. For virtual instruments, the buffer size determines how long it will take for MIDI information to be received, converted into audio by the virtual synthesizer, and then sent to the audio Out port. But during mixing, your computer will be generating the largest number of virtual devices and demanding the largest buffer size.

Adjusting the Buffer

During the mixing and mastering processes, I would recommend setting the buffer size to its maximum possible value. Don't be afraid of using 1,024 or even 2,048 samples. For this purpose, some control panels will have a drop-down box, while others will have sliders and even knobs. Use whatever appears on your control panel to increase the buffer size. Then, when you start recording your next project, repeat the process, but try to set it as low as possible. A modern computer should be able to handle 64 or 128 samples. But if you experience pops and clicks, try 256 or 384 samples, or whatever it takes to eliminate the anomalies.

Activating the Steinberg Audio
Power Scheme (Windows Only)

No matter where you are in your Cubase Project, it's a good idea, if you're using Windows, to activate the Steinberg Audio Power Scheme. This will prevent the CPUs and processor cores in your computer from being throttled. CPU throttling dynamically adjusts the speed of the CPU and the related cores based on load demand, but can cause problems for DAW programs such as Cubase. This power scheme will be active when Cubase is running, and return the computer to the Windows setting when you quit Cubase. All you need to do is enable the Activate Steinberg Audio Power Scheme checkbox on the Device Setup window, as shown in Figure C.3.

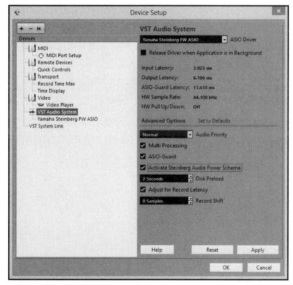

Figure C.3. The Device Setup window and Steinberg Audio Power Scheme checkbox.

Index

POWER TOOLS SERIES

POWER TOOLS FOR STUDIO ONE 2, VOLUME 1
DVD-ROM

by Larry the O

Power Tools for Studio One 2 shows the reader how to get around Studio One and perform recording, editing, mixing, and mastering.

Book/DVD-ROM Pack
978-1-4584-0226-4 ....$39.99

POWER TOOLS FOR STUDIO ONE 2, VOLUME 2
DVD-ROM

by Larry the O

Studio One maven Larry the O takes users even deeper into advanced applications, such as working with loops and video, mixing, mastering, and sharing your work with the world, exploring each topic in comprehensive detail.

Book/DVD-ROM Pack
978-1-4768-7468-5 ....$39.99

POWER TOOLS FOR LOGIC PRO 9
DVD-ROM

by Rick Silva

Power Tools for Logic Pro 9 unlocks Logic's immense capabilities to help you achieve amazing results for your audio and music productions with techniques you won't find in beginner-level books or videos.

Book/DVD-ROM Pack
978-1-4234-4345-2 ....$39.99

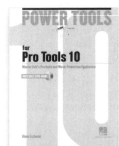

POWER TOOLS FOR PRO TOOLS 10
DVD-ROM

by Glenn Lorbecki

See and experience the new features incorporated in this powerful software offering, all the way from the new ways it handles data, memory, and gain functions to some seemingly small updates that make a huge difference in your productivity.

Book/DVD-ROM
978-1-4584-0035-2 ....$39.99

POWER TOOLS FOR REASON 6
DVD-ROM

by Andrew Eisele

Power Tools for Reason 6 is a comprehensive book that provides a quick-start tutorial that not only gets you up and running quickly, but also delves into advanced sequencing and mixing techniques.

Book/DVD-ROM Pack
978-1-4584-0227-1 ....$39.99

POWER TOOLS FOR CUBASE 7
DVD-ROM

by Matthew Loel T. Hepworth

Power Tools for Cubase 7 was written with the new user in mind. You'll learn the process all the way from installation and configuration to adding mastering treatments to your mix.

Book/DVD-ROM Pack
978-1-4584-1368-0 ....$39.99

POWER TOOLS FOR ABLETON LIVE 9
DVD-ROM

by Jake Perrine

Unlike other books about Live that simply explain its features like a second manual, this hands-on-centric book contains a series of exercises that walk you through all the features you need to produce professional-sounding music with Ableton Live 9.

Book/DVD-ROM Pack
978-1-4584-0038-3 ....$39.99

HAL•LEONARD
www.halleonardbooks.com

Prices, content, and availability subject to change without notice.

081